C٨   ﾉOVE
            ﾟCKET

Anton Bruckner

A Discography

Fallen Leaf Reference Books in Music
ISSN 8755–268X, No. 6

Anton Bruckner
A Discography

Lee T. Lovallo

Fallen Leaf Press

Published by Fallen Leaf Press
P.O. Box 10034
Berkeley, CA 94709 USA

Library of Congress Cataloging-in-Publication Data

Lovallo, Lee T., 1946-
   Anton Bruckner: a discography / Lee T. Lovallo.
      p. — (Fallen Leaf reference books in music ; 6)
   Foreword in German.
   Includes bibliographical references (p.) and indexes.
   ISBN 0-914913-05-0
   1. Bruckner, Anton, 1824-1896—Discography. I. Title.
  II. Series: Fallen Leaf reference books in music; no. 6.
ML 156.5.B78L7 1991
016.78'092—dc20   86-46229
                                       CIP
                                       MN

The paper used in this book meets the minimum requirements
of the American National Standard for Information Services—
Permanence of Paper for Printed Library Materials, ANSI
Z39.48-1984.

Contents

I. Choral and Vocal Works

Contents

Choral and Vocal Works, cont.

II. Chamber Music

III. Organ Works

IV. Orchestral Works

Preface

The length and technical demands of Anton Bruckner's major works, coupled with a long-standing prejudice against his music among many performers, delayed acceptance of his compositions in the United States. Augmented by open-reel tapes, cassette tapes, compact discs, and now videodiscs, phonograph records had much to do with making Bruckner's music better appreciated in this country. By cataloging information about commercial recordings of Bruckner's works, this discography documents the rapid surge in enthusiasm for a body of work that many listeners now rank with the finest musical art of the nineteenth century.

While my goal was to catalog all issues in all formats of all recordings of Bruckner's music, practical considerations have limited this catalog's scope. I have included all recordings known to me but have described in detail only the earliest issue physically available for my review. Reissues, earlier issues unaccessible to my research, and parallel issues in other formats are noted only by label, number, and format. Also, I have chosen to disregard the country of origin of each issue. Considering the truly international scope of most record distribution companies, it makes little sense to identify a particular item as French or Japanese when it is as readily obtainable in the U.S.A. or in Great Britain and when it may be distributed by a firm based in the Netherlands. I have included information about the location at which the recording was made, however.

This discography documents as fully as possible nearly eight hundred performances of Bruckner's music, ranging from 1930's recordings on 78-rpm discs through currently available digital video material. Preferring in all cases to deal with primary source material rather than to rely upon other discographies, I have drawn most heavily upon the extensive collection of recordings belonging to the California Friends of Bruckner. I have also inspected recorded materials at the libraries of the University of California at Berkeley and at Davis, at the California State University library in Sacramento, and at the Stanford University Library and Archive of Recorded Sound in Stanford, California.

Mr. Michael Grey of the Smithsonian Institution read, corrected, and amplified the entire working catalog in 1989, and I am most grateful to him for his generous and accurate assistance. Most of the information relating to recent Japanese recordings was contributed by Mr. Grey. The pioneering discography of J. F. Weber was invaluable to me, serving as the inspiration for this project and setting a high standard of quality that I have sought to emulate. Other secondary sources of information are noted in the bibliography.

In the main part of the discography, recordings are presented by performing medium: vocal and choral works, chamber music, organ pieces, and orchestral works. Within these groups, pieces appear in the same order as in Renate Grasberger's index (*Werkverzeichnis A. Bruckner*, Tutzing: Hans Schneider, 1977), resulting in a mostly alphabetical and logical sequence. Recordings of the same work by various performers are arranged alphabetically by conductor, or by ensemble in the case of chamber music, or by soloist in the case of organ music. This information appears in coded form as a catalog number preceding each entry. Individual entries give, as appropriate, the following information in this sequence:

- conductor (or soloist)
- principal performing ensemble
- secondary ensemble (usually a chorus)
- soloists (listed in normal score order)
- place and date of the original recording
- the editor's name
- year in which the version used was completed
- record label and number
- recording format ("digital" is reserved to describe the first stage of the recording process)
- number of sides used for this selection
- year in which this issue was released
- primary source location
- timings (total time followed by that of each movement)
- annotators
- other music appearing on the record
- parallel issues (LP disc(s) unless otherwise indicated)

Information about the sources for the dates of the original recording and its release is conveyed via abbreviations preceding each year cited: "W." refers to J. F. Weber's discography (*Discography Series X: Bruckner*, Utica, New York: J. F. Weber, 1975); "p." indicates a phonoright date, "©" a copyright date, usually appearing on the record package or associated notes; entries without abbreviations, often with a specific month given, draw on specific statements given on the record jacket; "ca." indicates an estimate, based usually on indirect evidence appearing on a recording, such as biographical information relating to a performer.

In the matter of the editions employed, I have given a brief description of the chief versions of each piece before the initial entry. This is limited to identifying the city where Bruckner completed each version, followed by the date, the Grasberger catalog number (WAB), and the formerly used catalog number from the Göllerich/Auer biography (G/A) (*Anton Bruckner: Ein Lebens- und Schaffensbild*, Regensburg: Gustav Bosse Verlag, 1922). Each individual entry then gives the year of the version employed in the recording and the editor's name, when known. In many cases identifying the edition is immaterial, because no significant differences exist among the various modern sources. This is true with respect to Symphonies Nos. 5, 6, 7, and 9, the chamber music, the organ pieces, and most of the choral music. Thus a lack of information in this regard should not be a cause for concern. I have otherwise identified editions by noting references on the record jacket or liner notes, by checking citations in other discographies, or by comparing the recording to published scores.

Richard Osborne provides an up-to-date, authoritative discussion of the editions, together with a selective, critical discography, in an article in *Gramophone* (August 1991).

Conductors tend to interpolate passages from several different scores, further complicating the identification of the version employed. The best that one can do under these circumstances is to identify the principal version and edition employed. Also, I have made no attempt to distinguish among relatively obscure variants, such as those found in the 1936 and 1944 printings of the Haas edition of the 1876 version of Symphony No. 5. Critics have used and continue to use a large vocabulary to cite various versions: "original version," "definitive version," "first definitive version," and "revised version" are among the most common terms. While such language may be employed with greater consistency now that the critical edition is nearing completion, I have elected to avoid such labels in favor of simply stating the year in which a version was completed, together with the editor's last name.

An index by conductor refers the user to all orchestral and choral recordings using the catalog numbers described above. Birth and death dates for conductors are given, together with the composition title, ensemble, record label, and year of recording. Also provided is an index of annotators, which lists the music discussed in each article, the record label and number, the release date of the recording, and the catalog number. A chronology of recordings based upon the year in which the performance was recorded cites title, performers, and catalog number. The orchestra index summarizes each ensemble's recording activity.

Names of performing ensembles are given in a standardized English format, except in cases like the Staatskapelle Dresden, for which no common English translations have appeared on records. Similarly (and despite the welter of mergers and acquisitions among record companies and the practice of sister firms distributing the same recordings in various countries under differing labels), label names are restricted to few variations and are given in full, with the exception of Deutsche Grammophon, which is abbreviated DG.

Timings may vary somewhat due to inherent difficulties in determining exactly when a movement begins and ends. Generally speaking, timings measured by me begin with the first audible tone of the composition and end when the last sound has died away. Audience applause and pauses between movements are not included in the timings. I have noted cases where timings vary significantly from information printed on the record jacket or liner notes.

Although my goal has been to provide a useable reference work, apprehendable without much explanation, I have included a list of abbreviations. The meaning of most of these will be obvious or at least entirely logical, I hope, to all readers. Suggestions for improvements in future editions of this work and, especially, corrections are most welcome. Please address such correspondence to the author, in care of Fallen Leaf Press, P.O. Box 10034, Berkeley, California 94709 USA.

Appreciation is also due my editor, Ann Basart, for her patience and guidance in seeing this project through, and to my wife, Helen, who assisted in timing many of the recordings and who encouraged me through fifty-eight performances of Symphony No. 4.

While it had occurred to me to provide the reader with my own recommendations on the various recordings cited herein, I have foregone such a personal indulgence. In an approach to justifying that decision let me cite my favorite recording, surely unrepresentative of the opinion of most critics, of Symphony No. 9: the 1965 performance of the Vienna Philharmonic Orchestra conducted by Zubin Mehta. To record collectors, recorded sound librarians, and to all listeners who have come to know the great diversity and beauty of Anton Bruckner's music, I dedicate this effort.

Lee T. Lovallo
Sacramento, California, August 1991

Vorwort

Die Länge und die technischen Anforderungen der Hauptwerke Anton Bruckners in Verbindung mit einem unter vielen Künstlern alten Vorurteil gegen seine Musik haben besonders in den U.S.A. den Empfang seiner Kompositionen gehindert. Nebst Tonbandaufnahmen, Musikkassetten, Compact Discs und jetzt Video Discs haben die Langspielplatten das hiesige Land so stark beeinflußt, daß Bruckners Musik allmählich viel höher geschätzt wird. Folgender Katalog lieferbarer Aufnahmen von Bruckners Musik dokumentiert den schnellen Aufschwung der Begeisterung über ein Gesamtwerk, das ein zahlreiches Publikum jetzt zu der schönsten musikalischen Kunst des neunzehnten Jahrhunderts zählt.

Obwohl es mein Ziel war, alle Aufnahmen von Bruckners Musik in allen Ausgaben und in allen Formaten in ein Verzeichnis aufzunehmen, ist der Bereich dieses Katalogs wegen praktischen Anforderungen beschränkt. Alle mir bekannten Aufnahmen sind eingeschlossen, aber nur die früheste vorhandene Ausgabe jeder Aufnahme wird ausführlich beschrieben. Neuausgaben, frühere aber nicht vorhandene Ausgaben, und Parallelausgaben in anderen Formaten erscheinen nur mit Schallplattenmarke und -nummer und Format. Auch wird das Land, wo die Ausgabe erscheint, nicht identifiziert. Weil die meisten Schallplattenfirmen jetzt wahrlich international handeln, ist es ziemlich sinnlos, eine einzelne Schallplatte z.B. als französisch oder als japanisch zu identifizieren, wenn derselbe Artikel in den USA oder in Großbritannien erhältlich ist, und wenn die Vertriebsfirma niederländisch sein mag. Genaue Auskünfte über Aufnahmeorte sind aber doch eingeschlossen.

Annähernd achthundert Aufführungen von Bruckners Musik werden so genau wie möglich dokumentiert, einschließlich Schallplatten von 78 Drehzahl pro Minute aus den dreißiger Jahren bis auf jetzt verfügbare Materialien in Digital-Video-Format. Wennmöglich und in allen Zwischenfällen habe ich mich auf ursprüngliche Quellen verlassen, insbesondere auf die ausgedehnte Aufnahmensammlung der California Friends of Bruckner in Sacramento. Auch habe ich Schallplatten in den Bibliotheken der University of California zu Berkeley und zu Davis, in der Musikbibliothek der California State University in Sacramento, und in der Stanford University Library and Archive of Recorded Sound in Stanford (Kalifornien) untersucht.

1989 hat Herr Michael Grey von der Smithsonian Institution die frühe Handschrift dieses Katalogs großmütig durchgehend geprüft, korrigiert, und weiter ausgeführt, wofür ich ihm herzlich danke. Die meisten Auskünfte über die neuerlichen japanischen Aufnahmen werden von Herrn Grey beigetragen. Die bahnbrechende Bruckner-Discographie von J.F. Weber war für die vorliegende Arbeit unentbehrlich. In ihrer Vollkommenheit und Genauigkeit diente sie mir sowohl als Motivation und als Vorbild. Andere Informationsquellen findet man in der Bibliographie.

Im Hauptteil der Discographie werden die Aufnahmen im allgemeinen nach Aufführungsmitteln präsentiert: Lieder und Chorwerke, Kammermusik, Orgelstücke, und Orchesterwerke. Innerhalb dieser Gruppen erscheinen die einzelnen Stücke serienmäßig nach dem Verzeichnis von Renate Grasberger, eine meistens alphabetische und logische Reihenfolge ergebend. Aufnahmen gleicher Werke von verschiedenen Aufführenden findet man hauptsächlich nach Dirigent, beziehungsweise bei Kammermusik nach Ensemble und bei Orgelmusik nach Solisten geordnet. Solche Angaben erscheinen verschlüsselt als Katalogziffern vor jedem Vermerk.

Einzelne Vermerke zeigen, wenn zweckmäßig, nach der nachstehenden Reihenfolge diese Informationen:
- Dirigent (oder Solist)
- aufführendes Ensemble
- eventuell mitwirkendes Ensemble
- Solisten (der normalen Partiturfolge nach)
- Ort und Datum der ursprünglichen Aufnahme
- Fertigungsjahr der gebrauchten Version und Herausgeber
- Quelle
- Schallplattenmarke und -nummer
- Aufnahmeformat ("digital" beschreibt ausschließlich die erste Phase des Aufnahmeverfahrens)
- Zahl der für dieses Stück benützten Plattenseiten
- Jahr der Plattenausgabe
- Zeitdauer (Totaldauer zuerst, dann die Dauer der einzelnen Sätze)
- Autor(en) der Erläuterungen
- andere Werke auf dem Tonträger

Quellenauskünfte für die Daten der ursprünglichen Aufnahme und für die Schallplattenausgaben versteht man durch die Abkürzungen, die vor jedem Datum stehen: "W." weist auf J.F. Webers Discographie hin; "p." bedeutet ein Phonorechts-Datum, "©" ein Urheberrechts-Datum, gewöhnlich auf dem Umschlag oder auf zugehörigen Bemerkungen; keine Abkürzung, oft mit genauem Monat vor dem Jahre, bedeutet ein auf exacter Anmerkung auf dem Umschlag basierendes Datum; "ca." heißt eine Vermutung, welche häufig auf einer indirekten Aufzeichnung beruht (z.B.: auf biographischen Informationen über einen Künstler).

Bezüglich der aufgenommenen Ausgaben wird dem Leser eine kurze Beschreibung der wichtigsten Fassungen jedes Stückes vor dessen erstem Vermerk gegeben. Solche Schilderungen beschränken sich auf den Ort, wo Bruckner die Version gefertigt hatte, das betreffende Datum, die Grasberger'sche Katalogziffer (WAB), und die Katalogziffer aus der Göllerich-Auer-Biographie (G/A). Danach zeigt jeder einzelne Vermerk nach dieser Werkbeschreibung das Herkunftsjahr der auf dieser Aufnahme gebrauchten Version und womöglich den Namen des Herausgebers. In manchen Fällen ist die Identifizierung der Ausgabe unwesentlich, denn die verschiedenen gedruckten modernen Quellen unterscheiden sich nur in geringstem Maße. Das gilt für die Sinfonien 5, 6, 7 und 9 sowie für die Kammermusik, die Orgelwerke, und die Mehrzahl der Chormusik. Also mag die Bezeichnung "n/a" (nicht vorhanden) an Stelle des Herausgebers im allgemeinen den Leser nicht beunruhigen. An anderen Stellen wurden die Ausgaben auf folgende Weise identifiziert: man bemerkt entsprechende Auskünfte auf dem Schallplattenumschlag oder auf beigelegten Notizen, man schlägt in früheren Discographien nach, oder man hört einfach der Musik zu und vergleicht dieselbe mit den gedruckten Partituren.

Eine neue, genaue Diskussion der Ausgaben samt einer kurzen, kritischen Diskographie erscheint in einem Artikel von Richard Osborne in der englischen Zeitschrift *Gramophone* (August 1991).

Der Identifizierungsprozeß wird noch komplizierter, da viele Dirigenten Passagen aus mehreren verschiedenen Partituren des gleichen Werks einfügen. Unter solchen Umständen führt man am besten die hauptsächlich gebrauchte Version und deren Herausgeber an. Übrigens versucht man nicht, verhältnismäßig obskure Variationen zu unterscheiden, wie z.B. die 1936 veröffentlichte Ausgabe und die 1944-Ausgabe der von Robert Haas herausgegebenen Partitur der Version 1876 der Sinfonie Nr. 5. Die Kritiker verwenden heute noch einen großen Wortschatz, um die vielen Versionen anzuführen: unter den am häufigsten gebrauchten Ausdrücken sind: ursprüngliche Fassung, endgültige Fassung, erste endgültige Fassung, revidierte Fassung, und Urtext. Obwohl man inskünftig solche Terminologie auf regelmäßigere Art benützen mag, im besonderen da die kritische Gesamtausgabe bald zu Ende gebracht wird, hat der Verfasser sich entschlossen, diese Bezeichnungen alle wegzulassen und an ihrer Stelle einfach das Fertigungsjahr der Fassung und den Familiennamen des Herausgebers zu erwähnen.

Das Dirigenten-Register umfaßt die Chor- und Orchesteraufnahmen und verwendet die oben erwähnten Katalogziffern. Samt dem Werktitel, dem Ensemblenamen und dem Jahre der Aufnahme erscheinen die Geburts- und Todesjahre der Dirigenten. Ein Register der Autoren der Erläuterungen verweist auf die Werktitel, die Erscheinungsdaten der Schallplatten, und die Katalogziffern. Eine Zeittafel stützt sich auf die Aufnahmedaten und bezeichnet den Titel, die Aufführenden und die Katalogziffer. Die Aktivität der verschiedenen Orchester wird durch das Orchester-Register dargelegt.

Trotz der heutigen Neigung vieler Ensembles ihre Namen in der einheimischen Sprache auszudrücken und ausgenommen von Fällen, wie z.B. bei der Staatskapelle Dresden, wobei früher keine englischen Übersetzungen auf Schallplatten erschienen sind, werden solche Bezeichnungen regelmäßig auf eine englische Art gegeben. Ungeachtet der Überfülle an geschäftlichen Verschmelzungen und Erwerbungen unter den Schallplattenunternehmen und trotz des Vertriebs der selben Aufnahmen unter verschiedenen Marken durch internationale, verwandte Firmen, beschränken sich die Schallplattenmarken auf wenige Variationen, welche mit der einzigen Ausnahme von "Deutsche Grammophon" ("DG") unverkürzt erscheinen.

Das Zeitmessen der Aufführungen ist nicht immer präzis, weil man manchmal auf Schwierigkeiten stößt, da der genaue Anfang und das genaue Ende einer Aufnahme sich nicht leicht feststellen lassen. Im allgemeinen beginnt die von dem Verfasser gemessene Dauer mit dem ersten hörbaren Ton und endet mit dem Ersterben des letzten Klangs. Das Beifallklatschen und die Pausen zwischen den Sätzen sind nicht eingeschlossen. In den Fällen, wenn die gemessene Dauer mit den auf dem Schallplattenumschlag oder beigelegten Anmerkungen gedruckten Zeiten nicht übereinstimmt, findet man brauchbare Vermerke.

Obwohl der Verfasser hier ein einfaches und leicht nützliches Nachschlagwerk anstrebt, das keiner längeren Einführung bedarf, folgt eine kurze Liste der gebrauchten Abkürzungen. Allen Lesern wird die Bedeutung der meisten dieser Zeichen hoffentlich selbstverständlich sein oder wenigstens ganz und gar logisch erscheinen. Vorschläge zum Verbessern dieses Katalogs sind höchst willkommen. Richten Sie bitte alle Korrespondenz an den Autor, c/o Fallen Leaf Press, P.O. Box 10034, Berkeley, California 94709, U.S.A.

Die Geduld und die zur Fertigstellung dieser Arbeit notwendige Beratung meiner Herausgeberin Frau Ann Basart verdient hohe Würdigung. Fräulein Eva Einstein und Herr und Frau René Stäldi haben sehr freundlich die deutsche Übersetzung durchgelesen und korrigiert. Danken möchte ich auch meiner Frau Helen für ihren Beistand, auch daß sie mir beim Zeitmessen der Aufnahmen half, und daß sie mich zum Zuhören von etwa fünfzig Aufführungen der Sinfonie Nr. 4 ermutigte.

Obwohl es mir eingefallen war, dem Leser mehrere eigene Empfehlungen über die Aufnahmen darzubieten, habe ich auf solch eine persönliche Befriedigung verzichtet. Um diesen Entschluß möglicherweise zu rechtfertigen, gebe ich hier meine Wahl—gewiß für die Meinung der meisten Kritiker nicht ausschlaggebend—zu der erhabensten Aufnahme der neunten Sinfonie: Zubin Mehta mit den Wiener Philharmonikern. Den Grammophonplattensammlern, den Schallplattenarchivisten, und allen Zuhörern, die die Vielfältigkeit und die Schönheit der Musik Anton Bruckners erlebt haben, widme ich bescheiden diesen Versuch.

Dr. Lee T. Lovallo
Sacramento, Kalifornien
im August 1991

Abbreviations

<	before the date given
b.	born
ca.	circa
CD	compact disc
CFB	California Friends of Bruckner
©	copyright
CST	Archive for Recorded Sound, Stanford
CSUS	California State University, Sacramento
DG	Deutsche Grammophon (Gesellschaft)
ed.	editor
G/A	Göllerich-Auer biography and list of works
LP	long-playing record
MG	Michael Grey, discographer
n/a	not available
p.	phonoright (recorded sound copyright)
rel.	released
s or ss	side(s)
SU	Stanford University
UCB	University of California, Berkeley
UCD	University of California, Davis
W.	*Bruckner*, Discography Series X, J. F. Weber
WAB	*Werkverzeichnis Anton Bruckner*, R. Grasberger
WERM	*The World's Encylopaedia of Recorded Music*, F. F. Clough and G. J. Cuming

Choral and Vocal Works

Afferentur regi (WAB 1, G/A 53)

Andante. In F Major. Composed in Linz in 1861 for four-part mixed choir. Originally a cappella, later with three trombones or organ accompaniment.

1001.BG0   Bertola, Giulio
Coro Polifonico Italiano
Recorded W. 1965, ed. n/a 1861
Issue: Musical Heritage Society MHS 1552, 1 stereo LP, 1 s [CFB], W. 1973
Timing: 1.56
Notes: Edward D. R. Neill
With Bruckner: Te Deum and four other motets
Other issues: Angelicum LPA 5989/STA 8989

1001.BM0   Best, Matthew
Corydon Singers
Recorded in St. Alban's Church, Holborn, London: May 1982, ed. n/a 1861
Issue: Hyperion A66062, 1 stereo LP, 1 s [CFB], p. 1983
Timing: 1.52
Notes: Douglas Hammond
With Bruckner: ten other motets
Other issues: Hyperion CD 66062 (CD)

1001.FA5   Flämig, Martin
Dresdner Kreuzchor; M. Zeumer, H. Kästner, H. Hombsch, tbns.
Recorded in Lukaskirche, Dresden: January 1985, ed. n/a 1861
Issue: Capriccio 10 081, 1 digital stereo CD, 1 s [CFB], p. 1987
Timing: 1.42
Notes: Hans Rutesame
With Bruckner: thirteen other motets
Other issues: Capriccio C 27 099, CC 27 099 (cassette), Delta 10 081 (CD), C 27 099, CC 27 099 (cassette)

1001.FJ0   Fuchs, Johannes
Zurich Chamber Choir, Slokar Trombone Quartet
Recorded in Reformed Church, Zürich-Altstetten: September 1984, ed. n/a 1861
Issue: Ex Libris CD 6009, 1 digital stereo CD, 1 s [CFB], p. 1985
Timing: 1.48
Notes: Alois Koch

With Bruckner: two Æquale and ten
other motets
Other issues: Koch Records Schwann
16 970

1001.GE0   Gronostay, Uwe
Denmark Radio Choir
Recorded in Trinitatis Church, Co-
penhagen: August 1985, ed. n/a
1861
Issue: Kontrapunkt 32022, 1 stereo CD,
1 s [CFB], p. 1989
Timing: 1.51
Notes: Knut Ketting
With Bruckner: nine other motets and
Werner: *Hommage à Bruckner*

1001.GG0   Guest, George
Choir of St. John's College, Cambridge
Recorded p. 1973, ed. n/a 1861
Issue: Argo ZRG 760, 1 stereo LP, 1 s
[CFB], W. 1974
Timing: 1.28
Notes: Peter Dennison
With Bruckner: four other motets and
Liszt: Missa choralis

1001.JE0   Jochum, Eugen
Chorus of the Bavarian Radio
Recorded 24-26 June 1966, ed. n/a 1861
Issue: DG 2720 054, 5 stereo LPs, 1 s
[CFB], ca. 1981
Timing: 2.00
Notes: Wolfgang Dömling
With Bruckner: Masses Nos. 1-3, Te
Deum, Psalm 150, motets
Other issues: DG 2530 139, 423 127-2
(CD)

1001.MJ0   Martini, Joachim
Junge Kantorei, Darmstadt
Recorded ca. 1973, ed. n/a 1861
Issue: BASF KMB 21336, 1 stereo LP,
1 s [CFB], W. 1973
Timing: 1.27
Notes: Lothar Hoffmann-Erbrecht
With Bruckner: Mass No. 2, two other
motets
Other issues: ABC AB-67021 [CFB]

1001.RT0   Rehmann, Theodor
Aachen Cathedral Choir
Recorded < 1945, ed. n/a 1861
Issue: Polydor 62892, 78, 1 s
With Bruckner: other choral works
Other issues: Polydor 32141 NL (45)

1001.RT5   Reichel, Helmuth
Zürcher Bach-Kantorei
Recorded in Reformed Church, Zürich-
Oerlikon: June 1981, ed. n/a 1861
Issue: Fono Schallplatten FCD 91 229,
1 stereo CD, 1 s [CFB], p. 1990
Timing: 1.55
Notes: Kurt Pahlen
With Bruckner: nine other motets
Other issues: Fono Schallplatten FSM
53 229

1001.SW0   Schäfer, Wolfgang
Freiburg Vocal Ensemble
Recorded in Church of St. Barbara,
Freiburg-Littenweiler: p. 1984, ed.
n/a 1861
Issue: Christophorus CD 74501, 1 digi-
tal stereo CD, 1 s [CFB], © 1984
Timing: 1.56
With Bruckner: nine other motets
Other issues: Christophorus SCGLX
74009

1001.ZH0   Zanotelli, Hans
   Philharmonisches Vocalensemble
   Stuttgart
   Recorded ca. 1987, ed. n/a 1861

Issue: Calig CAL 30 477, 1 stereo LP,
   1 s, ca. 1987
With Bruckner: eleven other motets

Asperges me (WAB 4, G/A 86)

Moderato. In F Major. Composed in Linz in 1868 for four-part mixed choir.

1004.BM0   Breitschaft, Mathias
   Limburger Dom-Singknaben
   Recorded ca. 1977, ed. n/a 1868

Issue: Carus FSM 53 1 18, 1 stereo LP,
   1 s, ca. 1977
With Bruckner: eight other motets and
   Palestrina: eight motets

Ave Maria (WAB 5, G/A 48)

Andante. In F Major. Composed at St. Florian in 1856 for four-part mixed choir with soprano and alto solos, organ and violoncello.

1005.FA5   Flämig, Martin
   Dresdner Kreuzchor
   Recorded in Lukaskirche, Dresden:
     January 1985, ed. n/a 1856
   Issue: Capriccio 10 081, 1 digital stereo
     CD, 1 s [CFB], p. 1987

Timing: 4.49
Notes: Hans Rutesame
With Bruckner: thirteen other motets
Other issues: Capriccio C 27 099, CC 27
   099 (cassette), Delta 10 081 (CD),
   C 27 099, CC 27 099 (cassette)

Ave Maria (WAB 6, G/A 52)

Andante (Sehr langsam). In F Major. Composed in Linz in 1861 for seven-part mixed choir.

1006.AJ0   Alldis, John
   John Alldis Choir
   Recorded p. 1967, ed. n/a 1861
   Issue: Argo ZRG 523, 1 stereo LP, 1 s
     [CFB], W. 1968
   Timing: 3.27
   Notes: Robert Henderson

With choral works by Bruckner,
   Schönberg, Debussy and Messiaen
Other issues: Decca SXL 21177

1006.AR0   Arndt, Günther
   Berlin Handel Chorus
   Recorded p. 1962, ed. n/a 1861

Issue: Musikfest 413 671-1, 1 stereo LP,
1 s [CFB], ca. 1980
Timing: 3.58
With works by nine other composers
Other issues: DG 19366/136366 (cassette), 415 892-2, 415 753-1, 415 892-
1 (cassette), 2535 682 (cassette), 2535
609 (cassette), 2310 255, and 17258
(45)

1006.BA5   Bader, Roland
St. Hedwig's Cathedral Choir, Berlin
Recorded ca. 1987, ed. n/a 1861
Issue: Ariola 202 180-366, 2 stereo LPs,
1 s, ca. 1987
With ten other choral works by various
composers

1006.BL0   Berberich, Ludwig
Munich Cathedral Choir
Recorded W. 1931, ed. n/a 1861
Issue: Christschall 118, 1 10" mono 78,
1 s [CST], 3.27
With Bruckner: Tantum ergo
Other issues: Homochord 2024

1006.BM0   Best, Matthew
Corydon Singers
Recorded in St. Alban's Church, Hol-
born, London: May 1982, ed. n/a
1861
Issue: Hyperion A66062, 1 stereo LP,
1 s [CFB], p. 1983
Timing: 4.00
Notes: Douglas Hammond
With Bruckner: ten other motets
Other issues: Hyperion CD 66 062 (CD)

1006.BM0h Böck, Herbert
Concentus Vocalis Wien
Recorded in Vienna: © 1988

Issue: Koch 317 008 H1, 1 stereo CD,
1 s [CFB], p. 1988
Timing: 3.25
With Distler: Totentanz

1006.BM1   Breitschaft, Mathias
Limburger Dom-Singknaben
Recorded ca. 1977, ed. n/a 1861
Issue: Carus FSM 53 1 18, 1 stereo LP,
1 s, ca. 1977
With Bruckner: eight other motets and
Palestrina: eight motets
Other issues: Carus 63 107

1006.BR0   Bradshaw, Richard
Saltarello Choir
Recorded in Church of St. Bartholo-
mew The Great, Smithfield, Lon-
don: p. 1974, ed. n/a 1861
Issue: CRD 1009, 1 stereo LP, 1 s [CFB],
p. 1974
Timing: 3.18
Notes: Anonymous
With Bruckner: four other motets and
works by Brahms and Verdi

1006.FA0   Flämig, Martin
Dresdner Kreuzchor
Recorded in Lukaskirche, Dresden:
January 1985, ed. n/a 1861
Issue: Capriccio 10 081, 1 digital stereo
CD, 1 s [CFB], p. 1987
Timing: 3.26
Notes: Hans Rutesame
With Bruckner: thirteen other motets
Other issues: Capriccio C 27 099, CC 27
099 (cassette), Delta 10 081 (CD), C
27 099, CC 27 099 (cassette),
Laserlight 15 278 (CD) [CFB]

1006.FE5   Forster, Karl
St. Hedwig's Cathedral Choir
Recorded < 1948, ed. n/a 1861
Issue: Electrola EG 8536, 78
Other issues: Electrola 17-8536 and E
40063 (45)

1006.FF0   Fries, Felix
Les Rossignols de Bruxelles
Recorded ca. 1960, ed. n/a 1861
Issue: Alpha 1002, 45, 1 s

1006.FH0   Froschauer, Hellmut
Singverein der Gesellschaft der Musik-
freunde
Recorded ca. 1958, ed. n/a 1861
Issue: Preiser SPR 3219, 1 LP, 1 s

1006.FU0   Fuchs, Johannes
Zurich Chamber Choir
Recorded in Reformed Church, Zürich-
Altstetten: September 1984, ed. n/a
1861
Issue: Ex Libris CD 6009, 1 digital ste-
reo CD, 1 s [CFB], p. 1985
Timing: 3.35
Notes: Alois Koch
With Bruckner: two Æquale and ten
other motets
Other issues: Koch Records Schwann
16 970

1006.GA5   Garbers, Wilfried
Herrenhäuser Chorgemeinschaft
Recorded ca. 1986, ed. n/a 1861
Issue: Sound Star Ton SST 0 152,
1 stereo LP, 1 s, ca. 1986
With Bruckner: Locus iste and four-
teen other choral works by various
composers

1006.GH0   Gillesberger, Hans
Vienna Kammerchor
Recorded ca. 1964, ed. n/a 1861
Issue: Lyrichord LLST 7136 (mono=LL
136), 1 stereo LP, 1 s [CFB], W. 1964
Timing: 3.35
Notes: Victor Chapin
With Bruckner: Mass No. 2 and Locus
iste
Other issues: Christophorus CGLP
75823/SCGLP 75824
Probably identical to 1006.GH1

1006.GH1   Gillesberger, Hans
Vienna Academy Chamber Choir
Recorded W. 1960, ed. n/a 1861
Issue: Austria Vanguard AVRS 6064, 1
mono LP, 1 s [UCB], W. 1963
Timing: 3.36
Notes: Anonymous
With Bruckner: four other motets and
Heiller: two motets
Other issues: Lyrichord LLST 7136,
Christophorus CGLP 75823, Record
Society RS 71, Amadeo AVRS 6064,
Amadeo 15084 (45)

1006.GH2   Gillesberger, Hans
Vienna Choir Boys, Chorus Viennensis
Recorded p. 1972, ed. n/a 1861
Issue: Acanta 41 232, 1 stereo CD, 1 s
[CFB], p. 1988
Timing: 3.25
Notes: Gerhard Schuhmacher
With Bruckner: four other motets and
Britten: Ceremonies of Carols
Other issues: BASF KBB 21232

1006.GH5   Günther, Hubert
Rhenish Choral Society
Recorded ca. 1976, ed. 1861

Issue: Garnet 40107, 1 stereo LP, 1 s, ca. 1976
With Bruckner: ten other brief pieces
Other issues: Garnet 40 170

1006.GH6 Gronostay, Uwe
Denmark Radio Choir
Recorded in Trinitatis Church, Copenhagen: August 1985, ed. n/a 1861
Issue: Kontrapunkt 32022, 1 stereo CD, 1 s [CFB], p. 1989
Timing: 3.23
Notes: Knut Ketting
With Bruckner: nine other motets and Werner: *Hommage à Bruckner*

1006.HA5 Hausmann, Elmar
Capella Vocale St. Aposteln, Cologne
Recorded ca. 1986, ed. n/a 1861
Issue: Aulos 53 569, 1 stereo LP, 1 s, ca. 1986
With Bruckner: Missa Solemnis and three motets

1006.HA5 Herreweghe, Philippe
La Chapelle Royale
Recorded November 1989
Issue: Harmonia mundi HMC 901322, 1 digital stereo CD, 1 ss [CFB], p. 1990
Timing: 3.35
Notes: Jean-Yves Bras
With Bruckner: Mass No. 2, Æquale I and II, four other motets

1006.HD0 Hellmann, Diethard
Bach Choir of Mainz
Recorded p. 1979, ed. n/a 1882
Issue: Calig CAL 30 469, 1 stereo LP, 1 s [CFB], p. 1979
Timing: 3.50

Notes: Anonymous "U.M."
With Bruckner: four other motets and Kodály: *Laudes organi*

1006.HE0 Herzog, Franz
Göttinger Boys' Choir
Recorded ca. 1960, ed. n/a 1861
Issue: Telefunken SMT 1110, LP, 1 s

1006.HL0 Hoch, Alphonse
Strasbourg Cathedral Choir
Recorded ca. 1940, ed. n/a 1861
Issue: Columbia RFX 71, 1 mono 78, 1 s
With Josquin: "Tu pauperum refugium"
Other issues: French release

1006.JE0 Jochum, Eugen
Chorus of the Bavarian Radio
Recorded 24-26 June 1966, ed. n/a 1861
Issue: DG 2720 054, 5 stereo LPs, 1 s [CFB], ca. 1981
Timing: 3.58
Notes: Wolfgang Dömling
With Bruckner: Masses 1-3, Te Deum, Psalm 150, motets
Other issues: DG 39134-5/139134-5, 2707 025, 136552, 423 127-2 (CD)

1006.KA0 Kalt, Pius
St. Hedwig's Cathedral Choir
Recorded < 1925, ed. n/a 1861
Issue: His Master's Voice HMV 66115, acoustic 78, 1 s

1006.KH0 Kramm, Herma
Münster Madrigal Choir
Recorded ca. 1970, ed. n/a 1861
Issue: Quadriga-Ton BBQ 2001, LP, 1 s
Other issues: Jubilate BBQ 2001

1006.LA0   Lippe, Anton
St. Hedwig's Cathedral Choir
Recorded ca. 1958, ed. n/a 1861
Issue: Telefunken SMT 1078, LP, 1 s
Other issues: Telefunken NT 261

1006.MA0   Martini, Joachim
Darmstadt Junge Kantorei
Recorded ca. 1971, ed. n/a 1861
Issue: Schwarzwald 13004, 1 stereo LP,
   1 s
Other issues: Schwarzwald CRO 833,
   2520833

1006.MA2   Matkowitz, Wolfgang
Heinrich-Schütz-Kreis Berlin
Recorded ca. 1986, ed. n/a 1861
Issue: Pape Nocturne NC 4, 1 stereo
   LP, 1 s, ca. 1986
With thirteen other choral works by
   various composers

1006.MA5   Mauersberger, Rudolf
Dresden Kreuzchor
Recorded < 1948, ed. n/a 1861
Issue: Electrola EG 3568, 1 mono 78,
   1 s
With a setting of "Innsbruck, ich muß
   dich lassen"

1006.ME0   Meyer, Xaver
Vienna Academy Kammerchor
Recorded ca. 1975, ed. n/a 1861
Issue: Mace MCS 9061, 1 stereo LP, 1 s
   [CFB], ca. 1975
Timing: 3.52
Notes: Hope Sheridan
With Bruckner: Os justi and choral
   works by four other composers
Other issues: Amadeo AVRS 6343

1006.ME1   Meyer, Xaver
Vienna Choir Boys
Recorded ca. 1958, ed. n/a 1861
Issue: Electrola C 048 28124, LP, 1 s
Other issues: Electrola E 20252 (45)

1006.MG0   Miller, Gary
New York City Gay Men's Chorus
Recorded in Flatbush Dutch Reformed
   Church, New York: May 1983, ed.
   n/a 1861
Issue: Pro Arte PAD 159, 1 digital ste-
   reo LP, 1 s [CFB], p. 1983
Timing: 3.19
Notes: Gary W. Miller
With choral works by ten other com-
   posers

1006.MT0   Mittergradnegger, Günther
Klagenfurt Madrigal Chorus
Recorded ca. 1975, ed. n/a 1861
Issue: Mace MCS 9078, 1 stereo LP, 1 s
   [CFB], ca. 1975
Timing: 3.44
Notes: Anonymous
With choral works by thirteen other
   composers
Other issues: Amadeo AVRS 5051

1006.MT1   Möller, Edith
Obernkirchen Children's Choir
Recorded ca. 1965, ed. n/a 1861
Issue: London 5895/OS 25895, LP, 1 s,
   W. 1965
Other issues: Telefunken SLE 14391

1006.PC0   Peloquin, C. Alexander
Peloquin Chorale
Recorded ca. 1960, ed. n/a 1861
Issue: Gregorian Institute EL 18, LP,
   1 s, W. 1960

Other issues: Gregorian Institute set
EL 100

1006.PP0   Pernoud, Pierre
La Psallette de Genève
Recorded ca. 1970, ed. n/a 1861
Issue: Disques VDE VDE 3044, 1 stereo
    LP, 1 s [CFB], ca. 1988
Timing: 3.35
Notes: Anonymous
With Bruckner: four other motets and
    Brahms: 3 motets
Schwann cites "Gallo" as record label.

1006.PW0   Pitz, Wilhelm
New Philharmonia Chorus
Recorded 16-18 November 1966, ed.
    n/a 1861
Issue: Angel S-36428, 1 stereo LP, 1 s
    [CFB], W. 1967
Timing: 3.08
Notes: Paul Jennings, W.A. Chislett
With Bruckner: four other motets and
    works by five other composers
Other issues: EMI ASD 2325, SME
    81046, EMI 037-30 954, 237-30 954
    (cassette)

1006.RT0   Rehmann, Theodor
Aachen Cathedral Choir
Recorded W. 1955, ed. n/a 1861
Issue: Polydor 62892, 1 mono 78, 1 s
Other issues: Polydor 32141 NL (45)

1006.RT5   Rinscheid, Michael
Singkreis Wehbach
Recorded ca. 1987, ed. n/a 1861
Issue: Elrec M 3 E 3177, 1 stereo LP, 1 s,
    ca. 1987
With Bruckner: Locus iste and fifteen
    other choral works by various com-
    posers

Other issues: Elrec CM 3 E 3177 (cassette)

1006.RT5   Reichel, Helmuth
Zürcher Bach-Kantorei
Recorded in Reformed Church, Zürich-
    Oerlikon: June 1981, ed. n/a 1861
Issue: Fono Schallplatten FCD 91 229, 1
    stereo CD, 1 s [CFB], p. 1990
Timing: 3.03
Notes: Kurt Pahlen
With Bruckner: nine other motets
Other issues: Fono Schallplatten FSM
    53 229

1006.SW0   Schäfer, Wolfgang
Freiburg Vocal Ensemble
Recorded in Church of St. Barbara,
    Freiburg-Littenweiler: p. 1984, ed.
    n/a 1861
Issue: Christophorus CD 74501, 1 digi-
    tal stereo CD, 1 s [CFB], © 1984
Timing: 3.52
With Bruckner: nine other motets
Other issues: Christophorus SCGLX
    74 009, 74 059F, CD74 539 (CD)

1006.SW1   Schrems, Theobald
Regensburger Domspatzen
Recorded ca. 1974, ed. n/a 1861
Issue: Musical Heritage Society MHS
    1935, 1 stereo LP, 1 s [UCD]
Timing: 3.02
With Bruckner: Virga Jesse and thir-
    teen other choral works by various
    composers
Other issues: Christophorus SCGLP
    75969, CV 75011 (45)

1006.SW3 Schweizer, Rolf
Pforzheim Motettenchor
Recorded W. 1976, ed. n/a 1861
Issue: Da Camera Magna SM 94048,
  1 stereo LP, 1 s, W. 1976
With Bruckner: Christus factus est and
  Os justi and Brahms: various works

1006.SW4 Smith, Jack
Keighly Vocal Union
Recorded ca. 1960, ed. n/a 1861
Issue: Calrec RF 352, LP, 1 s

1006.TK0 Thomas, Kelvin
Silver Ring Choir of Bath
Recorded ca. 1969, ed. n/a 1861
Issue: Music for Pleasure SMfP 1304,
  LP, 1 s, W. 1969

1006.WG0 Wilhelm, Gerhard
Stuttgarter Hymnus-Chorknaben
Recorded ca. 1986, ed. n/a 1861
Issue: Intercord 160 801, 1 stereo LP,
  1 s, ca. 1986

With Bruckner: Tantum ergo and
twelve other works by various composers
Other issues: Intercord K 29726, 185
815

1006.WH0 Wormsbächer, Hellmut
Bergedorfer Chamber Choir
Recorded ca. 1960, ed. n/a 1861
Issue: Telefunken SLT 43115, 1 stereo
  LP, 1 s [UCD]
Timing: 2.50
Notes: Anonymous
With fifteen other choral works by
  Romantic composers

1006.ZH0 Zanotelli, Hans
Philharmonisches Vocalensemble
Stuttgart
Recorded ca. 1987, ed. n/a 1861
Issue: Calig CAL 30 477, 1 stereo LP,
  1 s, ca. 1987
With Bruckner: eleven other motets

Ave regina coelorum (WAB 8, G/A without number)

Composed ca. 1886 for unison voices with organ accompaniment.

1008.L_0 Loré
Petit Chanteurs de la Notre-Dame de la
  Joie
Recorded W. 1968, ed. n/a 1886
Issue: R.C.A. 840 005, LP, 1 s

1008.PP0 Pernoud, Pierre
La Psallette de Genève
Recorded ca. 1970, ed. n/a 1886
Issue: Disques VDE VDE 3044, 1 stereo
  LP, 1 s [CFB], ca. 1988
Timing: 2.02

Notes: Anonymous
With Bruckner: four other motets and
  Brahms: three motets
Organ part is assigned to choir.

1008.RT0 Rehmann, Theodor
Aachen Cathedral Choir
Recorded < 1948, ed. n/a 1886
Issue: Polydor 62892, 78, 1 s
With Bruckner: other choral works
Other issues: Polydor 32141 NL (45)

Mass for Holy Thursday (WAB 9, G/A 8)

In F Major. Composed in 1844 for four-part mixed choir possibly at Kronstorf.

1009.PJ0   Peerik, Jan S.
Ensemble Vocal Raphael
Recorded ca. 1987, ed. Bauernfeind/
    Nowak 1844

Issue: Elrec G 3 E 3226, 1 stereo LP, 1 s,
    ca. 1987
With Bruckner: Locus iste and seven
    choral works by various composers

Christus factus est (WAB 11, G/A 112)

Moderato misterioso. In d minor. Composed in 1884 in Vienna for four-part mixed choir.

1011.AJ0   Alldis, John
John Alldis Choir
Recorded p. 1967, ed. n/a 1884
Issue: Argo ARG 523, 1 stereo LP, 1 s
    [CFB], W. 1968
Timing: 4.51
Notes: Robert Henderson
With choral works of Bruckner,
    Schönberg, Debussy, and Messiaen
Other issues: Decca SXL 21177

1011.BK0   Beringer, Karl-Friedrich
Windsbacher Knabenchor
Recorded ca. 1986, ed. n/a 1884
Issue: Bellaphon 680 05 001, 1 stereo
    LP, 1 s, ca. 1986
With Bruckner: Locus iste and Os justi
    and four other choral works by vari-
    ous composers

1011.BM0   Best, Matthew
Corydon Singers
Recorded in St. Alban's Church, Hol-
    born, London: May 1982, ed. n/a
    1884
Issue: Hyperion A66062, 1 stereo LP,
    1 s [CFB], p. 1983

Timing: 5.25
Notes: Douglas Hammond
With Bruckner: ten other motets
Other issues: Hyperion CD 66062 (CD)

1011.BO0   Böck, Herbert
Concentus Vocalis Wien
Recorded in Vienna: COP 1988
Issue: Koch 317 008 H1, 1 stereo CD,
    1 s [CFB], p. 1988
Timing: 5.05
With Distler: *Totentanz*

1011.BR0   Bradshaw, Richard
Saltarello Choir
Recorded in Church of St. Bartholo-
    mew The Great, Smithfield, Lon-
    don: p. 1974, ed. n/a 1884
Issue: CRD 1009, 1 stereo LP, 1 s [CFB],
    p. 1974
Timing: 4.25
Notes: Anonymous
With Bruckner: four other motets and
    works by Brahms and Verdi

1011.BT0   Breitschaft, Mathias
Limburger Dom-Singknaben

Recorded ca. 1977, ed. n/a 1868
Issue: Carus FSM 53118, 1 stereo LP,
1 s, ca. 1977
With Bruckner: seven other motets and
Palestrina: eight motets

1011.FA5   Flänig, Martin
Dresdner Kreuzchor
Recorded in Lukaskirche, Dresden:
January 1985, ed. n/a 1884
Issue: Capriccio 10 081, 1 digital stereo
CD, 1 s [CFB], p. 1987
Timing: 4.53
Notes: Hans Rutesame
With Bruckner: thirteen other motets
Other issues: Capriccio C 27 099, CC 27
099 (cassette), Delta 10 081 (CD), C
27 099, CC 27 099 (cassette)

1011.FJ0   Fuchs, Johannes
Zurich Chamber Choir
Recorded in Reformed Church, Zürich-
Altstetten: September 1984, ed. n/a
1884
Issue: Ex Libris CD 6009, 1 digital ste-
reo CD, 1 s [CFB], p. 1985
Timing: 6.48
Notes: Alois Koch
With Bruckner: two Æquale and ten
other motets
Other issues: Koch Records Schwann
16 970

1011.GH0   Gillesberger, Hans
Vienna Academy Chamber Choir
Recorded W. 1960, ed. n/a 1884
Issue: Austria Vanguard AVRS 6064,
1 mono LP, 1 s [UCB], W. 1963
Timing: 5.26
With Bruckner: four other motets and
Heiller: two motets

Other issues: Record Society RS 71,
Amadeo AVRS 6064, Amadeo 15085
(45)

1011.GH1   Gillesberger, Hans
Vienna Choir Boys, Chorus Viennensis
Recorded p. 1972, ed. n/a 1884
Issue: Acanta 41 232, 1 stereo CD, 1 s
[CFB], p. 1988
Timing: 5.07
Notes: Gerhard Schuhmacher
With Bruckner: four other motets and
Britten: Ceremonies of Carols
Other issues: BASF KBB 21232

1011.GR0   Graham, Melva Treffinger
Grace Church Choir of Gentlemen and
Boys
Recorded in Grace Church on-the-Hill,
Toronto: May 1990, ed. n/a
Issue: Grace Church GC 02, 1 digital
stereo CD, 1 s, November 1990
Timing: 4.25
With Bruckner: two other motets and
works by other composers
Other issues: Grace Church GC 02 (cas-
sette)

1011.GU0   Gronostay, Uwe
Denmark Radio Choir
Recorded in Trinitatis Church,
Copenhagen: August 1985, ed. n/a
1884
Issue: Kontrapunkt 32022, 1 stereo CD,
1 s [CFB], p. 1989
Timing: 4.43
Notes: Knut Ketting
With Bruckner: nine other motets and
Werner: *Hommage à Bruckner*

1011.GW0 Gönnenwein, Wolfgang
Stuttgart Madrigal Choir
Recorded in Ev. Frauenkirche, Ess-
lingen/Neckar: July 1962, ed. n/a
1884
Issue: Cantate 640 230, 1 mono LP, 1 s
[UCB]
Timing: 5.44
Notes: Cornelia Auerbach-Schröder
With Bruckner: three other motets and
Brahms: three motets
Other issues: Cantate 650 230, 656 013

1011.GW1 Guest, George
Berkshire Boy Choir
Recorded W. 1967, ed. n/a 1884
Issue: [private label] U3RS 8846, LP,
1 s

1011.HA5 Hahn, Hans Helmut
St. Jakobschor Rothenburg, Sing-
gemeinschaft Petersaurach
Recorded in St. Jacob's Church,
Rothenburg: ca. 1986, ed. n/a 1884
Issue: Pelca PSR 40 620, 1 stereo LP,
1 s, ca. 1986
With Bruckner: three other motets and
three works by various composers

1011.HD0 Hellmann, Diethard
Bach Choir of Mainz
Recorded p. 1979, ed. n/a 1884
Issue: Calig CAL 30 469, 1 stereo LP,
1 s [CFB], p. 1979
Timing: 4.53
Notes: Anonymous "U.M."
With Bruckner: four other motets and
Kodály: Laudes organi

1011.HP0 Herreweghe, Philippe
La Chapelle Royale
Recorded November 1989

Issue: Harmonia mundi HMC 901322,
1 digital stereo CD, 1 s [CFB], p.
1990
Timing: 6.05
Notes: Jean-Yves Bras
With Bruckner: Mass No. 2, Æquale I
and II, four other motets

1011.JE0   Jochum, Eugen
Chorus of the Bavarian Radio
Recorded 24-26 June 1966, ed. n/a 1884
Issue: DG 2720 054, 5 stereo LPs, 1 s
[CFB], W. 1966
Timing: 5.54
Notes: Wolfgang Dömling
With Bruckner: Masses Nos. 1-3, Te
Deum, Psalm 150, motets
Other issues: DG 39137-8/139137-8,
2707 026, 136552, 423 127-2 (CD),
SLGM 1412/4, MGX 9917/8, DG 15
MG 3030, DG 413 512-1

1011.MJ0   Martini, Joachim
Darmstadt Junge Kantorei
Recorded ca. 1971, ed. n/a 1884
Issue: Schwarzwald 13004, LP, 1 s
Other issues: Schwarzwald CRO 833
and 2520833

1011.PP0   Pernoud, Pierre
La Psallette de Genève
Recorded ca. 1970, ed. n/a 1884
Issue: Disques VDE VDE 3044, 1 stereo
LP, 1 s [CFB], ca. 1988
Timing: 5.35
Notes: Anonymous
With Bruckner: four other motets and
Brahms: three motets
Schwann gives "Gallo" as record label.

1011.PW0 Pitz, Wilhelm
New Philharmonia Chorus
Recorded 16-18 November 1966, ed.
n/a 1884
Issue: Angel S-36428, 1 stereo LP, 1 s
[CFB], W. 1967
Timing: 4.30
Notes: Paul Jennings, W.A. Chislett
With Bruckner: four other motets and
works by five other composers
Other issues: EMI ASD 2325, SME 81046

1011.RE5 Reichel, Helmuth
Zürcher Bach-Kantorei
Recorded in Reformed Church, Zürich-
Oerlikon: June 1981, ed. n/a 1884
Issue: Fono Schallplatten FCD 91 229,
1 stereo CD, 1 s [CFB], p. 1990
Timing: 5.55
Notes: Kurt Pahlen
With Bruckner: nine other motets
Other issues: Fono Schallplatten FSM
53 229

1011.RH0 Rilling, Helmut
Figuralchor Stuttgart
Recorded ca. 1986, ed. n/a 1884
Issue: Intercord 185 815, 5 stereo LPs,
1 s, ca. 1986
With Bruckner: three other motets and
26 other choral works by various
composers
Other issues: Intercord 722 05 SB

1011.SW0 Schäfer, Wolfgang
Freiburg Vocal Ensemble
Recorded in Church of St. Barbara,
Freiburg-Littenweiler: p. 1984, ed.
n/a 1884
Issue: Christophorus CD 74501, 1 digi-
tal stereo CD, 1 s [CFB], © 1984

Timing: 5.26
With Bruckner: nine other motets
Other issues: Christophorus SCGLX
74 009

1011.SW1 Schauerte, Gustav
Paderborn Cathedral Choir
Recorded W. 1928, ed. n/a 1884
Issue: Polydor 27137, 78, 1 s
Other issues: Grammophone J 65014
(78)

1011.SW3 Schweizer, Rolf
Pforzheim Motettenchor
Recorded W. 1976, ed. n/a 1879
Issue: Da Camera Magna SM 94048,
1 stereo LP, 1 s, W. 1976
With Bruckner: Ave Maria and Os justi
and Brahms: various works

1011.SW5 Sonnenschmidt, Jürgen
Bezirkskantorei Pirmasens
Recorded ca. 1986, ed. n/a 1884
Issue: Spirella Spi 2704 XC, 1 stereo LP,
1 s, ca. 1986
With Bruckner: Os justi and seven other
works by various composers

1011.WT0 Westphalian Trombone
Quartet
Recorded p. 1982, ed. n/a 1884
Issue: MD+G L 3094, 1 digital stereo
CD, 1 s [CFB], p. 1982
Timing: 5.41
Notes: Joachim Thalmann
With Bruckner: Locus iste and works
by Sweelinck, Serocki, Staden and
Bozza
Other issues: Mdg G 1094

1011.ZH0 Zanotelli, Hans
Philharmonisches Vocalensemble
Stuttgart
Recorded ca. 1987, ed. n/a 1884

Issue: Calig CAL 30 477, 1 stereo LP,
1 s, ca. 1987
With Bruckner: eleven other motets

Ecce sacerdos (WAB 13, G/A 115)

Maestoso. In a minor. Composed in 1885 in Vienna for eight-part mixed choir, three trombones and organ.

1013.BM0 Best, Matthew
Corydon Singers
Recorded in St. Alban's Church,
Holborn, London: May 1982, ed. n/
a 1885
Issue: Hyperion A66062, 1 stereo LP,
1 s [CFB], p. 1983
Timing: 5.05
Notes: Douglas Hammond
With Bruckner: ten other motets
Other issues: Hyperion CD 66062 (CD)

1013.FA5 Flämig, Martin
Dresdner Kreuzchor, M. Winkler, organ
Recorded in Lukaskirche, Dresden:
January 1985, ed. n/a 1885
Issue: Capriccio 10 081, 1 digital stereo
CD, 1 s [CFB], p. 1987
Timing: 5.54
Notes: Hans Rutesame
With Bruckner: thirteen other motets
Other issues: Capriccio C 27 099, CC
27 099 (cassette), Delta 10 081 (CD),
C 27 099, CC 27 099 (cassette)

1013.FJ0 Fuchs, Johannes
Zurich Chamber Choir, Slokar Trombone Quartet

Recorded in Reformed Church, Zürich-
Altstetten: September 1984, ed. n/a
1885
Issue: Ex Libris CD 6009, 1 digital stereo CD, 1 s [CFB], p. 1985
Timing: 5.03
Notes: Alois Koch
With Bruckner: two Æquale and ten
other motets
Other issues: Koch Records Schwann
16 970

1013.GE0 Gronostay, Uwe
Denmark Radio Choir
Recorded in Trinitatis Church,
Copenhagen: August 1985, ed. n/a
1885
Issue: Kontrapunkt 32022, 1 stereo CD,
1 s [CFB], p. 1989
Timing: 5.38
Notes: Knut Ketting
With Bruckner: nine other motets and
Werner: *Hommage à Bruckner*

1013.GG0 Guest, George
Choir of St. John's College, Cambridge
Recorded p. 1973, ed. n/a 1885
Issue: Argo ZRG 760, 1 stereo LP, 1 s
[CFB], W. 1974
Timing: 5.29
Notes: Peter Dennison

With Bruckner: four other motets and Liszt: Missa choralis

1013.GH0 Günther, Hubert
Rhenish Youth Choir, Rhenish Choral Society
Recorded ca. 1976, ed. n/a 1885
Issue: Garnet 40 107, 1 stereo LP, 1 s, ca. 1976
With Bruckner: ten other brief pieces

1013.JE0 Jochum, Eugen
Chorus of the Bavarian Radio
Recorded 24-26 June 1966, ed. n/a 1885
Issue: DG 2720 054, 5 stereo LPs, 1 s [CFB], ca. 1981
Timing: 6.08
Notes: Wolfgang Dömling
With Bruckner: Masses Nos. 1-3, Te Deum, Psalm 150, motets
Other issues: DG 39134-5/139134-5, 2707 025, 136552, 423 127-2 (CD), DG 15 MG 3030, SLGM 1413/4, MGX 9917/8

1013.MJ0 Martini, Joachim
Junge Kantorei, Darmstadt
Recorded ca. 1973, ed. n/a 1885
Issue: BASF KMB 21336, 1 stereo LP, 1 s [CFB], W. 1973
Timing: 4.38
Notes: Lothar Hoffmann-Erbrecht
With Bruckner: Mass No. 2, two other motets

Other issues: ABC AB-67021 [CFB]

1013.RH0 Reichel, Helmuth
Zürcher Bach-Kantorei
Recorded in Reformed Church, Zürich-Oerlikon: June 1981, ed. n/a 1885
Issue: Fono Schallplatten FCD 91 229, 1 stereo CD, 1 s [CFB], p. 1990
Timing: 7.10
Notes: Kurt Pahlen
With Bruckner: nine other motets
Other issues: Fono Schallplatten FSM 53 229

1013.SW0 Schäfer, Wolfgang
Freiburg Vocal Ensemble
Recorded in Church of St. Barbara, Freiburg-Littenweiler: p. 1984, ed. n/a 1885
Issue: Christophorus CD 74501, 1 digital stereo CD, 1 s [CFB], © 1984
Timing: 6.19
With Bruckner: nine other motets
Other issues: Christophorus SCGLX 74 009

1013.ZH0 Zanotelli, Hans
Philharmonisches Vocalensemble Stuttgart
Recorded ca. 1987, ed. n/a 1885
Issue: Calig CAL 30 477, 1 stereo LP, 1 s, ca. 1987
With Bruckner: eleven other motets

In jener letzten der Nächte (WAB 17, G/A 23)

Andante. In F Major. Composed ca. 1848 at St. Florian for four-part mixed choir.

1017.JJ0   Jürgens, Jürgen
Recorded in Dormition Abbey, Jerusalem: July 1984, ed. n/a 1848
Issue: Jerusalem Records ATD 8503, 1 digital stereo LP, 1 s [CFB], p. 1985
Timing: 1.06
Notes: David H. Aldeborgh

With Bruckner: Missa Solemnis, Magnificat, one more sacred song

1017.ME0   Möller, Edith
Obernkirchen Children's Choir
Recorded W. 1965, ed. T.B. Rehmann 1848
Issue: London 5895/OS 25895, LP, 1 s, W. 1965

In S. Angelum custodem (WAB 18, G/A 85)

Composed ca. 1868 for four-part mixed choir. Also known as "Iam lucis orto sidere."

1018.BM0   Breitschaft, Mathias
Limburger Dom-Singknaben
Recorded ca. 1977, ed. n/a 1868

Issue: Carus FSM 53 1 18, 1 stereo LP, 1 s, ca. 1977
With Bruckner: eight other motets and Palestrina: eight motets

Inveni David (WAB 19, G/A without number)

In f minor. Composed in Linz in 1868 for four-part male choir and four trombones.

1019.BM0   Best, Matthew
Corydon Singers
Recorded in St. Alban's Church, Holborn, London: May 1982, ed. n/a 1868
Issue: Hyperion A66062, 1 stereo LP, 1 s [CFB], p. 1983
Timing: 2.07
Notes: Douglas Hammond

With Bruckner: ten other motets
Other issues: Hyperion CD 66062 (CD)

1019.FA5   Flämig, Martin
Dresdner Kreuzchor; G. Eßbach, M. Zeumer, H. Kästner, H. Hombsch, tbns.
Recorded in Lukaskirche, Dresden: January 1985, ed. n/a 1868

Issue: Capriccio 10 081, 1 digital stereo CD, 1 s [CFB], p. 1987
Timing: 2.55
Notes: Hans Rutesame
With Bruckner: thirteen other motets
Other issues: Capriccio C 27 099, CC 27 099 (cassette), Delta 10 081 (CD), C 27 099, CC 27 099 (cassette)

1019.FJ0   Fuchs, Johannes
Zurich Chamber Choir, Slokar Trombone Quartet
Recorded in Reformed Church, Zürich-Altstetten: September 1984, ed. n/a 1868
Issue: Ex Libris CD 6009, 1 digital stereo CD, 1 s [CFB], p. 1985
Timing: 2.45
Notes: Alois Koch
With Bruckner: two Æquale and ten other motets
Other issues: Koch Records Schwann 16 970

1019.GG0   Guest, George
Choir of St. John's College, Cambridge
Recorded p. 1973, ed. n/a 1868
Issue: Argo ZRG 760, 1 stereo LP, 1 s [CFB], W. 1974
Timing: 1.44
Notes: Peter Dennison
With Bruckner: four other motets and Liszt: Missa choralis

1019.KM0   Koekelkoeren, Martin
Maastreechter Staar
Recorded W. 1966, ed. n/a 1868
Issue: Philips 402 155 NE, 45, 1 s

1019.MJ0   Martini, Joachim
Junge Kantorei, Darmstadt
Recorded ca. 1973, ed. n/a 1868
Issue: BASF KMB 21336, 1 stereo LP, 1 s [CFB], W. 1973
Timing: 2.04
Notes: Lothar Hoffmann-Erbrecht
With Bruckner: Mass No. 2, two other motets
Other issues: ABC AB-67021 [CFB]

1019.ZG0   Zapf, Gerd
Bavaria-Blechsolisten München
Recorded February 1984, ed. Philip Gordon ca.1984
Issue: Calig CAL 50837, 1 digital stereo CD, 1 s [CFB], p. 1984
Timing: 3.13
Notes: Bernd Edelmann, Karl Batz
Other issues: Calig CAL 30 837.
With eighteen other pieces by various composers
Arranged for brass ensemble and titled "Gebet und Alleluja"

1019.ZH0   Zanotelli, Hans
Philharmonisches Vocalensemble Stuttgart
Recorded ca. 1987, ed. n/a 1868
Issue: Calig CAL 30 477, 1 stereo LP, 1 s, ca. 1987
With Bruckner: eleven other motets

Libera me, Domine (WAB 22, G/A 41)

In f minor. Composed in 1854 probably at St. Florian for five-part mixed choir, three trombones, violoncello, string bass and organ.

1022.BM0   Best, Matthew
English Chamber Orchestra Wind Ensemble, Corydon Singers
Recorded in Church of St. Alban, Holborn, London: April 1985, ed. n/a 1854
Issue: Hyperion CDA66177, 1 digital stereo CD, 1 s [CFB], p. 1986
Timing: 9.04
Notes: Robert Simpson
With Bruckner: Mass No. 2 and two Æquale
Other issues: Hyperion 66177 (LP and cassette)

1022.FA5   Flämig, Martin
Dresdner Kreuzchor; M. Winkler, organ, M. Zeumer, H. Kästner, H. Hombsch, tbns.

Recorded in Lukaskirche, Dresden: January 1985, ed. n/a 1854
Issue: Capriccio 10 081, 1 digital stereo CD, 1 s [CFB], p. 1987
Timing: 5.27
Notes: Hans Rutesame
With Bruckner: thirteen other motets
Other issues: Capriccio C 27 099, CC 27 099 (cassette), Delta 10 081 (CD), C 27 099, CC 27 099 (cassette)

1022.ZH0   Zanotelli, Hans
Philharmonisches Vocalensemble Stuttgart
Recorded ca. 1987, ed. n/a 1854
Issue: Calig CAL 30 477, 1 stereo LP, 1 s, ca. 1987
With Bruckner: eleven other motets

Locus iste (WAB 23, G/A 92)

Allegro moderato. In C Major. Composed in 1869 probably at Vienna for four-part mixed choir.

1023.AA0   Anonymous
Vienna Hofmusikkapelle
Recorded W. 1909, ed. n/a 1869
Issue: His Master's Voice HMV 44762, acoustic 78, 1 s

1023.AJ0   Alldis, John
John Alldis Choir
Recorded p. 1967, ed. n/a 1869
Issue: Argo ZRG 523, 1 stereo LP, 1 s [CFB], W. 1968

Timing: 2.53
Notes: Robert Henderson
With choral works by Bruckner, Schönberg, Debussy and Messiaen
Other issues: Decca SXL 21177

1023.BE0   Berberich, Ludwig
Munich Cathedral Choir
Recorded W. 1931, ed. n/a 1869
Issue: Christschall 141, 1 10" mono 78, 1 s [CST]

Timing: 2.39
With Bruckner: Os justi

1023.BF0   Beringer, Karl-Friedrich
Windsbacher Knabenchor
Recorded ca. 1986, ed. n/a 1869
Issue: Bellaphon 680 05 001, 1 stereo
LP, 1 s, ca. 1987
With Bruckner: Christus factus est and
Os justi and four other choral works
by various composers

1023.BG0   Bertola, Giulio
Coro Polifonico Italiano
Recorded W. 1965, ed. n/a 1869
Issue: Musical Heritage Society MHS
1552, 1 stereo LP, 1 s [CFB], W. 1973
Timing: 2.29
Notes: Edward D. R. Neill
With Bruckner: Te Deum and four other
motets
Other issues: Angelicum LPA 5989/
STA 8989

1023.BM0   Best, Matthew
Corydon Singers
Recorded in St. Alban's Church, Hol-
born, London: May 1982, ed. n/a
1869
Issue: Hyperion A66062, 1 stereo LP,
1 s [CFB], p. 1983
Timing: 3.22
Notes: Douglas Hammond
With Bruckner: ten other motets
Other issues: Hyperion CD 66062 (CD)

1023.BR0   Bradshaw, Richard
Saltarello Choir
Recorded in Church of St. Bartholomew The Great, Smithfield, London: p. 1974, ed. n/a 1869

Issue: CRD 1009, 1 stereo LP, 1 s [CFB],
p. 1974
Timing: 2.30
Notes: Anonymous
With Bruckner: four other motets and
works by Brahms and Verdi

1023.BT0   Breitschaft, Mathias
Limburger Dom-Singknaben
Recorded ca. 1977, ed. n/a 1869
Issue: Carus FSM 53118, 1 stereo LP,
1 s, ca. 1977
With Bruckner: seven other motets and
Palestrina: eight motets

1023.FA0   Flämig, Martin
Dresdner Kreuzchor
Recorded in Lukaskirche, Dresden:
January 1985, ed. n/a 1869
Issue: Capriccio 10 081, 1 digital stereo
CD, 1 s [CFB], p. 1987
Timing: 2.21
Notes: Hans Rutesame
With Bruckner: thirteen other motets
Other issues: Capriccio C 27 099, CC 27
099 (cassette), Delta 10 081 (CD),
C 27 099, CC 27 099 (cassette)

1023.FH0   Froschauer, Helmuth
Singverein der Gesellschaft der
Musikfreunde
Recorded ca. 1958, ed. n/a 1869
Issue: Preiser SPR 3219, LP, 1 s
With Bruckner: other choral works

1023.FJ0   Fuchs, Johannes
Zurich Chamber Choir
Recorded in Reformed Church, Zürich-
Altstetten: September 1984, ed. n/a
1869
Issue: Ex Libris CD 6009, 1 digital ste-
reo CD, 1 s [CFB], p. 1985

Timing: 3.10
Notes: Alois Koch
With Bruckner: two Æquale and ten
　other motets
Other issues: Koch Records Schwann
　16 970

1023.GA5　Garbers, Wilfried
Herrenhäuser Chorgemeinschaft
Recorded ca. 1986, ed. n/a 1869
Issue: Sound Star Ton SST 0 152,
　1 stereo LP, 1 s, ca. 1986
With Bruckner: Ave Maria and four-
　teen other choral works by various
　composers

1023.GH0　Gillesberger, Hans
Vienna Kammerchor
Recorded ca. 1964, ed. n/a 1869
Issue: Lyrichord LLST 7136, 1 stereo
　LP, 1 s [CFB], W. 1964
Timing: 2.53
Notes: Victor Chapin
With Bruckner: Mass No. 2 and Ave
　Maria
Other issues: Christophorus CGLP
　75823/SCGLP 75824

1023.GH1　Gillesberger, Hans
Vienna Kammerchor
Recorded W. 1960, ed. n/a 1869
Issue: Austria Vanguard AVRS 6064,
　1 mono LP, 1 s [UCB], W. 1963
Timing: 2.28
Notes: Anonymous
With Bruckner: four other motets and
　Heiller: two motets
Other issues: Rec. Soc. RS 71, Amadeo
　AVRS 6064, Amadeo 15084 (45)

1023.GH2　Gillesberger, Hans
Vienna Choir Boys, Chorus Viennensis
Recorded p. 1972, ed. n/a 1869
Issue: Acanta 41 232, 1 stereo CD, 1 s
　[CFB], p. 1988
Timing: 2.45
Notes: Gerhard Schuhmacher
With Bruckner: four other motets and
　Britten: *Ceremony of Carols*
Other issues: BASF KBB 21232

1023.GR0　Graham, Melva Treffinger
Grace Church Choir of Gentlemen and
　Boys
Recorded in Grace Church on-the-Hill,
　Toronto: May 1990, ed. Peters
Issue: Grace Church GC 02, 1 digital
　stereo CD, 1 s, November 1990
Timing: 2.35
With Bruckner: two other motets and
　works by other composers
Other issues: Grace Church GC 02 (cas-
　sette)

1023.GW0　Gönnenwein, Wolfgang
Stuttgart Madrigal Choir
Recorded in Ev. Frauenkirche, Ess-
　lingen/Neckar: July 1962, ed. n/a
　1869
Issue: Cantate 640230, 1 mono LP, 1 s
　[UCB], W. 1963
Timing: 2.58
Notes: Cornelia Auerbach-Schröder
With Bruckner: three other motets and
　Brahms: three motets
Other issues: Cantate 650 230

1023.GW3　Gronostay, Uwe
Denmark Radio Choir
Recorded in Trinitatis Church, Co-
　penhagen: August 1985, ed. n/a
　1869

Issue: Kontrapunkt 32022, 1 stereo CD,
1 s [CFB], p. 1989
Timing: 2.34
Notes: Knut Ketting
With Bruckner: nine other motets and
Werner: *Hommage à Bruckner*

1023.GW5 Günther, Hubert
Rheinische Singgemeinschaft
Recorded ca. 1976, ed. n/a 1869
Issue: Garnet 41 107, 1 stereo LP, 1 s, ca.
1976
With Bruckner: ten other works

1023.HA5 Hahn, Hans Helmut
St. Jakobschor Rothenburg, Sing-
gemeinschaft Petersaurach
Recorded in St. Jacob's Church,
Rothenburg: ca. 1986, ed. n/a 1869
Issue: Pelca PSR 40 620, 1 stereo LP,
1 s, ca. 1986
With Bruckner: three motets, and three
works by other composers

1023.HD0 Hellmann, Diethard
Bach Choir of Mainz
Recorded p. 1979, ed. n/a 1869
Issue: Calig CAL 30 469, 1 stereo LP,
1 s [CFB], p. 1979
Timing: 3.05
Notes: Anonymous "U.M."
With Bruckner: four other motets and
Kodály: *Laudes organi*

1023.HP0 Herreweghe, Philippe
La Chapelle Royale
Recorded November 1989
Issue: Harmonia mundi HMC 901322,
1 digital stereo CD, 1 s [CFB],
p. 1990
Timing: 3.00
Notes: Jean-Yves Bras

With Bruckner: Mass No. 2, Æquale I
and II, four other motets

1023.IA0 Itai, Avner
Israel Kibbutz Choir
Recorded ca. 1986, ed. n/a 1869
Issue: Pick-Records PR 70 129, 1 stereo
LP, 1 s, ca. 1986
With nine choral works by various
composers

1023.JE0 Jochum, Eugen
Chorus of the Bavarian Radio
Recorded 24-26 June 1966, ed. n/a 1869
Issue: DG 2720 054, 5 stereo LPs, 1 s
[CFB], ca. 1981
Timing: 3.38
Notes: Wolfgang Dömling
With Bruckner: Masses Nos. 1-3, Te
Deum, Psalm 150, motets
Other issues: DG 39134-5/139134-5,
2707 025, 136552, 423 127-2 (CD)

1023.KF0 Klausing, Franz
Palestrina-Kreis
Recorded W. 1960, ed. n/a 1869
Issue: Christophorus C 72127, 45, 1 s

1023.LA0 Los Angeles Philharmonic
Trombone Ensemble
Recorded in Los Angeles: ca. 1976, ed.
Ralph Sauer 1869
Issue: Western International Music
WIMR-12, 1 stereo LP, 1 s [CFB],
ca. 1976
Timing: 2.08
Notes: Ralph Sauer
With Bruckner: two other motets and
thirteen other works by various
composers
Transcribed for trombone quartet.

1023.MJ0   Martini, Joachim
Junge Kantorei, Darmstadt
Recorded W. 1971, ed. n/a 1869
Issue: Schwarzwald 13004, LP, 1 s
With Bruckner: other choral works
Other issues: Schwarzwald CRO 833;
2520 833

1023.MT0   Mattmann, Erwin
Trinity Church Choir, Bern
Recorded ca. 1986, ed. n/a 1869
Issue: Fono FSM 30 4721, 1 stereo LP,
1 s, ca. 1986
With ten choral works by various com-
posers

1023.PJ0   Peerik, Jan S.
Ensemble Vocal Raphael
Recorded ca. 1987, ed. n/a 1869
Issue: Elrec G 3 E 3226, 1 stereo LP, 1 s,
ca. 1987
With Bruckner: Mass for Holy Thurs-
day and seven other choral works
by various composers

1023.PW0   Pitz, Wilhelm
New Philharmonia Chorus
Recorded 16-18 November 1966, ed.
n/a 1869
Issue: Angel S-36428, 1 stereo LP, 1 s
[CFB], W. 1967
Timing: 2.42
Notes: Paul Jennings, W.A. Chislett
With Bruckner: four other motets and
works by five other composers
Other issues: EMI ASD 2325, SME 81046

1023.RG0   Raabe, Gerson
Gerson Raabe Brass Ensemble
Recorded ca. 1986, ed. n/a 1869
Issue: Laudate 91 539, 1 stereo LP, 1 s,
ca. 1986

With fifteen other works arranged for
brass ensemble
Other issues: Laudate 96 939 (cassette)

1023.RT0   Rehmann, Theodor
Aachen Cathedral Choir
Recorded W. 1956, ed. n/a 1869
Issue: Mace MCS 9030, LP, 1 s
Other issues: Columbia C 80102, C 047
28072 M

1023.RT5   Reichel, Helmuth
Zürcher Bach-Kantorei
Recorded in Reformed Church, Zürich-
Oerlikon: June 1981, ed. n/a 1869
Issue: Fono Schallplatten FCD 91 229,
1 stereo CD, 1 s [CFB], p. 1990
Timing: 3.17
Notes: Kurt Pahlen
With Bruckner: nine other motets
Other issues: Fono Schallplatten FSM
53 229

1023.RT5   Rinscheid, Michael
Singkreis Wehbach
Recorded ca. 1987, ed. n/a 1869
Issue: Elrec M 3 E 3177, 1 stereo LP, 1 s,
ca. 1987
With Bruckner: Locus iste and fifteen
other choral works by various com-
posers
Other issues: Elrec CM 3 E 3177 (cas-
sette)

1023.SW0   Schäfer, Wolfgang
Freiburg Vocal Ensemble
Recorded in Church of St. Barbara,
Freiburg-Littenweiler: p. 1984, ed.
n/a 1869
Issue: Christophorus CD 74501, 1 digi-
tal stereo CD, 1 s [CFB], © 1984
Timing: 3.06

With Bruckner: nine other motets
Other issues: Christophorus SCGLX
74 009

1023.SW1   Schrems, Theobald
Regensburg Cathedral Choir
Recorded < 1948, ed. n/a 1869
Issue: Electrola EG 3903, 78, 1 s
With Liszt: Ave Maria

1023.VS0   Valen, Sverre
Valen Choir
Recorded in Sandefjord Kirke: April
1988, ed. n/a 1869
Issue: BD BD 7006 CD, 1 digital stereo
CD, 1 s [CFB], ca. 1989
Timing: 2.15
With fourteen other choral works by
various composers

1023.WT0   Westphalian Trombone
Quartet
Recorded p. 1982, ed. 1869
Issue: MD+G L 3094, 1 digital stereo
CD, 1 s [CFB], p. 1982
Timing: 3.37
Notes: Joachim Thalmann
With Bruckner: Christus factus est and
works by Sweelinck, Serocki, Staden
and Bozza
Other issues: Mdg G 1094

1023.ZH0   Zanotelli, Hans
Philharmonisches Vocalensemble
Stuttgart
Recorded ca. 1987, ed. n/a 1869
Issue: Calig CAL 30 477, 1 stereo LP,
1 s, ca. 1987
With Bruckner: eleven other motets

Magnificat in B flat Major (WAB 24, G/A 34)

Composed in 1852 at St. Florian for four soloists, four-part mixed choir, organ and orchestra.

1024.JJ0   Jürgens, Jürgen
Israel Chamber Orchestra, Monteverdi
Chorus, Hamburg
Recorded in Dormition Abbey, Jerusa-
lem: July 1984, ed. n/a 1852

Issue: Jerusalem Records ATD 8503,
1 digital stereo LP, 1 s [CFB],
p. 1985
Timing: 4.27
Notes: David H. Aldcborgh
With Bruckner: Missa Solemnis and
two sacred songs

Mass in C Major (WAB 25, G/A 4)

Composed ca. 1842 for alto, two horns and organ.

1025.RW0   Riedelbauch, Wolfgang
S. Aida and O. Rohrmeier, hns, W.
Riedelbauch, organ
Recorded ca. 1973, ed. n/a 1842

Issue: Colosseum SM 548, 1 stereo LP,
1 s [CFB], W. 1973
Timing: 10.51
Notes: Anonymous
With Bruckner: Psalm 146

Mass No. 1 in d minor (WAB 26, G/A 71)

Composed in 1864 in Linz, revised in 1876 in Vienna and again in 1881-1882. For soloists, four-part mixed choir, organ and orchestra.

1026.AA0　Anonymous [Gloria only]
Basilica Chorus
Recorded WERM 1935, ed. n/a 1864
Issue: Polydor 66116, mono 78

1026.AC0　Adler, F. Charles
Radio Vienna Chorus and Orchestra
Recorded W. 1957, ed. n/a 1864
Issue: S.P.A. 72, LP, ss, W. 1957
Other issues: Record Society RS 58,
Lumen AMS 7

1026.JE0　Jochum, Eugen
Bavarian Radio Symphony Orchestra,
Bavarian Radio Chorus
Recorded ca. 1973, ed. n/a 1876
Issue: DG 2530 314, 1 stereo LP, 2 ss
[CFB], ca. 1973
Timing: 46.12
Notes: Horst-Günther Scholz
Other issues: DG 2720 054 [CFB]

1026.KP0　Kalt, Pius
[Gloria only]
St. Hedwig's Cathedral Choir
Recorded < 1925, ed. n/a 1882
Issue: Polydor 66116, 1 acoustic 78, 1 s
Other issues: Polydor B 25048 (78) [1949]

Mass No. 2 in e minor (WAB 27, G/A 79)

Composed in 1866 in Linz, revised 1876, 1882, 1885 and in 1896 in Vienna. For eight-part mixed choir and wind ensemble.

1027.BD0　Barenboim, Daniel
English Chamber Orchestra, John
Alldis Choir
Recorded in Peterborough Cathedral:
2 and 4 May 1974
Issue: Angel S-37112, 1 quadraphonic
LP, 2 ss [CFB], W. 1976
Timing: 43.05
Notes: Hans-Hubert Schönzeler
Other issues: EMI EAC 80176, ASD
3079, 1C 063 02531

1027.BL0　Berberich, Ludwig
[Gloria, Et incarnatus, Sanctus and
Benedictus only]
Munich Cathedral Choir
Recorded ca. 1931, ed. 1882 n/a
Issue: Musica Sacra B 4521-3, 3 mono
78's, 6 ss [CST], 22.11
Other issues: Gloria only also on
Ultraphone EP 242, Royale 567

1027.BM0   Best, Matthew
English Chamber Orchestra Wind En-
semble, Corydon Singers
Recorded in Church of St. Alban,
Holborn, London: April 1985, ed.
n/a 1882
Issue: Hyperion CDA66177, 1 digital
stereo CD, 1 s [CFB], p. 1986
Timing: 40.40
Notes: Robert Simpson
With Bruckner: Libera me and two
Æquale
Other issues: Hyperion 66177 (LP and
cassette)

1027.FK0   Forster, Karl
Berlin Philharmonic Orchestra, St. Hed-
wig's Cathedral Choir
Recorded W. 1955, ed. n/a 1882
Issue: Odeon E. 80010, 1 mono LP, 2 ss
[SU], W. 1960
Timing: 31.43
With Bruckner: Te Deum
Other issues: Odeon ALP 1567, E 80010,
WCLP 530, EMI 047 01142 M

1027.GH0   Gillesberger, Hans
Vienna State Opera Orchestra, Vienna
Kammerchor
Recorded ca. 1964
Issue: Lyrichord LLST 7136, 1 stereo
LP, 2 ss [CFB], W. 1964
Timing: 21.28
Notes: Victor Chapin
With Bruckner: two motets
Other issues: Lyrichord LL 136,
Christophorus CGLP/SCGLP 75824

1027.GW0   Gönnenwein, Wolfgang
Southwest German Radio Orchestra,
South German Madrigal Choir
Recorded W. 1971, ed. n/a 1882

Issue: EMI 137-290 526-3, 2 stereo LPs,
2 ss, ca. 1986
With masses by Mozart and Schubert
Other issues: EMI 437-290 526-9 (cassette), Odeon C 063 29061

1027.HE0   Herreweghe, Philippe
Ensemble Musique Oblique, La Cha-
pelle Royale
Recorded November 1989, ed. 1868
Issue: Harmonia mundi HMC 901322,
1 digital stereo CD, 1 s [CFB],
p. 1990
Timing: 35.51
Notes: Jean-Yves Bras
With Bruckner: Æquale I and II and
five motets

1027.HJ0   Hömberg, Johannes
Pro Musica Köln
Recorded COP 1978, ed. n/a 1882
Issue: Opus Musicum OM 201/03,
3 stereo LPs, 1 s [SU], © 1978
Timing: 7.50
Notes: H.C. Schmidt, Johannes Höm-
berg
With Mass movements by nineteen
other composers

1027.JE0   Jochum, Eugen
Bavarian Radio Symphony Orchestra,
Bavarian Radio Symphony Chorus
Recorded ca. 1971, ed. n/a 1866
Issue: DG 2720 054, 5 stereo LPs, 2 ss
[CFB], ca. 1981
Timing: 43.22
Notes: Wolfgang Dömling
With Bruckner: Masses Nos. 1 and 3,
Te Deum, Psalm 150, motets
Other issues: DG 2530 139, 423 127-2
(CD)

1027.KL0   Kron, Leopold
Bruckner Chorus of Linz, Linz-
Windensemble
Recorded ca. 1977, ed. n/a 1882
Issue: Summit SUM 5034, 1 stereo LP,
2 ss [SU], p. 1978
Timing: 35.50
Notes: Maxwell Davies

1027.MJ0   Martini, Joachim
Vienna Symphony, Junge Kantorei,
Darmstadt
Recorded ca. 1973, ed. n/a 1866
Issue: BASF KMB 21336, 1 stereo LP,
2 ss [CFB], W. 1973
Timing: 28.58
Notes: Lothar Hoffmann-Erbrecht
With Bruckner: three motets
Other issues: ABC AB-67021 [CFB]

1027.MZ0   Mehta, Zubin
Vienna Philharmonic Orchestra, Cho-
rus of the Vienna Opera
Recorded in Sofiensaal, Vienna: 1976,
ed. n/a 1866
Issue: London OS 26506, 1 stereo LP,
1 s [CFB], © 1978
Timing: 34.05
Notes: Anonymous
With Bruckner: Te Deum
Other issues: SXL 6837

1027.NR0   Norrington, Roger
Philip Jones Wind Ensemble, Schütz
Choir of London
Recorded December 1973, ed. n/a 1866
Issue: Argo ZRG 710, 1 stereo LP, 2 ss
[CFB], W. 1974
Timing: 25.19
Notes: Derek Watson
Other issues: London K18 C945, GT
9290

1027.OH0   Odermath, Hermann
Gregorius-Chor and Orchestra of the
Liebfrauenkirche, Zürich
Recorded W. 1930, ed. n/a
Issue: Christschall 37-41, 78

1027.RE0   Rehmann, Theodor
Berlin Symphony Orchestra, Aachen
Cathedral Choir
Recorded W. 1938, ed. S.A. Reiss 1882
Issue: Victor DM 596, 6 mono 78s, 12 ss
[CST], ca. 1938
Timing: 42.49
Other issues: Victor 15583/8, DB 4525-
30, DB 8563-8

1027.RH0   Rilling, Helmuth
Bach-Collegium Stuttgart; Gächinger,
Gedächtniskirche and Spandauer
choirs
Recorded ca. 1972, ed. n/a 1882
Issue: Musical Heritage Society MHS
1801, 1 stereo LP, 2 ss [CFB], ca. 1973
Timing: 44.07
Notes: Joachim von Hecker
Other issues: Oryx 3C 320, Bärenreiter
Bmu 13 30, BM 30 SL 1330

1027.RZ0   Rögner, Heinz
Berlin Radio Symphony Orchestra,
Berlin Radio Chorus
Recorded in Studio Christuskirche,
Berlin: 1988, ed. n/a 1882
Issue: Ars Vivendi 2100172, 1 digital
stereo CD, 1 s [CFB], p. 1990
Timing: 35.02
Notes: Mathias Hansen
With Bruckner: Te Deum

1027.TM0   Thurn, Max
Hamburg State Opera Orchestra, Hamburg State Opera Chorus

Recorded ca. 1938, ed. n/a
Issue: Capitol EEL 2504, 5 mono 78's,
   10 ss [CFB], W. 1949
Timing: 23.57
Notes: Anonymous
Other issues: Capitol P-8004 [CFB],
   KEM 8004 (45), Telefunken E 2607-
   11 (78), T 161-5 (78), LGX 66033
   (LP), LSK 7029 (LP)

1027.WH0 Wormsbächer, Hellmut
Hamburg State Philharmonic Orches-
   tra, Bergedorf Chamber Choir
Recorded p. 1973, ed. n/a 1866
Issue: Telefunken 6.41297 AS, 1 stereo
   LP, 2 ss [CFB], W. 1974
Timing: 35.59
Notes: Winfried Kirsch
With Schubert: Deutsche Messe
Other issues: Telefunken SAT 22545

Mass No. 3 in f minor (WAB 28, G/A 80)

Composed in 1868 in Linz, revised 1876, 1877, 1881, and 1890-1893 in Vienna. For soloists, four-part mixed choir, organ and orchestra.

1028.AT0 Asahina, Takashi
Osaka Philharmonic Orchestra, T.C.F.
   Chorus
Recorded live: 16 September 1983, ed.
   n/a 1868
Issue: JVC Victor SJX-9578, 1 digital
   stereo LP, 2 ss, ca. 1988
Other issues: JVC Victor VDC-521 (CD),
   VDC-1195 (CD)

1028.BD0 Barenboim, Daniel
New Philharmonia Orchestra, New
   Philharmonia Chorus
Recorded p. 1972, ed. Nowak 1868
Issue: Angel S-36921, 1 stereo LP, 2 ss
   [CFB], W. 1973
Timing: 58.03
Notes: Hans-Hubert Schönzeler
Other issues: ASD 2836, EMI 063-02318,
   C 069 02318

1028.DC0 Davis, Colin
Bavarian Radio Symphony Orchestra,
   Bavarian Radio Chorus

Recorded in Munich: June 1988, ed.
   1883
Issue: Philips 422 358-2 PH, 1 digital
   stereo CD, 1 s [CFB], © 1989
Timing: 1.04.50
Notes: Michael Kennedy
Organ: E. Schloter

1028.FK0 Forster, Karl
Berlin Symphony Orchestra, St.
   Hedwig's Cathedral Choir
Recorded in Grünewaldkirche, Berlin:
   March 1962, ed. Haas 1868
Issue: EMI 237 29 0640 4, 1 stereo cas-
   sette, 2 ss [CFB], ca. 1988
Timing: 53.43
Notes: Sigurd Schimpf
Weber gives 1963 as the date of the
   original LP.
Other issues: Angel 35982, EMI 037-
   290 640-1 (LP and cassette), EMI
   137-291 125-3, ALP 1964/ASD 515,
   E/STE 80715, FALP/ASDF 757

1028.GF0   Grossmann, Ferdinand
  Vienna State Philharmonia, Akademie
    Kammerchor
  Recorded in Vienna: ca. 1953, ed. n/a
    1893
  Issue: Vox PL 7940, 1 mono LP, 2 ss
    [CFB], W. 1953
  Timing: 57.51
  Notes: Helen H. Less

1028.JE0   Jochum, Eugen
  Bavarian Radio Symphony Orchestra,
    Bavarian Radio Chorus
  Recorded W. 1962, ed. Nowak 1868
  Issue: DG 138 829, 1 stereo LP, 2 ss
    [CFB], W. 1963
  Timing: 57.11
  Notes: Anonymous
  Other issues: DG 2720 054 [CFB]

Missa solemnis in B flat Major (WAB 29, G/A 42)

Composed at St. Florian in 1854 for soloists, four-part mixed choir, organ and orchestra.

1029.GH0   Günther, Hubert
  BRT Symphony Orchestra, Brussels,
    Rheinische Singgemeinschaft
  Recorded ca. 1986, ed. n/a 1854
  Issue: Garnet 40170, 1 stereo LP, 1 s, ca.
    1986
  With Bruckner: Ave Maria

1029.HE0   Hausmann, Elmar
  Capella Vocale St. Aposteln, Cologne
  Recorded ca. 1986, ed. n/a 1854
  Issue: Aulos 53 569, 1 stereo LP, 1 s, ca.
    1986
  With Bruckner: four motets

1029.JJ0   Jürgens, Jürgen
  Israel Chamber Orchestra, Monteverdi
    Chorus, Hamburg
  Recorded in Dormition Abbey, Jerusa-
    lem: July 1984, ed. n/a 1854
  Issue: Jerusalem Records ATD 8503,
    1 digital stereo LP , 2 ss [CFB],
    p. 1985
  Timing: 36.45
  Notes: David H. Aldeborgh
  With Bruckner: Magnificat and two
    sacred songs

Os justi (WAB 30, G/A 105)

Nicht schnell. Composed in Vienna in 1879 for eight-part mixed choir.

1030.BL0   Berberich, Ludwig
  Munich Cathedral Choir
  Recorded W. 1931, ed. n/a 1879
  Issue: Christschall 141, 1 10" mono 78,
    1 s [CST], ca. 1931
  Timing: 3.15
  With Bruckner: Locus iste

1030.BL5   Beringer, Karl-Friedrich
  Windsbacher Knabenchor
  Recorded ca. 1986, ed. n/a 1879
  Issue: Bellaphon 680 05 001, 1 stereo
    LP, 1 s, ca. 1987
  With Bruckner: Christus factus est and
    Locus iste and four other works by
    various composers

1030.BM0 Best, Matthew
Corydon Singers
Recorded in St. Alban's Church, Hol-
  born, London: May 1982, ed. n/a
  1879
Issue: Hyperion A66062, 1 stereo LP,
  1 s [CFB], p. 1983
Timing: 4.56
Notes: Douglas Hammond
With Bruckner: ten other motets
Other issues: Hyperion CD 66062 (CD)

1030.BN0 Böck, Herbert
Concentus Vocalis Wien
Recorded in Vienna: © 1988
Issue: Koch 317 008 H1, 1 stereo CD,
  1 s [CFB], p. 1988
Timing: 3.20
With Distler: Totentanz

1030.BO0 Boles, Frank Woodhouse
Choir of St. Paul's Episcopal Church
Recorded in St. Joan of Arc R.C. Church,
  Indianapolis: p. 1984, ed. n/a 1879
Issue: BDC Records BDB-1101, 1 stereo
  LP, 1 s [CFB], p. 1984
Timing: 3.47
With ten other choral pieces by various
  composers
The final Alleluia is omitted.

1030.BR0 Bradshaw, Richard
Saltarello Choir
Recorded in Church of St. Bartholo-
  mew The Great, Smithfield, Lon-
  don: p. 1974, ed. n/a 1879
Issue: CRD 1009, 1 stereo LP, 1 s [CFB],
  p. 1974
Timing: 4.04
Notes: Anonymous
With Bruckner: four other motets and
  works by Brahms and Verdi

1030.BT0 Breitschaft, Mathias
Limburger Dom-Singknaben
Recorded ca. 1977, ed. 1879
Issue: Carus FSM 53 1 18, 1 stereo LP,
  1 s
With Bruckner: eight other motets and
  Palestrina: eight motets

1030.CF0 Clausing, Franz
Palestrina-Kreis
Recorded W. 1960, ed. n/a 1879
Issue: Christophorus C 72127, 45, 1 s

1030.FA5 Flämig, Martin
Dresdner Kreuzchor
Recorded in Lukaskirche, Dresden:
  January 1985, ed. n/a 1879
Issue: Capriccio 10 081, 1 digital stereo
  CD, 1 s [CFB], p. 1987
Timing: 4.00
Notes: Hans Rutesame
With Bruckner: thirteen other motets
Other issues: Capriccio C 27 099, CC
  27 099 (cassette), Delta 10 081 (CD),
  C 27 099, CC 27 099 (cassette)

1030.FK0 Forster, Karl
St. Hedwig's Cathedral Choir
Recorded < 1948, ed. n/a 1879
Issue: Electrola EG 8536, 78, 1 s
Other issues: Electrola 17-8536 (45), E
  40063

1030.FU0 Fuchs, Johannes
Zurich Chamber Choir
Recorded in Reformed Church, Zürich-
  Altstetten: September 1984, ed. n/a
  1879
Issue: Ex Libris CD 6009, 1 digital ste-
  reo CD, 1 s [CFB], p. 1985
Timing: 4.20
Notes: Alois Koch

With Bruckner: two Æquale and ten other motets
Other issues: Koch Records Schwann 16 970

1030.GE0   Gillesberger, Hans
Vienna Academy Chamber Choir
Recorded W. 1960, ed. n/a 1879
Issue: Austria Vanguard AVRS 6064, 1 mono LP, 1 s [UCB], W. 1963
Timing: 4.57
Notes: Anonymous
With Bruckner: four other motets and Heiller: two motets
Other issues: Amadeo AVRS 6064, 15085 (45)

1030.GE2   Gillesberger, Hans
Vienna Academy Chamber Choir
Recorded W. 1964, ed. n/a 1879
Issue: Vox DL 1040, 1 mono LP, 1 s [SU], W. 1964
Timing: 4.57
Notes: Harry Halbreich
With Liszt: Missa choralis
Other issues: Vox STDL 501040, Christophorus SCGLP 75855

1030.GE3   Gillesberger, Hans
Vienna Choir Boys, Chorus Viennensis
Recorded p. 1972, ed. n/a 1879
Issue: Acanta 41 232, 1 stereo CD, 1 s [CFB], p. 1988
Timing: 4.32
Notes: Gerhard Schuhmacher
With Bruckner: four other motets and Britten: *Ceremony of Carols*
Other issues: BASF KBB 21232

1030.GG0   Guest, George
Choir of St. John's College, Cambridge
Recorded p. 1973, ed. n/a 1879

Issue: Argo ZRG 760, 1 stereo LP, 1 s [CFB], W. 1974
Timing: 4.56
Notes: Peter Dennison
With Bruckner: four other motets and Liszt: Missa choralis

1030.GH0   Günther, Hubert
Männergesangverein Concordia Hamm, Rheinisches Kinder- und Jugendchor
Recorded ca. 1976, ed. n/a 1879
Issue: Garnet 40 107, 1 stereo LP, 1 s
With Bruckner: ten other pieces

1030.GO0   Gronostay, Uwe
Denmark Radio Choir
Recorded in Trinitatis Church, Copenhagen: August 1985, ed. n/a 1879
Issue: Kontrapunkt 32022, 1 stereo CD, 1 s [CFB], p. 1989
Timing: 4.22
Notes: Knut Ketting
With Bruckner: nine other motets and Werner: Hommage à Bruckner

1030.GO0   Gönnenwein, Wolfgang
Stuttgart Madrigal Choir
Recorded in Ev. Frauenkirche, Esslingen / Neckar: July 1962, ed. n/a 1879
Issue: Cantate 640230, 1 mono LP, 1 s [UCB], W. 1963
Timing: 4.44
Notes: Cornelia Auerbach-Schröder
With Bruckner: 3 motets and Brahms: 3 motets
Other issues: Cantate 650 230, Cantate 656 013

1030.GR0   Graham, Melva Treffinger
Grace Church Choir of Gentlemen and
Boys
Recorded in Grace Church on-the-Hill,
Toronto: May 1990, ed. Peters
Issue: Grace Church GC 02, 1 digital
stereo CD, 1 s, November 1990
Timing: 4.30
With Bruckner: two other motets and
works by other composers
Other issues: Grace Church GC 02 (cassette)

1030.HA5   Harrassowitz, Hermann
Bach-Chor St. Lorenz Nürnberg
Recorded in St. Laurence Church,
Nuremberg: ca. 1986, ed. n/a 1879
Issue: Carus 53 130, 1 stereo LP, 1 s,
ca. 1986
With nine choral works by various
composers

1030.HA5   Hausmann, Elmar
Capella Vocale St. Aposteln, Cologne
Recorded ca. 1986, ed. n/a 1879
Issue: Aulos 53 569, 1 stereo LP, 1 s, ca.
1986
With Bruckner: Missa Solemnis and
three other motets

1030.HA5   Hahn, Hans Helmut
St. Jakobschor Rothenburg, Sing-
gemeinschaft Petersaurach
Recorded in St. Jacob's Church,
Rothenburg: ca. 1986, ed. n/a 1879
Issue: Pelca PSR 40 620, 1 stereo LP,
1 s, ca. 1986
With Bruckner: three motets and three
works by other composers

1030.HD0   Hellmann, Diethard
Bach Choir of Mainz
Recorded p. 1979, ed. n/a 1879
Issue: Calig CAL 30 469, 1 stereo LP,
1 s [CFB], p. 1979
Timing: 4.00
Notes: Anonymous "U.M."
With Bruckner: four other motets and
Kodály: Laudes organi

1030.HP0   Herreweghe, Philippe
La Chapelle Royale
Recorded November 1989
Issue: Harmonia mundi HMC 901322,
1 digital stereo CD, 1 s [CFB],
p. 1990
Timing: 4.39
Notes: Jean-Yves Bras
With Bruckner: Mass No. 2, Æquale I
and II, four other motets

1030.HR0   Holliday, Robert
Hamline Choir
Recorded < 1948, ed. n/a 1879
Issue: Hamline H.U. 3, 1 mono 78, 1 s

1030.JE0   Jochum, Eugen
Chorus of the Bavarian Radio
Recorded 24-26 June 1966, ed. n/a 1879
Issue: DG 2720 054, 5 stereo LPs, 1 s
[CFB], ca. 1981
Timing: 5.02
Notes: Wolfgang Dömling
With Bruckner: Masses 1-3, Te Deum,
Psalm 150, motets
Other issues: DG 39137-8/139137-8,
2707 026, 136552, 423 127-2 (CD)

1030.KH0   Kramm, Herma
Münster Madrigal Choir
Recorded ca. 1970, ed. n/a 1879
Issue: Carillon ST 105, LP, 1 s

1030.MJ0   Martini, Joachim
Junge Kantorei, Darmstadt
Recorded W. 1971, ed. n/a 1879
Issue: Schwarzwald 13004, LP, 1 s
Other issues: Schwarzwald CRO 833,
2520833

1030.MR0   Mauersberger, Rudolf
Dresden Kreuzchor
Recorded < 1948, ed. n/a 1879
Issue: Polydor 10281, 78, 1 s
Other issues: Brunswick 35034 (78)

1030.MX0   Meyer, Xaver
Vienna Academy Kammerchor
Recorded ca. 1975, ed. n/a 1879
Issue: Mace MCS 9061, 1 stereo LP, 1 s
[CFB], ca. 1975
Timing: 4.24
Notes: Hope Sheridan
With Bruckner: Ave Maria and choral
works by four other composers
Other issues: Amadeo AVRS 6343

1030.PP0   Pernoud, Pierre
La Psallette de Genève
Recorded ca. 1970, ed. n/a 1879
Issue: Disques VDE VDE 3044, 1 stereo
LP, 1 s [CFB], ca. 1988
Timing: 4.28
Notes: Anonymous
With Bruckner: four other motets and
Brahms: three motets
Schwann cites "Gallo" as record label;
this performance omits final Alle-
luia

1030.PW0   Pitz, Wilhelm
New Philharmonia Chorus
Recorded 16-18 November 1966, ed.
n/a 1879

Issue: Angel S-36428, 1 stereo LP, 1 s
[CFB], W. 1967
Timing: 3.32
Notes: Paul Jennings, W.A. Chislett
With Bruckner: four other motets and
works by five other composers
Other issues: EMI ASD 2325, SME
81046, EMI 037-30 954 (LP and cas-
sette)

1030.RE5   Reichel, Helmuth
Zürcher Bach-Kantorei
Recorded in Reformed Church, Zürich-
Oerlikon: June 1981, ed. n/a 1879
Issue: Fono Schallplatten FCD 91 229, 1
stereo CD, 1 s [CFB], p. 1990
Timing: 4.27
Notes: Kurt Pahlen
With Bruckner: nine other motets
Other issues: Fono Schallplatten FSM
53 229

1030.RH0   Rilling, Helmuth
Gächinger Kantorei Stuttgart
Recorded ca. 1986, ed. n/a 1879
Issue: Intercord 185 815, 5 stereo LPs,
1 s, ca. 1986
With Bruckner: three other motets and
twenty-six other choral works by
various composers
Other issues: Intercord 722 05 SB

1030.SW0   Schäfer, Wolfgang
Freiburg Vocal Ensemble
Recorded in Church of St. Barbara,
Freiburg-Littenweiler: p. 1984, ed.
n/a 1879
Issue: Christophorus CD 74501, 1 digi-
tal stereo CD, 1 s [CFB],© 1984
Timing: 4.54
With Bruckner: nine other motets

Other issues: Christophorus SCGLX 74 009

1030.SZ0   Schweizer, Rolf
Pforzheim Motettenchor
Recorded W. 1976, ed. n/a 1879
Issue: Da Camera Magna SM 94048, 1 stereo LP, 1 s, W. 1976
With Bruckner: Ave Maria and Christus factus est and Brahms: various works

1030.SZ5   Sonnenschmidt, Jürgen
Bezirkskantorei Pirmasens
Recorded ca. 1986, ed. n/a 1879

Issue: Spirella Spi 2704 XC, 1 stereo LP, 1 s, ca. 1986
With Bruckner: Christus factus est and seven works by various composers

1030.ZH0   Zanotelli, Hans
Philharmonisches Vocalensemble Stuttgart
Recorded ca. 1987, ed. n/a 1879
Issue: Calig CAL 30 477, 1 stereo LP, 1 s, ca. 1987
With Bruckner: eleven other motets

Pange lingua et Tantum ergo (WAB 33, G/A 84)

Composed in 1868 at Linz for four-part mixed choir.

1033.BG0   Bertola, Giulio
Coro Polifonico Italiano
Recorded W. 1965, ed. n/a 1868
Issue: Musical Heritage Society MHS 1552, 1 stereo LP, 1 s [CFB], W. 1973
Timing: 5.02
Notes: Edward D. R. Neill
With Bruckner: Te Deum and four other motets
Other issues: Angelicum LPA 5989/ STA 8989

1033.BM0   Best, Matthew
Corydon Singers
Recorded in St. Alban's Church, Holborn, London: May 1982, ed. n/a 1868
Issue: Hyperion A66062, 1 stereo LP, 1 s [CFB], p. 1983
Timing: 4.34

Notes: Douglas Hammond
With Bruckner: ten other motets
Other issues: Hyperion CD 66062 (CD)

1033.BM5   Breitschaft, Mathias
Limburger Dom-Singknaben
Recorded ca. 1977, ed. 1868
Issue: Carus FSM 53 1 18, 1 stereo LP, 1 s, ca. 1977
With Bruckner: eight other motets and Palestrina: eight motets

1033.FA5   Flämig, Martin
Dresdner Kreuzchor
Recorded in Lukaskirche, Dresden: January 1985, ed. n/a 1868
Issue: Capriccio 10 081, 1 digital stereo CD, 1 s [CFB], p. 1987
Timing: 6.01
Notes: Hans Rutesame

With Bruckner: thirteen other motets
Other issues: Capriccio C 27 099, CC 27 099 (cassette), Delta 10 081 (CD), C 27 099, CC 27 099 (cassette)

1033.FJ0   Fuchs, Johannes
Zurich Chamber Choir
Recorded in Reformed Church, Zürich-Altstetten: September 1984, ed. n/a 1868
Issue: Ex Libris CD 6009, 1 digital stereo CD, 1 s [CFB], p. 1985
Timing: 5.12
Notes: Alois Koch
With Bruckner: two Æquale and ten other motets
Other issues: Koch Records Schwann 16 970

1033.GG0   Guest, George
Choir of St. John's College, Cambridge
Recorded p. 1973, ed. n/a 1868
Issue: Argo ZRG 760, 1 stereo LP, 1 s [CFB], W. 1974
Timing: 5.44
Notes: Peter Dennison
With Bruckner: four other motets and Liszt: *Missa choralis*

1033.GH0   Günther, Hubert
Rheinische Singgemeinschaft
Recorded ca. 1976, ed. n/a 1868
Issue: Garnet 40 107, 1 stereo LP, 1 s, ca. 1976
With Bruckner: ten other works

1033.GO0   Gronostay, Uwe
Denmark Radio Choir
Recorded in Trinitatis Church, Copenhagen: August 1985, ed. n/a 1868
Issue: Kontrapunkt 32022, 1 stereo CD, 1 s [CFB], p. 1989

Timing: 2.24
Notes: Knut Ketting
With Bruckner: nine other motets and Werner: *Hommage à Bruckner*

1033.HF0   Habel, Ferdinand
St. Stephen's Cathedral Choir of Vienna
Recorded W. 1931, ed. n/a 1868
Issue: Christschall 130, 78, 1 s

1033.JE0   Jochum, Eugen
Chorus of the Bavarian Radio
Recorded 24-26 June 1966, ed. n/a 1868
Issue: DG 2720 054, 5 stereo LPs, 1 s [CFB], ca. 1981
Timing: 4.22
Notes: Wolfgang Dömling
With Bruckner: Masses 1-3, Te Deum, Psalm 150, motets
Other issues: DG 2530 139, 423 127-2 (CD)

1033.LA0   Los Angeles Philharmonic Trombone Ensemble
Recorded in Los Angeles: ca. 1976, ed. Ralph Sauer 1868
Issue: Western International Music WIMR-12, 1 stereo LP, 1 s [CFB], ca. 1976
Timing: 1.47
Notes: Ralph Sauer
With Bruckner: two other motets and thirteen other works by various composers
Transcribed for trombone quartet

1033.MJ0   Martini, Joachim
Junge Kantorei, Darmstadt
Recorded W. 1971, ed. n/a 1868
Issue: Schwarzwald 13004, LP, 1 s
Other issues: Schwarzwald CRO 833, 2520833

1033.RH0   Reichel, Helmuth
Zürcher Bach-Kantorei
Recorded in Reformed Church, Zürich-
Oerlikon: June 1981, ed. n/a 1868
Issue : Fono Schallplatten FCD 91 229,
1 stereo CD, 1 s [CFB], p. 1990
Timing: 5.03
Notes: Kurt Pahlen
With Bruckner: nine other motets
Other issues: Fono Schallplatten FSM
53 229

1033.SW0   Schäfer, Wolfgang
Freiburg Vocal Ensemble
Recorded in Church of St. Barbara,
Freiburg-Littenweiler: p. 1984, ed.
n/a 1868

Issue: Christophorus CD 74501, 1 digi-
tal stereo CD, 1 s [CFB], © 1984
Timing: 5.10
With Bruckner: nine other motets
Other issues: Christophorus SCGLX
74 009

1033.ZH0   Zanotelli, Hans
Philharmonisches Vocalensemble
Stuttgart
Recorded ca. 1987, ed. n/a 1868
Issue: Calig CAL 30 477, 1 stereo LP,
1 s, ca. 1987
With Bruckner: eleven other motets

Psalm 112 (WAB 35, G/A 65)

In B flat Major. Composed in 1863 at Linz for eight-part mixed choir and orchestra.

1035.BM0   Best, Matthew
English Chamber Orchestra, Corydon
Singers
Recorded in All Hallows, Gospel Oak,
London: February 1987, ed. n/a
1863
Issue: Hyperion CDA66245, 1 digital
stereo CD, 1 s [CFB], © 1987
Timing: 10.04
Notes: Robert Simpson
With Bruckner: Requiem and Psalm
114
Other issues: Hyperion A66245, KA
66245 (cassette)

1035.SH0   Swoboda, Henry
Vienna Symphony Orchestra, Vienna
Academy Kammerchor

Recorded ca. 1951, ed. n/a 1863
Issue: Westminster W-9600, 1 mono
LP, 1 s [CFB], W. 1963
Timing: 13.35
Notes: Gabriel Engel
With Bruckner: Psalm 150 and Strauss:
Wanderers Sturmlied
Other issues: Westminster WL 5055-6
[CFB], XWN 18075, WAL 201, Nixa
WLP 6201

1035.SH0a Swoboda, Henry
Vienna Symphony Orchestra, Vienna
Academy Kammerchor
Recorded in Austria: © 1950, ed. n/a
1863
Issue: Westminster WL 5055-6, 2 mono
LPs, 1 s [CFB], W. 1951

Timing: 13.35
Notes: Gabriel Engel
With Bruckner: Symphony No. 6 and
   Psalm 150

Other issues: Westminster W-9600 (see
   1035.SH0)

Psalm 114 (WAB 36, G/A 36)

*In G Major. Composed in 1852 at St. Florian for five-part mixed choir and
orchestra.*

1036.BM0   Best, Matthew
   Corydon Singers
   Recorded in All Hallows, Gospel Oak,
      London: February 1987, ed. Mat-
      thew Best 1852
   Issue: Hyperion CDA66245, 1 digital
      stereo CD, 1 s [CFB], © 1987

Timing: 9.05
Notes: Robert Simpson
With Bruckner: Requiem and Psalm
   112
Other issues: Hyperion A66245,
   KA66245 (cassette)

Psalm 146 (WAB 37, G/A 50)

*In A Major. Composed in 1860 at St. Florian or in Linz for soloists, four-part
mixed choir and orchestra.*

1037.RW0   Riedelbauch, Wolfgang
   Nuremberg Symphony Orchestra,
      Hans Sachs Choir and Teachers'
      Choir of Nuremberg
   Recorded ca. 1973, ed. Riedelbauch
      1860

Issue: Colosseum SM 548, 1 stereo LP,
   1+ ss [CFB], W. 1973
Timing: 33.26
Notes: Anonymous
With Bruckner: Mass in C Major

Psalm 150 (WAB 38, G/A 122)

*In C Major. Composed in 1892 and revised later that year in Vienna, for
soloists, four-part mixed choir and orchestra.*

1038.BD0   Barenboim, Daniel
   Chicago Symphony Orchestra, Chicago
      Symphony Chorus
   Recorded March 1979, ed. n/a 1892

Issue: DG 2707 116, 2 stereo LPs, 1 s
   [CFB], p. 1980
Timing: 8.40
Notes: Siegfried Kross, Robert Simpson

With Bruckner: Symphony No. 7 and
  Helgoland
Other issues: DG410 650-1, MG8430/1

1038.SH0   Swoboda, Henry
  Vienna Symphony Orchestra, Vienna
    Academy Kammerchor
  Recorded ca. 1951, ed. n/a 1892
  Issue: Westminster W-9600, 1 mono
    LP, 1 s [CFB], W. 1963
  Timing: 11.32
  Notes: Gabriel Engel
  With Bruckner: Psalm 112 and Strauss:
    Wanderers Sturmlied
  Other issues: Westminster WL 5055-6
    (q.v.), WAL 201, XWN 18075, Nixa
    WLP 6201

1038.SH0a Swoboda, Henry
  Vienna Symphony Orchestra, Vienna
    Academy Kammerchor
  Recorded in Austria: © 1950, ed. n/a
    1892
  Issue: Westminster WL 5055-6, 2 mono
    LPs, 1 s [CFB], W. 1951
  Timing: 11.32
  Notes: Gabriel Engel
  With Bruckner: Symphony No. 6 and
    Psalm 112
  Other issues: Westminster W-9600
    [CFB]

Requiem in d minor (WAB 39, G/A 22)

Composed at St. Florian in 1849 and revised in Vienna in 1892, for soloists, four-part mixed choir and orchestra.

1039.BE0   Best, Matthew
  English Chamber Orchestra, Corydon
    Singers
  Recorded in All Hallows Church, Gos-
    pel Oak, London: February 1987,
    ed. n/a 1849
  Issue: Hyperion CDA66245, 1 digital
    stereo CD, 1 s [CFB], © 1987
  Timing: 36.32
  Notes: Robert Simpson
  With Bruckner: Psalms 114 and 112
  Other issues: Hyperion A66245,
    KA66245 (cassette)

1039.BH0   Beuerle, Hans Michael
  Werner Keltsch Instrumental En-
    semble, Laubacher Kantorei
  Recorded ca. 1973, ed. Haas 1849
  Issue: Nonesuch H-71327, 1 stereo LP,
    2 ss [CFB], © 1976
  Timing: 35.27
  Notes: Bernard Jacobson
  Other issues: Cantate 658 231

1039.EH0   Ermert, Herbert
  Siegerland-Orchester, Bach-Gemein-
    schaft Bonn
  Recorded ca. 1986, ed. n/a 1849
  Issue: Aulos 53 552, 1 stereo LP, 2 ss, ca.
    1986

1039.GH0   Günther, Hubert
Rhenish Symphony Orchestra, Rhenish
   Youth Choir and Rhenish Choral
   Society
Recorded ca. 1976, ed. n/a 1892
Issue: Garnet 40 104, 1 stereo LP, 2 ss

1039.SH0   Schönzeler, Hans-Hubert
London Philharmonic Orchestra, Alex-
   andra Choir

Recorded in Holy Trinity, Brompton,
   London: June 1970, ed. n/a 1849
Issue: Unicorn UNS 210, 1 stereo LP,
   2 ss [CFB], W. 1971
Timing: 37.02
Notes: Hans-Hubert Schönzeler
With Bruckner: Three Orchestral
   Pieces, March in d minor

Tantum ergo, D Major (WAB 42, G/A 15)

*Composed at St. Florian in 1846 and revised in Vienna in 1888, for five-part
mixed choir and organ.*

1042.BL0   Berberich, Ludwig
Munich Cathedral Choir
Recorded W. 1931, ed. n/a
Issue: Christschall 118, 1 10" mono 78,
   1 s [CST], ca. 1931
Timing: 2.26
Notes: Anonymous
With Bruckner: Ave Maria

1042.BM0   Breitschaft, Mathias
Limburger Dom-Singknaben
Recorded ca. 1977, ed. n/a 1888
Issue: Carus FSM 53 1 18, 1 stereo LP,
   1 s, ca. 1977
With Bruckner: eight other motets and
   Palestrina: eight motets

1042.FA5   Flämig, Martin
Dresdner Kreuzchor, M. Winkler, or-
   gan
Recorded in Lukaskirche, Dresden:
   January 1985, ed. n/a 1888
Issue: Capriccio 10 081, 1 digital stereo
   CD, 1 s [CFB], p. 1987
Timing: 3.38

Notes: Hans Rutesame
With Bruckner: thirteen other motets
Other issues: Capriccio C 27 099, CC 27
   099 (cassette), Delta 10 081 (CD),
   C 27 099, CC 27 099 (cassette)

1042.GW0   Gönnenwein, Wolfgang
Stuttgart Madrigal Choir
Recorded in Ev. Frauenkirche, Essling-
   en/Neckar: July 1962, ed. n/a 1888
Issue: Cantate 640 230, 1 mono LP, 1 s
   [UCB], W. 1963
Timing: 3.16
Notes: Cornelia Auerbach-Schröder
With Bruckner: three other motets and
   Brahms: three motets
Other issues: Cantate 650 230

1042.GW5   Günther, Hubert
Rheinische Singgemeinschaft
Recorded ca. 1976, ed. n/a 1888
Issue: Garnet 40 107, 1 stereo LP, 1 s,
   ca. 1976
With Bruckner: ten other works

1042.HH0   Hahn, Hans Helmut
St. Jakobschor Rothenburg, Sing-
gemeinschaft Petersaurach
Recorded in St. Jacob's Church,
Rothenburg: ca. 1986, ed. n/a 1888
Issue: Pelca PSR 40 620, 1 stereo LP,
1 s, ca. 1986
With Bruckner: three motets and three
works by other composers

1042.RT0   Rehmann, Theodor
Aachen Cathedral Choir
Recorded in Gregorius-Haus, Aachen:
< 1948, ed. n/a
Issue: Musica Sacra B4525, 1 mono 78,
1 s

1042.WG0   Wilhelm, Gerhard
Stuttgarter Hymnus-Chorknaben
Recorded ca. 1986, ed. n/a 1888
Issue: Intercord 160 801, 1 stereo LP,
1 s, ca. 1986
With Bruckner: Ave Maria and twelve
other choral works by various com-
posers
Other issues: Intercord 185 815

1042.WH0   Wollenweider, Hans
Haselbach [Choir]
Recorded ca. 1958, ed. n/a
Issue: Concert Hall SMS 2299, LP, 1 s

Te Deum (WAB 45, G/A 109)

In C Major. Composed in Vienna in 1881, revised in 1883 and 1884, for four
soloists, four-part mixed choir, organ (ad lib.) and orchestra. Only the version
of 1884 has been published.

1045.BD0   Barenboim, Daniel
New Philharmonia Orchestra, New
Philharmonia Chorus
Recorded ca. 1969, ed. n/a 1881
Issue: Angel S-36615, 1 stereo LP, 1 s
[CFB], W. 1970
Timing: 22.45
Notes: Anonymous
With J.S. Bach: Magnificat in D Major
Other issues: EMI ASD 2533, C 063
01991, Seraphim 4XG-60427 (cas-
sette), EMI 037-769 259-1 (LP and
cassette)

1045.BD1   Barenboim, Daniel
Chicago Symphony Orchestra, Chicago
Symphony Chorus
Recorded 28 March 1981, ed. n/a 1881

Issue: DG 2741 007, 2 digital stereo LPs,
1 s [CFB], 28 March 1981
Timing: 22.26
Notes: Stefan Kunze, Robert Simpson
With Bruckner: Symphony No. 8
Other issues: DG 410 650-1, 415 616-4
GW (cassette), 52 MG 0214/5

1045.BL0   Bernardi, Lorenzo
Leipzig Bach Festival Orchestra,
Leipzig Bach Festival Chorus
Recorded ca. 1970, ed. n/a 1881
Issue: Orion 6913, 1 stereo LP, 1 s [CFB],
W. 1970
Timing: 22.22
Notes: Anonymous
With Handel: Laudate pueri Dominum
Other issues: Odeon 638 (cassette)

1045.FK0   Forster, Karl
Berlin Philharmonic Orchestra, St.
Hedwig's Cathedral Choir, Berlin
Recorded ca. 1955, ed. n/a 1881
Issue: Arabesque 8007-2, 2 mono LPs,
1 s [CFB], ca. 1977
Timing: 21.42
Notes: Andrew Porter
With Brahms: German Requiem
Other issues: Odeon E 80010, ALP 1567,
XLP 30073-4, EMI C 047 01142 M,
Arabesque A-9007-2 (cassette)

1045.GF0   Gatz, Felix
[Te Deum and Tu Rex only]
Berlin Staatskapelle, Bruckner Choir
Recorded W. 1928, ed. n/a 1884
Issue: Decca 25159, 78
Other issues: Parlaphone E 10710, A
5006, Odeon O 6572, Odeon 170059
(78)

1045.HB0   Haitink, Bernard
Concertgebouw Orchestra, Amster-
dam, Netherlands Radio Chorus
Recorded 19-20 September 1966, ed.
n/a 1884
Issue: Philips 802 759/60 AY, 2 stereo
LPs, 1 s [CFB], W. 1967
Timing: 22.20
Notes: Conrad Wilson
With Bruckner: Symphony No. 7
Other issues: Philips PHM 2 598/PHS
2 998, SAL 3624-5, 6700 038, 802 759-
60 AY, 13PC 98, SFX 7662/3

1045.HB1   Haitink, Bernard
Vienna Philharmonic Orchestra, Bavarian Radio Chorus
Recorded in Musikverein, Vienna: December 1988

Issue: Philips 422 342-2 PH2, 2 digital
stereo CDs, 1 s [CFB], p. 1989
Timing: 23.46
Notes: Michael Kennedy, Hans
Christoph Worbs
With Bruckner: Symphony No. 5

1045.HW0   Helbich, Wolfgang
Bremen Bach Orchestra, Bremen Ca-
thedral Choir
Recorded in Bremen: ca. 1986, ed. n/a
1881
Issue: Mdg J 1064/65, 2 stereo LPs, 1 s,
ca. 1986
With Brahms: German Requiem

1045.JA0   Janigro, Antonio
Angelicum Orchestra of Milan, Coro
Polifonico Italiano
Recorded W. 1975, ed. n/a 1881
Issue: Musical Heritage Society MHS
1552, 1 stereo LP, 2 ss [CFB], W.
1973
Timing: 19.29
Notes: Edward D. R. Neill
With Bruckner: five motets
Other issues: Angelicum LPA 5989/
STA 8989

1045.JE0   Jochum, Eugen
Munich Radio Symphony Orchestra,
Munich Radio Symphony Chorus
Recorded ca. 1948, ed. n/a 1881
Issue: Decca DX-109, 3 mono LPs, 1 s
[CFB], W. 1951
Timing: 22.42
Notes: Irving Kolodin
With Bruckner: Symphony No. 8
Other issues: Polydor 72020-1 (78), DG
16002, 17155, 18247-8

1045.JE1   Jochum, Eugen
Berlin Philharmonic Orchestra, Chorus of the Deutsche Oper Berlin
Recorded 28 June and 1-2 July 1965, ed. Nowak 1884
Issue: DG 2707 024, 2 stereo LPs, 1 s [CFB], W. 1973
Timing: 21.43
Notes: Constantin Floros
With Bruckner: Symphony No. 9
Other issues: DG 2720 054 [CFB], 39117-8/139117-8, 139399, 423 127-2 (CD)

1045.JE1   Jochum, Eugen
Berlin Philharmonic Orchestra, Chorus of the Deutsche Oper Berlin
Recorded 28 June and 1-2 July 1965, ed. n/a 1881
Issue: DG 2707 024, 2 stereo LPs, 2 ss [CFB], W. 1966
Timing: 21.43
Notes: Constantin Floros
With Bruckner: Symphony No. 9
Other issues: DG 39117-8/139117-8, 139399, 2727 011, 2740 136, 2720 054 [CFB]

1045.JE2   Jochum, Eugen
Bavarian Radio Symphony Orchestra, Bavarian Radio Chorus
Recorded live 14 May 1954
Issue: Orfeo CD-195892, 1 mono CD, 1 s, ca. 1990
Other issues: Orfeo MC-195892 (cassette)

1045.KH0   Karajan, Herbert von
Berlin Philharmonic Orchestra, Wiener Singverein
Recorded 26, 29 September 1976, ed. n/a 1881

Issue: DG 2530 704, 1 stereo LP, 2 ss [CFB], W. 1977
Timing: 25.01
Notes: K.H. Ruppel
With Mozart: Mass No. 14, "Coronation"
Other issues: DG 2530 704 (cassette), DG MG 1041

1045.KH1   Karajan, Herbert von
Vienna Philharmonic Orchestra, Vienna Singverein
Recorded in Großer Musikvereinssaal, Vienna: 22 September 1984, ed. n/a 1881
Issue: DG 410 521-2, 2 digital stereo CDs, 1 s [CFB], p. 1985
Timing: 26.08
Notes: Thomas Kohlhase, John Warrack
With Brahms: A German Requiem
Other issues: DG 410 521-1, 410 5214 (cassette), DG F66 G 50187/8 (CD), S2MG 0870/1

1045.KH2   Karajan, Herbert von
Vienna Symphony Orchestra, Vienna Singverein
Recorded live 29 September 1952
Issue: Hunt HUNT CD 705, 1 mono CD, 1 s, ca. 1990

1045.MZ0   Mehta, Zubin
Vienna Philharmonic Orchestra, Chorus of the Vienna State Opera
Recorded in Sofiensaal, Vienna: 15-16 June 1976, ed. n/a 1881
Issue: London OS 26506, 1 stereo LP, 1 s [CFB], © 1978
Timing: 20.56
Notes: Anonymous
With Bruckner: Mass No. 2

Other issues: SXL 6837, King set SOL 1014/26, London set LDOC1326/38

1045.MZ5 Messner, Josef
Salzburg Festival Orchestra and Chorus
Recorded W. 1949, ed. n/a 1884
Issue: Festival FLP 101, LP, W. 1950

1045.OE0 Ormandy, Eugene
Philadelphia Orchestra, Temple University Choirs
Recorded 13 April 1966, ed. n/a 1881
Issue: Columbia M2S 768, 2 stereo LPs, 1 s [CFB], W. 1968
Timing: 18.30
Notes: Jack Diether
With Bruckner: Symphony No. 5
Other issues: Columbia CM2S 768, 77222

1045.RH0 Rögner, Heinz
Berlin Radio Symphony Orchestra, Berlin Radio Chorus
Recorded in Studio Christuskirche, Berlin: 1988, ed. n/a 1884
Issue: Ars Vivendi 2100172, 1 digital stereo CD, 1 s [CFB], p. 1990
Timing: 23.25
Notes: Mathias Hansen
With Bruckner: Mass No. 2

1045.SM0 Stephani, Martin
[In te Domine speravi only]
Philharmonia Hungarica, Chor des Musikvereins, Bielefeld
Recorded 2-3 February 1976, ed. n/a 1881
Issue: Teldec 8.44068, 1 stereo CD, 1 s [CFB], © 1988

Timing: 6.09
With Bruckner: Symphony No. 9
Other issues: Telefunken 6.42037 [complete timing: 23.36], Telefunken SLA 6187

1045.WA0 Wallberg, Heinz
Vienna National Orchestra, Jeunesses Musicales Chorus
Recorded W. 1967, ed. n/a 1884
Issue: Guilde Int. du Disque SMS 2442, LP
Other issues: Guilde Int. du Disque SMS 2604

1045.WB0 Walter, Bruno
New York Philharmonic, Westminster Choir
Recorded 7 March 1953, ed. Mahler 1884
Issue: Columbia Y2 35238, 2 stereo LPs, this selection mono, 1 s [CFB], © 1979
Timing: 20.05
Notes: Anonymous
With Bruckner: Symphony No. 7
Other issues: Columbia ML 4980, CBS 72317, Philips GBL 5629, L 09407-8 L, Melodiya D 028225-8, CBS 39 651

1045.WB1 Walter, Bruno
Vienna Philharmonic Orchestra, Vienna State Opera Chorus
Recorded live 13 November 1955
Issue: Nuova era 2303, 1 mono CD, 1 s, ca. 1990
With Brahms: Symphony No. 4

Tota pulchra es (WAB 46, G/A 101)

Composed in 1878 at Vienna for tenor solo, four-part mixed choir and organ.

1046.BL0   Berberich, Ludwig
Munich Cathedral Choir
Recorded W. 1929, ed. n/a 1878
Issue: Polydor 27119, 1 mono 78, 1 s
Other issues: Polydor J 65006 (78)

1046.BM0   Best, Matthew
Corydon Singers
Recorded in St. Alban's Church, Hol-
born, London: May 1982, ed. n/a
1878
Issue: Hyperion A66062, 1 stereo LP,
1 s [CFB], p. 1983
Timing: 5.44
Notes: Douglas Hammond
With Bruckner: ten other motets
Other issues: Hyperion CD 66062 (CD)

1046.BO0   Böck, Herbert
Concentus Vocalis Wien
Recorded in Vienna: © 1988
Issue: Koch 317 008 H1, 1 stereo CD,
1 s [CFB], p. 1988
Timing: 4.50
With Distler: Totentanz

1046.EJ0   Eichorn, Joachim
Jugendkantorei Wetzlar
Recorded ca. 1988, ed. 1878
Issue: Mitra 16 206, 1 digital stereo LP,
1 s, ca. 1988
With ten other choral works by various
composers

1046.FA0   Flämig, Martin
Dresdner Kreuzchor
Recorded in Lukaskirche, Dresden:
January 1985, ed. n/a 1878

Issue: Capriccio 10 081, 1 digital stereo
CD, 1 s [CFB], p. 1987
Timing: 4.25
Notes: Hans Rutesame
With Bruckner: thirteen other motets
Other issues: Capriccio C 27 099, CC
27 099 (cassette), Delta 10 081 (CD),
C 27 099, CC 27 099 (cassette),
Laserlight 15 278 (CD) [CFB]

1046.FJ0   Fuchs, Johannes
Zurich Chamber Choir
Recorded in Reformed Church, Zürich-
Altstetten: September 1984, ed. n/a
1878
Issue: Ex Libris CD 6009, 1 digital ste-
reo CD, 1 s [CFB], p. 1985
Timing: 5.02
Notes: Alois Koch
With Bruckner: two Æquale and ten
other motets
Other issues: Koch Records Schwann
16 970

1046.GU0   Gronostay, Uwe
Denmark Radio Choir
Recorded in Trinitatis Church, Copen-
hagen: August 1985, ed. n/a 1878
Issue: Kontrapunkt 32022, 1 stereo CD,
1 s [CFB], p. 1989
Timing: 4.43
Notes: Knut Ketting
With Bruckner: nine other motets and
Werner: Hommage à Bruckner

1046.HE0   Hausmann, Elmar
Capella Vocale St. Aposteln, Cologne
Recorded ca. 1986, ed. n/a 1878

Issue: Aulos 53 569, 1 stereo LP, 1 s, ca. 1986
With Bruckner: Missa Solemnis and three other motets

1046.JE0   Jochum, Eugen
Chorus of the Bavarian Radio
Recorded 24-26 June 1966, ed. n/a 1878
Issue: DG 2720 054, 5 stereo LPs, 1 s [CFB], ca. 1981
Timing: 5.13
Notes: Wolfgang Dömling
With Bruckner: Masses Nos. 1-3, Te Deum, Psalm 150, motets
Other issues: DG 39134-5/139134-5, 2707 025, 136552, 2561 221, 423 127-2 (CD)

1046.MJ0   Martini, Joachim
Junge Kantorei, Darmstadt
Recorded W. 1971, ed. n/a 1878
Issue: Schwarzwald 13004, LP, 1 s
Other issues: Schwarzwald CRO 833, 2520833

1046.MJ0   Messner, Joseph
Salzburg Cathedral Choir
Recorded W. 1930, ed. n/a 1878
Issue: Christschall 90, 78, 1 s

1046.PP0   Pernoud, Pierre
La Psallette de Genève
Recorded ca. 1970, ed. n/a 1878
Issue: Disques VDE VDE 3044, 1 stereo LP, 1 s [CFB], ca. 1988
Timing: 5.06
Notes: Anonymous
With Bruckner: four other motets and Brahms: three motets
Schwann gives "Gallo" as record label

1046.RH0   Reichel, Helmuth
Zürcher Bach-Kantorei
Recorded in Reformed Church, Zürich-Oerlikon: June 1981, ed. n/a 1878
Issue: Fono Schallplatten FCD 91 229, 1 stereo CD, 1 s [CFB], p. 1990
Timing: 4.55
Notes: Kurt Pahlen
With Bruckner: nine other motets
Other issues: Fono Schallplatten FSM 53 229

1046.SW0   Schäfer, Wolfgang
Freiburg Vocal Ensemble
Recorded in Church of St. Barbara, Freiburg-Littenweiler: p. 1984, ed. n/a 1878
Issue: Christophorus CD 74501, 1 digital stereo CD, 1 s [CFB], © 1984
Timing: 4.40
With Bruckner: nine other motets
Other issues: Christophorus SCGLX 74 009, 74 059F, CD74 539 (CD)

1046.WF0   Wasner, Franz
Trapp Family Singers
Recorded W. 1956, ed. n/a 1878
Issue: Decca DL 9838, 1 mono LP, 1 s [CSUS], W. 1956
Timing: 3.56
With sixteen other works by various composers
Other issues: Decca MG 4708

1046.ZH0   Zanotelli, Hans
Philharmonisches Vocalensemble Stuttgart
Recorded ca. 1987, ed. n/a 1878
Issue: Calig CAL 30 477, 1 stereo LP, 1 s, ca. 1987
With Bruckner: eleven other motets

Vexilla regis (WAB 51, G/A 120)

Composed in 1892 at Vienna for four-part mixed choir.

1051.BG0   Bertola, Giulio
Coro Polifonico Italiano
Recorded W. 1965, ed. n/a 1892
Issue: Musical Heritage Society MHS
1552, 1 stereo LP, 1 s [CFB], W. 1973
Timing: 4.16
Notes: Edward D. R. Neill
With Bruckner: Te Deum and four other
motets
Other issues: Angelicum LPA 5989/
STA 8989

1051.BM0   Best, Matthew
Corydon Singers
Recorded in St. Alban's Church, Hol-
born, London: May 1982, ed. n/a
1892
Issue: Hyperion A66062, 1 stereo LP,
1 s [CFB], p. 1983
Timing: 4.48
Notes: Douglas Hammond
With Bruckner: ten other motets
Other issues: Hyperion CD 66 062 (CD)

1051.BM5   Breitschaft, Mathias
Limburger Dom-Singknaben
Recorded ca. 1977, ed. 1892
Issue: Carus FSM 53118, 1 stereo LP,
1 s, ca. 1977
With Bruckner: seven other motets and
Palestrina: eight motets

1051.FA5   Flämig, Martin
Dresdner Kreuzchor
Recorded in Lukaskirche, Dresden:
January 1985, ed. n/a 1892

Issue: Capriccio 10 081, 1 digital stereo
CD, 1 s [CFB], p. 1987
Timing: 4.41
Notes: Hans Rutesame
With Bruckner: thirteen other motets
Other issues: Capriccio C 27 099, CC 27
099 (cassette), Delta 10 081 (CD),
C 27 099, CC 27 099 (cassette)

1051.FJ0   Fuchs, Johannes
Zurich Chamber Choir
Recorded in Reformed Church, Zürich-
Altstetten: September 1984, ed. n/a
1892
Issue: Ex Libris CD 6009, 1 digital ste-
reo CD, 1 s [CFB], p. 1985
Timing: 5.23
Notes: Alois Koch
With Bruckner: two Æquale and ten
other motets
Other issues: Koch Records Schwann
16 970

1051.GU0   Gronostay, Uwe
Denmark Radio Choir
Recorded in Trinitatis Church, Co-
penhagen: August 1985, ed. n/a
1892
Issue: Kontrapunkt 32022, 1 stereo CD,
1 s [CFB], p. 1989
Timing: 6.09
Notes: Knut Ketting
With Bruckner: nine other motets and
Werner: *Hommage à Bruckner*

1051.HF0   Habel, Ferdinand
St. Stephen's Cathedral Choir of Vienna
Recorded W. 1931, ed. n/a 1892
Issue: Christschall 130, 78, 1 s

1051.HP0   Herreweghe, Philippe
La Chapelle Royale
Recorded November 1989
Issue: Harmonia mundi HMC 901322,
   1 digital stereo CD, 1 s [CFB],
   p. 1990
Timing: 4.50
Notes: Jean-Yves Bras
With Bruckner: Mass No. 2, Æquale I
   and II, four other motets

1051.JE0   Jochum, Eugen
Chorus of the Bavarian Radio
Recorded 24-26 June 1966, ed. n/a 1892
Issue: DG 2720 054, 5 stereo LPs, 1 s
   [CFB], ca. 1981
Timing: 6.03
Notes: Wolfgang Dömling
With Bruckner: Masses Nos. 1-3, Te
   Deum, Psalm 150, motets
Other issues: DG 423 127-2 (CD), SLGM
   1413/4, MGX 9917/8

1051.LA0   Los Angeles Philharmonic
   Trombone Ensemble
Recorded in Los Angeles: ca. 1976, ed.
   R. Sauer 1892
Issue: Western International Music
   WIMR-12, 1 stereo LP, 1 s [CFB], ca.
   1976
Timing: 2.13
Notes: Ralph Sauer

With Bruckner: two other motets and
   thirteen other works by various
   composers
Transcribed for trombone quartet

1051.RH0   Reichel, Helmuth
Zürcher Bach-Kantorei
Recorded in Reformed Church, Zürich-
   Oerlikon: June 1981, ed. n/a 1892
Issue: Fono Schallplatten FCD 91 229,
   1 stereo CD, 1 s [CFB], p. 1990
Timing: 4.27
Notes: Kurt Pahlen
With Bruckner: nine other motets
Other issues: Fono Schallplatten FSM
   53 229

1051.SW0   Schäfer, Wolfgang
Freiburg Vocal Ensemble
Recorded in Church of St. Barbara,
   Freiburg-Littenweiler: p. 1984, ed.
   n/a 1892
Issue: Christophorus CD 74501, 1 digi-
   tal stereo CD, 1 s [CFB], © 1984
Timing: 4.36
With Bruckner: nine other motets
Other issues: Christophorus SCGLX
   74 009

1051.ZH0   Zanotelli, Hans
Philharmonisches Vocalensemble
   Stuttgart
Recorded ca. 1987, ed. n/a 1892
Issue: Calig CAL 30 477, 1 stereo LP,
   1 s, ca. 1987
With Bruckner: eleven other motets

Virga Jesse (WAB 52, G/A 116)

Alla breve. Feierlich langsam. In e minor. Composed in 1885 at Vienna for four-part mixed choir.

1052.AJ0   Alldis, John
John Alldis Choir
Recorded p. 1967, ed. n/a 1885
Issue: Argo ZRG 523, 1 stereo LP, 1 s
  [CFB], W. 1968
Timing: 2.58
Notes: Robert Henderson
With choral works by Bruckner, Schönberg, Debussy and Messiaen
Other issues: Decca SXL 21177

1052.AR0   Arndt, Günther
Berlin Motet Choir
Recorded < 1948, ed. n/a 1885
Issue: Decca LW 5131, LP, 1 s
With Schnabel: Transeamus
Other issues: Decca D 17805 (45),
  F 43805 (78)

1052.BG0   Bertola, Giulio
Coro Polifonico Italiano
Recorded W. 1965, ed. n/a 1885
Issue: Musical Heritage Society MHS
  1552, 1 stereo LP, 1 s [CFB], W. 1973
Timing: 3.08
Notes: Edward D. R. Neill
With Bruckner: Te Deum and four other motets
Other issues: Angelicum LPA 5989/
  STA 8989

1052.BM0   Best, Matthew
Corydon Singers
Recorded in St. Alban's Church, Holborn, London: May 1982, ed. n/a 1885

Issue: Hyperion A66062, 1 stereo LP,
  1 s [CFB], p. 1983
Timing: 4.23
Notes: Douglas Hammond
With Bruckner: ten other motets
Other issues: Hyperion CD 66 062 (CD)

1052.BM0h Böck, Herbert
Concentus Vocalis Wien
Recorded in Vienna: © 1988
Issue: Koch 317 008 H1, 1 stereo CD,
  1 s [CFB], p. 1988
Timing: 3.30
With Distler: *Totentanz*

1052.BM1   Brandstetter, Manfred
Bach Choir Hannover
Recorded ca. 1970, ed. n/a 1885
Issue: Psallite PET 124 030772, 1 stereo
  LP, 1 s

1052.BR0   Bradshaw, Richard
Saltarello Choir
Recorded in Church of St. Bartholomew The Great, Smithfield, London: p. 1974, ed. n/a 1885
Issue: CRD 1009, 1 stereo LP, 1 s [CFB],
  p. 1974
Timing: 3.16
Notes: Anonymous
With Bruckner: four other motets and works by Brahms and Verdi

1052.FA5   Flämig, Martin
Dresdner Kreuzchor
Recorded in Lukaskirche, Dresden: January 1985, ed. n/a 1885

Issue: Capriccio 10 081, 1 digital stereo CD, 1 s [CFB], p. 1987
Timing: 4.47
Notes: Hans Rutesame
With Bruckner: thirteen other motets
Other issues: Capriccio C 27 099, CC 27 099 (cassette), Delta 10 081 (CD), C 27 099, CC 27 099 (cassette), Laserlight 15 278 [CFB]

1052.FW0   Faure, William
William Faure Kammerchor
Recorded < 1948, ed. n/a 1885
Issue: Telefunken A 10046, 78, 1 s
With Schnabel: Transeamus

1052.FX0   Fuchs, Johannes
Zurich Chamber Choir
Recorded in Reformed Church, Zürich-Altstetten: September 1984, ed. n/a 1885
Issue: Ex Libris CD 6009, 1 digital stereo CD, 1 s [CFB], p. 1985
Timing: 5.05
Notes: Alois Koch
With Bruckner: two Æquale and ten other motets
Other issues: Koch Records Schwann 16 970

1052.GH0   Gillesberger, Hans
Vienna Academy Chamber Choir
Recorded W. 1960, ed. n/a 1885
Issue: Austria Vanguard AVRS 6064, 1 mono LP, 1 s [UCB], W. 1963
Timing: 4.09
Notes: Anonymous
With Bruckner: four other motets and Heiller: two motets
Other issues: Record Society RS 71, Amadeo AVRS 6064, 15084 (45)

1052.GH1   Gillesberger, Hans
Vienna Choir Boys, Chorus Viennensis
Recorded p. 1972, ed. n/a 1885
Issue: Acanta 41 232, 1 stereo CD, 1 s [CFB], p. 1988
Timing: 3.58
Notes: Gerhard Schuhmacher
With Bruckner: four other motets and Britten: *Ceremony of Carols*
Other issues: BASF KBB 21232

1052.GU0   Gronostay, Uwe
Denmark Radio Choir
Recorded in Trinitatis Church, Copenhagen: August 1985, ed. n/a 1892
Issue: Kontrapunkt 32022, 1 stereo CD, 1 s [CFB], p. 1989
Timing: 3.57
Notes: Knud Ketting
With Bruckner: nine other motets and Werner: *Hommage à Bruckner*

1052.HA0   Habel, Ferdinand
St. Stephen's Choir of Vienna
Recorded W. 1931, ed. n/a 1885
Issue: Christschall 129, 1 mono 78, 1 s [CST]
Timing: 3.45
Notes: Anonymous
With Haydn: "Du bist's, dem Ruhm und Ehre gebühret"

1052.HA5   Hausmann, Elmar
Capella Vocale St. Aposteln, Cologne
Recorded ca. 1986, ed. n/a 1885
Issue: Aulos 53 569, 1 stereo LP, 1 s, ca. 1986
With Bruckner: Missa Solemnis and three other motets

1052.HD0   Hellmann, Diethard
Bach Choir of Mainz
Recorded p. 1979, ed. n/a 1885
Issue: Calig CAL 30 469, 1 stereo LP,
     1 s [CFB], p. 1979
Timing: 4.15
Notes: Anonymous "U.M."
With Bruckner: four other motets and
     Kodály: Laudes organi

1052.JE0   Jochum, Eugen
Chorus of the Bavarian Radio
Recorded 24-26 June 1966, ed. n/a 1885
Issue: DG 2720 054, 5 stereo LPs, 1 s
     [CFB], ca. 1981
Timing: 4.28
Notes: Wolfgang Dömling
With Bruckner: Masses 1-3, Te Deum,
     Psalm 150, motets
Other issues: DG 39134-5/139134-5,
     2707 025, 136552, 423 127-2 (CD)

1052.MR0   Mauersberger, Rudolf
Dresden Kreuzchor
Recorded < 1948, ed. n/a 1885
Issue: Polydor 10281, 78, 1 s
Other issues: Brunswick 35034 (78)

1052.PW0   Pitz, Wilhelm
New Philharmonia Chorus
Recorded 16-18 November 1966, ed.
     n/a 1885
Issue: Angel S-36428, 1 stereo LP, 1 s
     [CFB], W. 1967
Timing: 3.10
Notes: Paul Jennings, W.A. Chislett
With Bruckner: four other motets and
     works by five other composers
Other issues: EMI ASD 2325, SME
     81046

1052.RH0   Reichel, Helmuth
Zürcher Bach-Kantorei
Recorded in Reformed Church, Zürich-
     Oerlikon: June 1981, ed. n/a 1885
Issue: Fono Schallplatten FCD 91 229,
     1 stereo CD, 1 s [CFB], p. 1990
Timing: 4.39
Notes: Kurt Pahlen
With Bruckner: nine other motets
Other issues: Fono Schallplatten FSM
     53 229

1052.SW0   Schäfer, Wolfgang
Freiburg Vocal Ensemble
Recorded in Church of St. Barbara,
     Freiburg-Littenweiler: p. 1984, ed.
     n/a 1885
Issue: Christophorus CD 74501, 1 digi-
     tal stereo CD, 1 s [CFB], © 1984
Timing: 3.45
With Bruckner: nine other motets
Other issues: Christophorus SCGLX
     74 009

1052.SW1   Schrems, Theobald
Regensburger Domspatzen
Recorded ca. 1974, ed. n/a 1885
Issue: Musical Heritage Society MHS
     1935, 1 stereo LP, 1 s [UCD]
Timing: 3.20
With Bruckner: Ave Maria and thir-
     teen other choral works by various
     composers
Other issues: Christophorus SCGLP
     75969, CV 75011 (45)

1052.ZH0   Zanotelli, Hans
  Philharmonisches Vocalensemble
  Stuttgart
  Recorded ca. 1987, ed. n/a 1885

Issue: Calig CAL 30 477, 1 stereo LP,
  1 s, ca. 1987
With Bruckner: eleven other motets

Helgoland (WAB 71, G/A 123)

In g minor. Composed in 1893 in Vienna for four-part male choir and orchestra.

1071.BD0   Barenboim, Daniel
  Chicago Symphony Orchestra, Chicago
  Symphony Chorus
  Recorded March 1979, ed. n/a 1893
  Issue: DG 2707 116, 2 stereo LPs, 1 s
  [CFB], p. 1980
  Timing: 13.46
  Notes: Siegfried Kross, Robert Simpson
  With Bruckner: Symphony No. 7 and
  Psalm 150
  Other issues: DG 410 650-1, MG 8430/1

1071.MW0 Morris, Wyn
  Symphonica of London, Ambrosian
  Male Voice Chorus
  Recorded W. 1977, ed. n/a 1893
  Issue: Peters PLE 043, 1 stereo LP, 1 s
  [CFB], p. 1978
  Timing: 14.50
  Notes: Jack Diether
  With Wagner: *Das Liebesmahl der Apostel*

Herbstlied (WAB 73, G/A 70)

In f# minor. Composed in Linz in 1864 for four-part male choir, two sopranos and piano.

1073.RT0   Rehmann, Theodor
  Aachen Cathedral Choir
  Recorded ca. 1955, ed. n/a 1864
  Issue: Electrola EG 6530, 78, 1 s
  With Bruckner: other choral works

1073.ST0   Schrems, Theobald
  Regensburg Cathedral Choir
  Recorded < 1948, ed. n/a 1864
  Issue: Electrola EG 6530, 78, 1 s
  With Reger: Im Himmelreich

Trösterin Musik (WAB 88, G/A 99)

Maestoso. In c minor. Composed in 1877 in Vienna for four-part male choir and organ.

1088.GH0 Günther, Hubert
Männergesangverein Concordia
Hamm
Recorded ca. 1976, ed. n/a 1877

Issue: Garnet 40 107, 1 stereo LP, 1 s, ca. 1976
With Bruckner: ten other pieces
Music is identical to "Nachruf," WAB 81.

Um Mitternacht (WAB 89, G/A 69)

Feierlich, doch nicht schleppend. In f minor. Composed in 1864 in Linz for four-part male choir, alto solo and piano.

1089.KR0 Kühbacher, Robert
Vienna Choir Boys
Recorded W. 1955, ed. J. Böhm 1864
Issue: Philips N 00726 R, LP, 1 s, ca. 1955

With works by Brahms, Reger, Buxtehude, etc.
Other issues: Philips P 08496 L, NBR 6024
This may be version No. 2 (WAB 90).

Um Mitternacht (WAB 90, G/A 93)

Ziemlich langsam, feierlich. In f minor. Composed in 1886 in Vienna and revised in 1887, for tenor solo and four-part male choir.

1090.AA0 Anonymous
Essen Schubertbund
Recorded ca. 1960, ed. n/a 1887
Issue: Polydor 249208, LP, 1 s

1090.GI0 Günther, Hubert
Rheinische Singgemeinschaft
Recorded ca. 1976, ed. n/a 1887

Issue: Garnet 40 107, 1 stereo LP, 1 s, ca. 1976
With Bruckner: ten other works

1090.SW0 Schneider, Walther
Stuttgart Liederkreis
Recorded ca. 1950, ed. n,'a 1886
Issue: Odeon O/STO 41453, 45, 1 s

O du liebes Jesu Kind (WAB 145, G/A 11)

Andante. In B flat Major. Composed ca. 1845 at St. Florian for solo voice with organ accompaniment.

1145.JJ0   Jürgens, Jürgen
Recorded in Dormition Abbey, Jerusalem: July 1984, ed. n/a 1855
Issue: Jerusalem Records ATD 8503, 1 digital stereo LP, 1 ss [CFB], p. 1985

Timing: 2.36
Notes: David H. Aldeborgh
With Bruckner: Missa Solemnis, Magnificat, one additional sacred song

Hostias

Not in WAB or G/A, possibly from Requiem in d minor, WAB 39.

1999.GH0   Günther, Hubert
Männergesangverein Concordia Hamm, Rheinisches Kinder- und Jugendchor
Recorded ca. 1976

Issue: Garnet 40107, 1 stereo LP, 1 s, ca. 1976
With Bruckner: eight other choral works

Chamber Music

String Quartet in c minor (WAB 111, not in G/A)

I. Allegro moderato, II. Andante, III. Scherzo (Presto), IV. Rondo (schnell).
For two violins, viola and cello. Composed in Linz in 1862.

2111.BQ0 Bamberg Cathedral Quartet
Recorded ca. 1988, ed. n/a 1862
Issue: Cavalli Records CLP 203, 1 stereo LP, 1 ss, ca. 1988
With Haydn: String Quartet No. 78

2111.KQ0 Keller Quartet
E. Keller, H. Ziehe, F. Schessl, G. Schmid, M. Braun
Recorded ca. 1967, ed. n/a 1862

Issue: Oryx 1808, 1 stereo LP, 2 ss [CFB], ca. 1970
Timing: 19.21 (6.22, 6.02, 3.06, 3.51)
Notes: Anonymous
With Bruckner: Intermezzo
Other issues: Musical Heritage Society MHS 1363-4, Da Camera SM 92707-8

String Quintet in F Major (WAB 112, G/A 103)

I. Gemäßigt, Moderato; II. Scherzo: Schnell, Trio: Langsamer; III. Adagio; IV.
Finale: Lebhaft bewegt, Langsamer. For two violins, two violas and cello.
Composed in Vienna in 1879 and first performed with the Intermezzo (WAB
113) in place of the Scherzo.

2112.AQ0 Amadeus Quartet
N. Brainin, S. Nissel, P. Schidlof, C. Aronowitz, M. Lovett
Recorded ca. 1965, ed. n/a 1879
Issue: DG 138 963, 1 stereo LP, 2 ss [CFB], W. 1965

Timing: 44.30 (13.04, 7.40, 13.41, 9.35)
Notes: Constantin Floros
Other issues: DG LPM 18963

2112.HQ0 Heutling Quartet, with Heinz-
Otto Graf, viola
Recorded W. 1974, ed. n/a 1879
Issue: Electrola 1C 063 29100, LP

2112.HW5 Horn, Erwin
[Adagio only] Recorded on the organ
of the Basilica, Waldsassen: ca. 1986,
ed. n/a
Issue: Mitra 16 170, 1 digital stereo LP,
1 ss, ca. 1986
With Bruckner: Symphony No. 2
[Scherzo only] and Guilmant: Sonata No. 1 for organ

2112.KA0 Kammermusiker Zürich
Recorded W. 1973, ed. n/a 1879
Issue: Pelca PSR 40 562, 1 stereo LP,
2 ss, W. 1973

2112.KE0 Keller Quartet
with G. Schmid, viola
Recorded W. 1967, ed. n/a 1879
Issue: Musical Heritage Society MHS
1363-4, 1 stereo LP, 2 ss
Other issues: Oryx ORX 1807, Da Camera SM 92707-8

2112.KO0 Kocian Quartet
P. Hula, J. Odstrcil, L. Maly, J. Najnar,
V. Bernasek
Recorded at Domovina studio, Prague:
December 1983, ed. n/a 1879
Issue: Supraphon CO-1744, 1 stereo
CD, 1 ss [CFB], p. 1986
Timing: 48.15 (13.42, 8.17, 16.45, 9.31)
Notes: Milos Pokora
Other issues: Supraphon 3360 1744

2112.KQ0 Koeckert Quartet
R. Koeckert, W. Buchner, O. Riedl,
G. Schmid, J. Merz

Recorded W. 1955, ed. n/a 1879
Issue: Decca DL 9796, 1 mono LP, 2 ss
[UCB], W. 1955
Timing: 40.59 (12.09, 7.16, 13.32, 8.02)
Notes: Egon Kenton
Other issues: DG LPM 18042

2112.MQ0 Melos Quartet
W. Melcher, G. Voss, H. Voss, E. San-
tiago, P. Buck
Recorded ca. 1969, ed. n/a 1879
Issue: Candide CE 31014, 1 stereo LP,
2 ss [CFB], W. 1969
Timing: 43.22 (12.07, 8.07, 13.00, 10.04)
Notes: Anonymous
With Wolf: Italian Serenade
Other issues: Intercord 180854, 820 744
(CD), Turnabout CT-7005 (cassette)

2112.OP0 Soloists of the Orchestra of
Paris
L. Yordanoff, Y. Boico, A. Chaves,
J. Dupouy, A. Tetard
Recorded in Paris: 1982, ed. n/a 1879
Issue: Ades 14.037, 1 stereo LP, 2 ss
[CFB], p. 1983
Timing: 47.05 (13.30, 7.00, 16.55, 9.40)
Notes: Paul-Gilbert Langevin

2112.PQ0 Prisca Quartet, with S. Mein-
cke, viola
Recorded < 1948, ed. n/a 1879
Issue: Polydor 15165-70, 6 mono 78s,
11 ss
With Haydn: Serenade
Other issues: Decca X 220-5

2112.SO0 Sonare Quartet
J. Klimkiewicz, L. Bonitz, H. Ko-
bayashi, V. Mendelssohn, E. Klein
Recorded at Orangerie, Darmstadt:
January 1990, ed. 1879

Issue: Claves CD 50-9006, 1 digital stereo CD, 1 s [CFB], p. 1990
Timing: 40.51 (12.44, 7.00, 12.50, 8.17)
Notes: Georg-Albrecht Eckle
With Bruckner: Intermezzo

2112.SQ0   Strub Quartet, with H. Münch-Holland, viola
Recorded < 1948, ed. n/a 1879
Issue: Electrola DB 5541-5, 5 mono 78s, 10 ss

2112.VK0   Vienna Konzerthaus Quartet, with F. Stangler, viola
Recorded W. 1956, ed. n/a 1879
Issue: Vanguard VRS 480, LP, W. 1956
Other issues: Amadeo AVRS 6030

2112.VP0   Vienna Philharmonia Quintet
W. Poduschka, A. Staar, J. Staar, H. Weis, W. Herzer
Recorded Sofiensaal, Vienna: April 1974, ed. Nowak 1879
Issue: London STS 15400, 1 stereo LP, 2 ss [CFB], © 1977
Timing: 43.32 (12.06, 7.30, 15.25, 8.31)
Notes: Leopold Nowak
With Bruckner: Intermezzo
Other issues: Decca SDD 490, 6.42160 AP

2112.VP1   Vienna Philharmonic Quintet
Recorded W. 1950, ed. n/a 1879
Issue: Vox PL 6330, LP, W. 1950

Intermezzo (WAB 113, G/A 104)

Moderato. In d minor, for two violins, two violas and cello. Composed in 1879 as a substitute for the original Scherzo of the String Quintet (WAB 112).

2113.AS0   Alberni String Quartet
H. Davis, P. People, B. Evans, R. Best, D. Smith
Recorded Unitarian Church, Rosslyn Hill, Hampstead, England: p. 1978, ed. n/a 1879
Issue: CRD 1046, 1 stereo LP, 1 s [CFB], p. 1978
Timing: 8.55
Notes: Max Harrison
With Brahms: Sextet in G, op. 36
Other issues: [Helikon] CRD CD-3346 (CD), 4046 (cassette)

2113.KQ0   Keller Quartet
E. Keller, H. Ziehe, F. Schessl, G. Schmid, M. Braun
Recorded ca. 1967, ed. n/a 1879

Issue: Oryx 1808, 1 stereo LP, 1 s [CFB], ca. 1970
Timing: 4.06
Notes: Anonymous
With Bruckner: String Quartet in c minor
Other issues: Musical Heritage Society MHS 1363-4, Da Camera SM 92707-8

2113.SO0   Sonare Quartet
J. Klimkiewicz, L. Bonitz, H. Kobayashi, V. Mendelssohn, E. Klein
Recorded Orangerie, Darmstadt: January 1990, ed. 1879
Issue: Claves CD 50-9006, 1 digital stereo CD, 1 s [CFB], p. 1990
Timing: 7.46

Notes: Georg-Albrecht Eckle
With Bruckner: Quintet in F Major

2113.VK0   Vienna Konzerthaus Quartet,
with F. Stangler, viola
Recorded W. 1956, ed. n/a 1879
Issue: Vanguard VRS 480, LP, W. 1956
With Bruckner: String Quintet in F
Other issues: Amadeo AVRS 6030

2113.VP0   Vienna Philharmonia Quintet
W. Poduschka, A. Staar, J. Staar,
H. Weis, W. Herzer

Recorded in Sofiensaal, Vienna: April
1974, ed. Nowak 1879
Issue: London STS 15400, 1 stereo LP,
2 ss [CFB], © 1977
Timing: 7.50
Notes: Leopold Nowak
With Bruckner: String Quintet in F
Major
Other issues: Decca SDD 490, 6.42160
AP

Æquale I (WAB 114, G/A 21)

In c minor. For three trombones, composed at St. Florian in 1847.

2114.BE0   Berlin Trombone Quartet
Recorded in Japan: W. 1971, ed. n/a
1847
Issue: CBS Sony SONC 16015, LP, 1 s

2114.BM0   Best, Matthew
English Chamber Orchestra Wind En-
semble
Recorded in Church of St. Alban, Hol-
born, London: April 1985, ed. n/a
1847
Issue: Hyperion CDA66177, 1 digital
stereo CD, 1 s [CFB], p. 1986
Timing: 1.50
Notes: Robert Simpson
With Bruckner: Mass No. 2, Libera me,
and Æquale II
Other issues: Hyperion 66177 (LP and
cassette)

2114.EM0   Herreweghe, Philippe
Ensemble Musique Oblique
J. Raffard, T. Guilbert, L. Milhiet, trom-
bones
Recorded November 1989
Issue: Harmonia mundi HMC 901322,
1 digital stereo CD, 1 s [CFB],
p. 1990
Timing: 1.55
Notes: Jean-Yves, Bras
With Bruckner: Mass No. 2, Aequale
II, five motets

2114.FJ0   Fuchs, Johannes
Slokar Trombone Quartet
Recorded Reformed Church, Zürich-
Altstetten: September 1984, ed. n/a
1847
Issue: Ex Libris CD 6009, 1 digital ste-
reo CD, 1 s [CFB], p. 1985

Timing: 2.00
Notes: Alois Koch
With Bruckner: Æquale II and eleven
  motets
Other issues: Koch Records Schwann
  16 970

2114.SP0   P. Schreckenburger Posaun-
  enensemble
Recorded W. 1976, ed. n/a 1847
Issue: R.B.M. RBM 3036, 1 stereo LP,
  1 s
With ten other works for trombone by
  various composers
Other issues: RBM 6 3036 (CD)

Apollo March (WAB 115) *See under IV. Orchestral works*

Erinnerung (WAB 117, G/A 87)

Langsam, innig. In A flat Major. For piano solo, composed in Linz ca. 1860.

2117.DJ0   Demus, Jörg
Recorded W. 1961, ed. n/a 1860
Issue: Music Guild M/S 23, 1 stereo
  LP, 1 s, W. 1962
Other issues: Intercord 180 812, 820 724
  (CD)

2117.HL0   Howard, Leslie
Recorded ca. 1986, ed. n/a 1986
Issue: Hyperion 66 090 TW, 1 stereo
  LP, 1 s, ca. 1986
With thirteen other piano pieces by
  various composers
Other issues: Hyperion CD 66 090 WP
  (CD)

Quadrille (WAB 121, G/A 26)

Pantalon. In A Major. For piano four hands, composed at St. Florian ca. 1854.

2121.WS0   Wikman, Solveig and Wikman, Bertil
Recorded W. 1976, ed. n/a 1854
Issue: Sterling S 1001-2, 1 stereo LP, 1 s,
  ca. 1976

Æquale II (WAB 149, not in G/A)

In c minor. For three trombones, composed at St. Florian ca. 1847.

2149.BM0   Best, Matthew
English Chamber Orchestra Wind Ensemble
Recorded Church of St. Alban, Holborn, London: April 1985, ed. n/a 1847
Issue: Hyperion CDA66177, 1 digital stereo CD, 1 s [CFB], p. 1986
Timing: 1.55
Notes: Robert Simpson
With Bruckner: Mass No. 2, Libera me and one other Æquale
Other issues: Hyperion 66177 (LP and cassette)

2149.EM0   Herreweghe, Philippe
Ensemble Musique Oblique
J. Raffard, T. Guilbert, L. Milhiet, trombones
Recorded November 1989
Issue: Harmonia mundi HMC 901322, 1 digital stereo CD, 1 s [CFB], p. 1990

Timing: 1.35
Notes: Jean-Yves Bras
With Bruckner: Mass No. 2, Æquale I, five motets

2149.FJ0   Fuchs, Johannes
Slokar Trombone Quartet
Recorded Reformed Church, Zurich-Altstetten: September 1984, ed. n/a 1847
Issue: Ex Libris CD 6009, 1 digital stereo CD, 1 s [CFB], p. 1985
Timing: 1.35
Notes: Alois Koch
With Bruckner: Æquale I and eleven motets
Other issues: Koch Records Schwann 16 970

Organ Works

Fugue in d minor (WAB 125, G/A 54)

Langsame Halbe. Composed in Linz in 1861.

3125.FA0   Forer, Alois
Recorded in the Hofburgkapelle, Vienna: ca. 1975, ed. n/a 1861
Issue: Elite Special PLPS 30 093, 1 stereo LP, 1 s [CSUS]
Timing: 3.22
Notes: Rudolf Scholz
With Bruckner: nine other organ works and Schmidt: Variations and Fugue
Organ: Walcker-Mayer

3125.GJ0   Galard, Jean
Recorded in the Cathedrale St. Pierre de Beauvais: May 1980, ed. n/a 1861
Issue: Solstice SOL 16, 1 stereo LP, 1 s [CFB], ca. 1980
Timing: 4.19
Notes: Jean Galard
With Bruckner: organ works, and works by Reubke and Barblan
Organ: Danion-Gonzalez, 1979

3125.HF0   Haselböck, Franz
Recorded in the Piaristenkirche, Vienna: ca. 1975, ed. n/a 1861
Issue: Musical Heritage Society MHS 1972, 1 stereo LP, 1 s [CFB], ca. 1975
Timing: 3.39
Notes: Franz Haselböck
With Bruckner and S. Sechter: organ works
Organ: Carl Buckow, 1856-58
Other issues: Corona 30059, Carus 33 107

3125.HO0   Horn, Erwin
Recorded in the Frauenkirche, Nuremburg: April 1990, ed. n/a
Issue: Novalis 150 071-2, 1 digital stereo CD, 1 s [CFB], p. 1990
Timing: 3.07
Notes: Erwin Horn
With Bruckner: organ works
Organ: Klais

3125.KI0   Knitl, Irmengard
Recorded ca. 1986, ed. n/a 1861
Issue: Pelca PSR 40 615, 1 stereo LP, 1 s, ca. 1986

With Bruckner: Prelude in d minor
and nineteen organ works by various composers

3125.LH0   Lohmann, Heinz
Recorded in the Jesuitenkirche,
Mannheim: ca. 1982, ed. n/a 1861
Issue: RBM 3004, 1 stereo LP, 1 s [CFB],
ca. 1982
Timing: 3.04
Notes: Heinz Lohmann
With Bruckner: complete organ works
and works by Mendelssohn
Organ: Johannes Klais, 1965

3125.RH0   Ruegenberg, Helmut
Recorded ca. 1976, ed. n/a 1861
Issue: Garnet 40 107, 1 stereo LP, 1 s, ca.
1976
With Bruckner: ten other brief pieces

3125.RL0   Roizman, Leonid
Recorded ca. 1960, ed. n/a 1861
Issue: Melodiya CM 04059-60, 1 stereo
LP, 1 s [UCD]
Timing: 5.38
Notes: Anonymous
With Bruckner: Postlude in d minor
and seven organ works by Haydn,
Mozart and Beethoven

Postlude in d minor (WAB 126, G/A 16)

Composed at St. Florian ca. 1852.

3126.DH0   Davies, Hazel
Recorded W. 1971, ed. n/a 1852
Issue: Qualiton SQUAD 107, LP, 1 s,
W. 1971
With Bruckner: Prelude in d minor

3126.FA0   Forer, Alois
Recorded in the Hofburgkapelle, Vien-
na: ca. 1975, ed. n/a 1852
Issue: Elite Special PLPS 30 093, 1 ste-
reo LP, 1 s [CSUS]
Timing: 3.29
Notes: Rudolf Scholz
With Bruckner: nine other organ works
and Schmidt: Variations and Fugue
Organ: Walcker-Mayer

3126.GJ0   Galard, Jean
Recorded in the Cathedrale St. Pierre
de Beauvais: May 1980, ed. n/a 1852

Issue: Solstice SOL 16, 1 stereo LP, 1 s
[CFB], ca. 1980
Timing: 2.33
Notes: Jean Galard
With Bruckner: organ works, and
works by Reubke and Barblan
Organ: Danion-Gonzalez, 1979

3126.HF0   Haselböck, Franz
Recorded in the Piaristenkirche, Vien-
na: ca. 1975, ed. n/a 1852
Issue: Musical Heritage Society MHS
1972, 1 stereo LP, 1 s [CFB], ca. 1975
Timing: 2.59
Notes: Franz Haselböck
With Bruckner and S. Sechter: organ
works
Organ: Carl Buckow, 1856-58
Other issues: Corona 30059, Carus 33
107

3126.HO0 Horn, Erwin
Recorded in the Frauenkirche, Nuremburg: April 1990, ed. n/a
Issue: Novalis 150 071-2, 1 digital stereo CD, 1 s [CFB], p. 1990
Timing: 3.34
Notes: Erwin Horn
With Bruckner: organ works

3126.LH0 Lohmann, Heinz
Recorded in the Jesuitenkirche, Mannheim: ca. 1982, ed. n/a 1852
Issue: RBM 3004, 1 stereo LP, 1 s [CFB], ca. 1982

Timing: 3.05
Notes: Heinz Lohmann
With Bruckner: complete organ works and works by Mendelssohn
Organ: Johannes Klais, 1965

3126.RL0 Roizman, Leonid
Recorded ca. 1960, ed. n/a 1852
Issue: Melodiya CM 04059-60, 1 stereo LP, 1 s [UCD]
Timing: 5.59
Notes: Anonymous
With Bruckner: Fugue in d minor and seven organ works by Haydn, Mozart and Beethoven

Prelude in E flat Major (WAB 127, G/A 3)

Andante. Composed in Hörsching ca. 1837.

3127.FA0 Forer, Alois
Recorded in the Hofburgkapelle, Vienna: ca. 1975, ed. n/a 1837
Issue: Elite Special PLPS 30093, 1 stereo LP, 1 s [CSUS]
Timing: 1.57
Notes: Rudolf Scholz
With Bruckner: nine other organ works and Schmidt: Variations and Fugue
Organ: Walcker-Mayer

3127.HF0 Haselböck, Franz
Recorded in the Piaristenkirche, Vienna: ca. 1975, ed. n/a 1837
Issue: Musical Heritage Society MHS 1972, 1 stereo LP, 1 s [CFB], ca. 1975
Timing: 1.49
Notes: Franz Haselböck
With Bruckner and S. Sechter: organ works
Organ: Carl Buckow, 1856-58

Other issues: Corona 30059, Carus 33 107

3127.HO0 Horn, Erwin
Recorded in the Frauenkirche, Nuremburg: April 1990, ed. n/a
Issue: Novalis 150 071-2, 1 digital stereo CD, 1 s [CFB], p. 1990
Timing: 1.59
Notes: Erwin Horn
With Bruckner: organ works
Organ: Klais

3127.LH0 Lohmann, Heinz
Recorded in the Jesuitenkirche, Mannheim: ca. 1982, ed. n/a 1837
Issue: RBM 3004, 1 stereo LP, 1 s [CFB], ca. 1982
Timing: 1.31
Notes: Heinz Lohmann

With Bruckner: complete organ works and works by Mendelssohn
Organ: Johannes Klais, 1965

3127.RH0 Ruegenberg, Helmut
Recorded ca. 1976, ed. n/a 1837
Issue: Garnet 40 107, 1 stereo LP, 1 s, ca. 1976
With Bruckner: ten other works

Four Preludes in E flat Major (WAB 128, G/A 2)

Composed in Hörsching ca. 1837. Preludes Nos. 1 and 2 have brief, apparently optional codas.

3128.FA0 Forer, Alois
Recorded in the Hofburgkapelle, Vienna: ca. 1975, ed. n/a 1837
Issue: Elite Special PLPS 30 093, 1 stereo LP, 1 s [CSUS]
Timing: 6.20 (2.43, 1.05, 0.40, 1.42)
Notes: Rudolf Scholz
With Bruckner: nine other organ works and Schmidt: Variations and Fugue
Organ: Walcker-Mayer

3128.GJ0 Galard, Jean
[Preludes Nos. 2 and 4 only]
Recorded in the Cathedrale St. Pierre de Beauvais: May 1980, ed. n/a 1837
Issue: Solstice SOL 16, 1 stereo LP, 1 s [CFB], ca. 1980
Timing: 2.16 (1.16, 1.00)
Notes: Jean Galard
With Bruckner: organ works, and works by Reubke and Barblan
Organ: Danion-Gonzalez, 1979

3128.HF0 Haselböck, Franz
Recorded in the Piaristenkirche, Vienna: ca. 1975, ed. n/a 1837
Issue: Musical Heritage Society MHS 1972, 1 stereo LP, 1 s [CFB], ca. 1975
Timing: 4.31 (1.54, 0.49, 0.32, 1.16)
Notes: Franz Haselböck
With Bruckner and S. Sechter: organ works
Organ: Carl Buckow, 1856-58
Other issues: Corona 30059, Carus 33 107, Magna 93 001 (?)

3128.HO0 Horn, Erwin
Recorded in the Frauenkirche, Nuremburg: April 1990, ed. n/a
Issue: Novalis 150 071-2, 1 digital stereo CD, 1 s [CFB], p. 1990
Timing: 5.58 (2.12, 0.46, 0.37, 2.23)
Notes: Erwin Horn
With Bruckner: organ works
Organ: Klais

3128.LH0 Lohmann, Heinz
Recorded in the Jesuitenkirche, Mannheim: ca. 1982, ed. n/a 1837
Issue: RBM 3004, 1 stereo LP, 1 s [CFB], ca. 1982
Timing: 5.59 (2.28, 1.02, .040, 1.19)
Notes: Heinz Lohmann
With Bruckner: complete organ works and works by Mendelssohn
Organ: Johannes Klais, 1965

Prelude in C Major (WAB 129, G/A 114)

Feierlich, langsam. Composed at St. Florian in 1884, sometimes referred to as the "Perger Präludium."

3129.BG0   Bovet, Guy
Recorded in the Church of Sainte-Claire, Vevey, Switzerland: ca. 1986, ed. n/a 1884
Issue: Gallo 30-325, 1 stereo LP, 1 s
With Brahms: chorale preludes

3129.FA0   Forer, Alois
Recorded in the Hofburgkapelle, Vienna: ca. 1975, ed. n/a 1884
Issue: Elite Special PLPS 30 093, 1 stereo LP, 1 s [CSUS]
Timing: 1.39
Notes: Rudolf Scholz
With Bruckner: nine other organ works and Schmidt: Variations and Fugue
Organ: Walcker-Mayer

3129.GJ0   Galard, Jean
Recorded in the Cathedrale St. Pierre de Beauvais: May 1980, ed. n/a 1884
Issue: Solstice SOL 16, 1 stereo LP, 1 s [CFB], ca. 1980
Timing: 1.28
Notes: Jean Galard
With Bruckner: organ works, and works by Reubke and Barblan
Organ: Danion-Gonzalez, 1979

3129.HF0   Haselböck, Franz
Recorded in the Piaristenkirche, Vienna: ca. 1975, ed. n/a 1884
Issue: Musical Heritage Society MHS 1972, 1 stereo LP, 1 s [CFB], ca. 1975
Timing: 1.49
Notes: Franz Haselböck
With Bruckner and S. Sechter: organ works
Organ: Carl Buckow, 1856-58

Other issues: Corona 30059, Carus 33 107, Schwann PVW 20 375

3129.HW5   Horn, Erwin
Recorded ca. 1986
Issue: Christophorus SCGLX 73 904, 1 stereo LP, 1 s, ca. 1986
With seven organ works by various composers

3129.HW6   Horn, Erwin
Recorded in the Frauenkirche, Nuremburg: April 1990, ed. n/a
Issue: Novalis 150 071-2, 1 digital stereo CD, 1 s [CFB], p. 1990
Timing: 1.58
Notes: Erwin Horn
With Bruckner: organ works
Organ: Klais

3129.KW0   Kuhlman, William
Recorded in St. Boniface Church, New Vienna, Iowa: 1986, ed. 1889
Issue: Organ Historical Society C-8, 1 stereo cassette, 1 s, ca. 1987
With works by nine other composers
Organ: Wm. Schuelke, 1891

3129.LH0   Lohmann, Heinz
Recorded in the Jesuitenkirche, Mannheim: ca. 1982, ed. n/a 1884
Issue: RBM 3004, 1 stereo LP, 1 s [CFB], ca. 1982
Timing: 1.58
Notes: Heinz Lohmann
With Bruckner: complete organ works and works by Mendelssohn
Organ: Johannes Klais, 1965

Prelude in d minor (WAB 130, G/A 16)

Andante. Composed at St. Florian ca. 1846-1852, often paired with the Postlude in d minor (WAB 126).

3130.DH0   Davies, Hazel
Recorded W. 1971, ed. n/a 1846
Issue: Qualiton SQUAD 107, LP, 1 s, W. 1971
With Bruckner: Postlude in d minor

3130.FA0   Forer, Alois
Recorded in the Hofburgkapelle, Vienna: ca. 1975, ed. n/a 1846
Issue: Elite Special PLPS 30 093, 1 stereo LP, 1 s [CSUS]
Timing: 1.28
Notes: Rudolf Scholz
With Bruckner: nine other organ works and Schmidt: Variations and Fugue
Organ: Walcker-Mayer

3130.GJ0   Galard, Jean
Recorded in the Cathedrale St. Pierre de Beauvais: May 1980, ed. n/a 1852
Issue: Solstice SOL 16, 1 stereo LP, 1 s [CFB], ca. 1980
Timing: 1.38
Notes: Jean Galard
With Bruckner: organ works, and works by Reubke and Barblan
Organ: Danion-Gonzalez, 1979

3130.HF0   Haselböck, Franz
Recorded in the Piaristenkirche, Vienna: ca. 1975, ed. n/a 1852
Issue: Musical Heritage Society MHS 1972, 1 stereo LP, 1 s [CFB], ca. 1975
Timing: 1.39
Notes: Franz Haselböck
With Bruckner and S. Sechter: organ works
Organ: Carl Buckow, 1856-58

Other issues: Corona 30059, Carus 33 107

3130.HO0   Horn, Erwin
Recorded in the Frauenkirche, Nuremburg: April 1990, ed. n/a
Issue: Novalis 150 071-2, 1 digital stereo CD, 1 s [CFB], p. 1990
Timing: 2.08
Notes: Erwin Horn
With Bruckner: organ works

3130.KI0   Knitl, Irmengard
Recorded ca. 1986, ed. n/a 1846
Issue: Pelca PSR 40 615, 1 stereo LP, 1 s, ca. 1986
With Bruckner: Fugue in d minor and nineteen works by various composers

3130.LH0   Lohmann, Heinz
Recorded in the Jesuitenkirche, Mannheim: ca. 1982, ed. n/a 1852
Issue: RBM 3004, 1 stereo LP, 1 s [CFB], ca. 1982
Timing: 1.50
Notes: Heinz Lohmann
With Bruckner: complete organ works and works by Mendelssohn
Organ: Johannes Klais, 1965

3130.WG0   Wachowski, Gerd
Recorded in St. Jacob's Church, Rothenburg: ca. 1988, ed. n/a 1846
Issue: Axel-Gerhard-Kühl Verlag AGK 30 211, 1 stereo LP, 1 s, ca. 1988
With three other organ works by various composers

Prelude and Fugue in c minor (WAB 131, G/A 18)

Composed at St. Florian in 1847.

3131.FA0   Forer, Alois
Recorded in the Hofburgkapelle, Vienna: ca. 1975, ed. n/a 1847
Issue: Elite Special PLPS 30 093, 1 stereo LP, 1 s [CSUS]
Timing: 5.40
Notes: Rudolf Scholz
With Bruckner: nine other organ works and Schmidt: Variations and Fugue
Other issues: Elite Special PLPS 30094
Organ: Walcker-Mayer

3131.GJ0   Galard, Jean
Recorded in the Cathedrale St. Pierre de Beauvais: May 1980, ed. n/a 1847
Issue: Solstice SOL 16, 1 stereo LP, 1 s [CFB], ca. 1980
Timing: 3.32
Notes: Jean Galard
With Bruckner: organ works, and works by Reubke and Barblan
Organ: Danion-Gonzalez, 1979

3131.HF0   Haselböck, Franz
Recorded in the Piaristenkirche, Vienna: ca. 1975, ed. n/a 1847
Issue: Musical Heritage Society MHS 1972, 1 stereo LP, 1 s [CFB], ca. 1975
Timing: 4.27
Notes: Franz Haselböck
With Bruckner and S. Sechter: organ works
Organ: Carl Buckow, 1856-58
Other issues: Corona 30059, Carus 33 107, Schwann PVW 20 375

3131.HO0   Horn, Erwin
Recorded in the Frauenkirche, Nuremburg: April 1990, ed. n/a
Issue: Novalis 150 071-2, 1 digital stereo CD, 1 s [CFB], p. 1990
Timing: 6.24
Notes: Erwin Horn
With Bruckner: organ works
Organ: Klais

3131.HU0   Humer, August
Recorded in the Old Cathedral, Linz: May 1981, ed. n/a 1847
Issue: Extempore AC 81-04, 1 stereo LP, 1 s [CFB], ca. 1981
Timing: 6.43
Notes: Otto Biba
With organ works by five other composers
Organ: Chrismann-Breinbauer, 1867

3131.KE0   Kaufmann, Eduard
Recorded in the Hofkirche, Lucerne: ca. 1986, ed. n/a 1847
Issue: Fono Schallplatten Arm 122, 1 stereo LP, 1 s, ca. 1986
With five organ works by various composers

3131.LH0   Lohmann, Heinz
Recorded in the Jesuitenkirche, Mannheim: ca. 1982, ed. n/a 1847
Issue: RBM 3004, 1 stereo LP, 1 s [CFB], ca. 1982
Timing: 3.48
Notes: Heinz Lohmann
With Bruckner: complete organ works and works by Mendelssohn
Organ: Johannes Klais, 1965

Orchestral Works

Apollo March (WAB 115, G/A 60)

Allegro moderato, E flat Major. Composed in Linz ca. 1862 for military band.

4115.GR0   Goldman, Richard Franko
Goldman Band
Recorded W. 1958, ed. Erik Leidzen
1862
Issue: Decca DL 78633, 1 stereo LP
[CSUS], W. 1958

Timing: 1.51
Notes: Anonymous
With seven other works for band by
various composers
Other issues: Decca DL 8633

March in d minor (WAB 96, G/A 61)

Composed in Linz in 1862.

4096.ML0   Mayer, Ludwig Karl
Berlin Municipal Orchestra
Recorded < 1948, ed. n/a 1862
Issue: Polydor 57215, 78, ca. 1948
With Bruckner: Three Orchestral Pieces
(WAB 97), Overture in g minor
Other issues: Grammophone 57361,
15540

4096.SH0   Schönzeler, Hans-Hubert
London Philharmonic Orchestra
Recorded in Barking Assembly Hall,
London: July 1970, ed. n/a 1862
Issue: Unicorn UNS 210, 1 stereo LP,
1 s [CFB], W. 1971

Timing: 4.28
Notes: Hans-Hubert Schönzeler
With Bruckner: Requiem, Three Or-
chestral Pieces (WAB 97)

4096.WF0   Walter, Friedrich
Hamburg New Symphony Orchestra
Recorded ca. 1960, ed. n/a 1862
Issue: Family Records FLP 141, 1 mono
LP, 1 s [CFB], ca. 1960
Timing: 4.43
With Bruckner: Three Orchestral Pieces
(WAB 97) and works by four other
composers
Other issues: Family Records SFLP 541

Three Orchestral Pieces (WAB 97, G/A 62)

I. Moderato, E flat Major, II. E minor, III. F Major. Composed in Linz in 1862.

4097.ML0   Mayer, Ludwig Karl
Berlin Municipal Orchestra
Recorded < 1948, ed. n/a 1862
Issue: Polydor 57215, 78
With Bruckner: March in d minor,
    Overture in g minor
Other issues: Polydor 57359, 15538

4097.SH0   Schönzeler, Hans-Hubert
London Philharmonic Orchestra
Recorded in Barking Assembly Hall,
    London: July 1970, ed. n/a 1862
Issue: Unicorn UNS 210, 1 stereo LP,
    1 s [CFB], W. 1971

Timing: 7.31 (2.01, 2.30, 3.00)
Notes: Hans-Hubert Schönzeler
With Bruckner: Requiem, March in d
    minor

4097.WF0   Walter, Friedrich
Hamburg New Symphony Orchestra
Recorded ca. 1960, ed. n/a 1862
Issue: Family Records FLP 141, 1 ste-
    reo LP, 1 s [CFB], ca. 1960
Timing: 7.45 (1.50, 2.26, 3.29)
With Bruckner: March and works of
    four other composers
Other issues: Family Records SFLP 541

Overture in g minor (WAB 98, G/A 63)

Adagio. Composed in 1863 and revised later that year.

4098.AF0   Adler, F. Charles
Vienna Philharmonia Orchestra
Recorded W. 1952, ed. Orel 1863
Issue: S.P.A. 24-25, 2 mono LPs, 1 s
    [UCB], W. 1952
Timing: 12.09
Notes: Edward Lawton
With Bruckner: Symphony No. 9

4098.CR0   Chailly, Riccardo
Berlin Radio Symphony Orchestra
Recorded in Jesus-Christus-Kirche,
    Berlin: February 1988, ed. 1863
Issue: London 421 593-2 10 LH, 1 digi-
    tal stereo CD, 1 s [CFB], © 1989

Timing: 11.37
Notes: Anonymous
With Bruckner: Symphony No. 0

4098.HL0   Hager, Leopold
Southwest German Radio Symphony
    Orchestra
Recorded in Hans-Rosbaud-Studio,
    Baden-Baden: 1988, ed. 1863
Issue: Amati SRR 8904/1, 1 digital ste-
    reo CD, 1 s [CFB], ca. 1989
Timing: 11.02
Notes: Paul Fiebig
With Schumann: Violin Concerto and
    Spohr: Symphony No. 3

4098.JM0   Janowski, Marek
Radio France Philharmonic Orchestra
Recorded at Radio France, Studio 104,
Paris: June 1990, ed. Nowak 1863
Issue: Virgin Classics VC 7 91206-2,
1 digital CD, 1 s [CFB], p. 1991
Timing: 9.36
Notes: Jonathan Freeman-Attwood
With Bruckner: Symphony No. 4

4098.MA0   Matacic, Lovro von
Philharmonia Orchestra
Recorded 12-13 October and 11-14
December 1954, ed. n/a 1863
Issue: Angel 35359, 2 mono LPs, 1 s
[UCB], W. 1956
Timing: 10.37
Notes: Michael Rose, Mosco Carner
With Bruckner: Symphony No. 4 and
Symphony No. 0 [Scherzo only]
Other issues: Angel 3548 B

4098.ML0   Mayer, Ludwig Karl
Berlin Municipal Orchestra
Recorded < 1948, ed. n/a 1863
Issue: Polydor 57214-5, 78
With Bruckner: Three Orchestral Pie-
ces (WAB 97), March in d minor
Other issues: Polydor 57360-1, 15539-
40

4098.OW0   Otterloo, Willem van
Vienna Symphony Orchestra
Recorded ca. 1955, ed. n/a 1863
Issue: Epic SC 6006, 2 mono LPs, 1 s, W.
1955
With Bruckner: Symphony No. 7
Other issues: Philips A 00249-50 L

4098.PL0   Pesek, Libor
Czech Philharmonic Orchestra
Recorded in Dvorak Hall, Prague: Janu-
ary-November 1986, ed. n/a 1863
Issue: Supraphon CO-72647, 1 digital
stereo CD, 1 s [CFB], p. 1988
Timing: 12.03
Notes: Jiri Vyslouzil
With Bruckner: Symphony No. 7

4098.SE0   Shapirra, Elyakum
London Symphony Orchestra
Recorded p. 1972, ed. Wöss 1863
Issue: EMI Odeon ASD 2808, 1 stereo
LP, 1 s [CFB], p. 1972
Timing: 11.02
Notes: Hans-Hubert Schönzeler
With Bruckner: Symphony in f minor
Other issues: EMI C 063 02309

4098.SW0   Steinberg, William
Pittsburgh Symphony Orchestra
Recorded in Soldiers and Sailors Me-
morial Hall, Pittsburgh: April 1968,
ed. n/a 1863
Issue: Command 12002 S, 2 stereo LPs,
1 s [CFB], W. 1970
Timing: 9.53
Notes: F.B. Weille
With Bruckner: Symphony No. 7

4098.WH0   Wood, Henry J.
Queen's Hall Orchestra
Recorded W. 1937, ed. n/a 1863
Issue: Decca 7, 2 mono 78s, 3 ss [CST]
Timing: 8.40
With Glinka: Ruslan and Ludmilla
Overture
Other issues: Decca X 192-3, 2771-2

Symphony No. 00 in f minor (WAB 99, G/A 64)

*I. Allegro molto vivace, II. Andante molto, III. Scherzo: Schnell, Trio:
Langsamer, IV. Finale: Allegro. Composed in Linz in 1863.*

4099.HE0   Horn, Erwin
[Scherzo only]
Recorded on the Klais organ of the
Frauenkirche, Nuremburg: April
1990, ed. Horn
Issue: Novalis 150 071-2, 1 digital ste-
reo CD, 1 s [CFB], p. 1990
Timing: 5.52
Notes: Erwin Horn
With Bruckner: organ works

4099.RG0   Rozhdestvensky, Gennady
USSR Symphony Orchestra
Recorded in Moscow: 1983, ed. n/a
1863
Issue: Chant du Monde LDX 78.851/
52, 2 stereo LPs, 2 ss [CFB], p. 1986

Timing: 44.31 (15.07, 12.47, 6.52, 9.45)
Notes: Jean Gallois
With Bruckner: Symphony No. 0
Other issues: Chant du Monde CM
460, K 478.851/52 (cassette), CM
278 851/2 (CD)

4099.SE0   Shapirra, Elyakum
London Symphony Orchestra
Recorded p. 1972, ed. Schönzeler 1863
Issue: Odeon ASD 2808, 1 stereo LP,
2 ss [CFB], p. 1972
Timing: 46.02 (15.42, 14.10, 5.37, 10.33)
Notes: Hans-Hubert Schönzeler
With Bruckner: Overture in g minor
Other issues: His Master's Voice ASD
2808, C 063 02309

Symphony No. 0 in d minor (WAB 100, G/A 68)

*I. Allegro, II. Andante, III. Scherzo: Presto, Trio: Langsamer und ruhiger, IV.
Finale: Moderato. Composed in Linz in 1864 and revised in Vienna in 1869.
There are slight differences between the 1924 edition of Joseph Wöss and the
1969 edition of Leopold Nowak. Both are based on the 1869 score.*

4100.BD0   Barenboim, Daniel
Chicago Symphony Orchestra
Recorded 3 March 1979, ed. Nowak
1869
Issue: DG 2531 319, 1 stereo LP, 2 ss
[CFB], p. 1981
Timing: 45.22 (15.02, 12.38, 6.42, 11.00)
Notes: Stefan Kunze, Robert Simpson
Other issues: DG 2740 253 [CFB], 28
MG 0091

4100.CR0   Chailly, Riccardo
Berlin Radio Symphony Orchestra
Recorded in Jesus-Christus-Kirche,
Berlin: February 1988, ed. 1869
Issue: London 421 593-2 10 LH, 1 digi-
tal stereo CD, 1 s [CFB], © 1989
Timing: 46.24 (15.15, 13.47, 6.47, 10.35)
Notes: Anonymous
With Bruckner: Overture in g minor
Other issues: London F32 L20195

4100.GH0 Gelmini, Hortense von
Nuremburg Symphony Orchestra
Recorded W. 1975, ed. Nowak 1869
Issue: Colosseum SM 558, LP

4100.HB0 Haitink, Bernard
Concertgebouw Orchestra, Amsterdam
Recorded June 1966, ed. n/a 1869
Issue: Philips 802 724 LY, 1 stereo LP,
2 ss [CFB], W. 1967
Timing: 43.29 (14.22, 12.56, 6.29, 9.42)
Notes: Anonymous
With Philips PHM 500131/PHS 900131,
802724, AL/SAL 3602, 6717 002,
SFX 7660/X5651

4100.HE0 Horn, Erwin
[Andante only]
Recorded on the Klais organ of St.
Maria Magdalena, Münnerstadt: ca.
1986, ed. Horn
Issue: Mitra 16 180, 1 digital stereo LP,
1 s, ca. 1986
With Bruckner: Symphony No. 7 [Adagio only] and four other works for
organ by various composers

4100.HE1 Horn, Erwin
[Andante only]
Recorded on the Klais organ of the
Frauenkirche, Nuremburg: April
1990, ed. Horn
Issue: Novalis 150 071-2, 1 digital stereo CD, 1 s [CFB], p. 1990
Timing: 14.33
Notes: Erwin Horn
With Bruckner: organ works

4100.ME0 Märzendorfer, Ernst
Austrian Broadcast Symphony Orchestra
Recorded p. 1978, ed. n/a 1869
Issue: Classical Excellence C 11022,
1 stereo cassette tape, 2 ss [CFB],
p. 1978
Timing: 44.20 (14.57, 11.14, 6.50, 11.19)

4100.ML0 Matacic, Lovro von
Philharmonia Orchestra
Recorded 12-13 October and 11-14
December 1954, ed. Wöss 1869
Issue: Angel 35359, 2 mono LPs, 1 s
[UCB], W. 1956
Timing: 6.13
Notes: Michael Rose, Mosco Carner
With Bruckner: Symphony No. 4 and
Overture in g minor
Other issues: Angel 35481B

4100.RG0 Rozhdestvensky, Gennady
USSR Symphony Orchestra
Recorded 1983, ed. n/a 1869
Issue: Chant du Monde LDX 78.851/
52, 2 stereo LPs, 2 ss [CFB], p. 1986
Timing: 51.28 (19.06, 15.06, 6.13, 11.03)
Notes: Jean Gallois
With Bruckner: Symphony No. 00
Other issues: Chant du Monde CM
460, K 478.851/52 (cassette), LDC-
278.851/52 (CD)

4100.SH0 Spruit, Henk
Concert Hall Symphony Orchestra
Recorded ca. 1952, ed. Wöss 1869
Issue: Concert Hall CHS 1142, 1 mono
LP, 2 ss [UCB], W. 1952
Timing: 42.00 (13.01, 11.57, 5.54, 11.08)
Notes: H. Ross Arnold
Other issues: Nixa CLP 1142, Classic
6225

4100.ZF0   Zaun, Fritz
[Scherzo only]
Berlin State Opera Orchestra
Recorded < 1948, ed. Wöss 1869
Issue: Victor 11726, 1 mono 78, 1 s
[CST]

Timing: 4.04
With Bruckner: Symphony No. 3
[Scherzo only]
Other issues: Victor C 2659, EH 844

Symphony No. 1 in c minor (WAB 101, G/A 78)

I. Allegro, II. Adagio, III. Scherzo: Schnell, Trio: Langsamer, IV. Finale:
Bewegt, feurig. Composed in Linz in 1866 and revised in Vienna in 1891. The
score published in 1893 of the Vienna revision is unreliable, whereas the Haas
and Nowak editions of both versions are accepted as accurate.

4101.AC0   Abbado, Claudio
Vienna Philharmonic Orchestra
Recorded November 1969, ed. n/a Linz,
1866
Issue: London CS 6706, 1 stereo LP, 2 ss
[CFB], © 1971
Timing: 47.13 (11.45, 12.40, 8.52, 13.56)
Notes: Geoffrey Crankshaw
Other issues: London SXL 6494, SXL
21217, LODC 1326/38, SLC 2103,
KISC-9013

4101.AF0   Adler, F. Charles
Vienna Orchestral Society
Recorded ca. 1955, ed. Schalk 1892
Issue: Unicorn LA 1015, 1 mono LP,
2 ss [UCB], W. 1955
Timing: 50.52 (13.48, 13.02, 7.44, 16.18)
Notes: Warren Storey Smith
Other issues: Siena 100 1, Delta DEL
12010, Summit LSU 3017

4101.AV0   Andreae, Volkmar
Austrian State Symphony Orchestra
Recorded ca. 1951, ed. Schalk 1891
Issue: Masterseal MW 40, LP, 1 s, W.
1951

4101.AV1   Andreae, Volkmar
Vienna Symphony Orchestra
Recorded W. 1953, ed. Haas 1866
Issue: Amadeo AVRS 5040, LP, W.
1965
[Probably identical with 4101.AV0]
Other issues: Philips GL 5845, Amadeo
12083

4101.AX0   Asahina, Takashi
Japan Philharmonic Orchestra
Recorded 29 January 1983, ed. 1866
Issue: Victor SJX 9571, 1 stereo LP, 2 ss
[MG], ca. 1983
Timing: 49.10 (13.38, 11.46, 8.56, 14.50)

4101.BD0   Barenboim, Daniel
Chicago Symphony Orchestra
Recorded p. 1981, ed. Nowak 1866
Issue: DG 2740 253, 12 digital stereo
LPs, 2 ss [CFB], p. 1981
Timing: 46.33 (12.11, 12.05, 9.00, 13.17)
Notes: Hans-Günter Klein
With Bruckner: nine other sympho-
nies
Other issues: DG 28 MG 0091

4101.CR0   Chailly, Riccardo
Berlin Radio Symphony Orchestra
Recorded in Jesus-Christus-Kirche,
Berlin: February 1987, ed. n/a 1891
Issue: London 421 091-2, 1 digital CD,
1 s [CFB], p. 1988
Timing: 54.14 (13.13, 13.45, 9.11, 18.05)
Notes: Andrew Huth
Other issues: London F32 L20195

4101.HB0   Haitink, Bernard
Concertgebouw Orchestra, Amster-
dam
Recorded June 1972, ed. Haas, 1866
Issue: Philips 6500 439, 1 stereo LP, 2 ss
[CFB], W. 1973
Timing: 46.18 (11.57, 13.00, 8.46, 12.35)
Notes: Deryck Cooke
Other issues: Philips set 6717 002, SFX
8635

4101.IE0   Inbal, Eliahu
Frankfurt Radio Symphony Orchestra
Recorded in Alte Oper, Frankfurt/
Main: 29-30 January 1987, ed. n/a
1866
Issue: Teldec 8.43619, 1 digital stereo
CD, 1 s [CFB], © 1987
Timing: 48.05 (13.10, 12.24, 8.21, 14.10)
Notes: Anonymous
Other issues: Teldec 6.43619, 4.43619
AZ (cassette), K28C-10030, K33Y-
10187

4101.JE0   Jochum, Eugen
Berlin Philharmonic Orchestra
Recorded 16-19 October 1965, ed.
Nowak 1866
Issue: DG SKL 929-939, 11 stereo LPs,
2 ss [CFB], W. 1968
Timing: 46.41 (12.24, 12.25, 8.50, 13.02)

Notes: Leopold Nowak, Eugen Joch-
um, Constantin Floros
With Bruckner: Symphonies 2-9
Other issues: DG 39131/139131, 2721
010, 2720 047, 2740 136, Hören und
Lernen HL 00 212 [Allegro only],
DG MGX 7056, MG 9813/4

4101.JE1   Jochum, Eugen
Staatskapelle Dresden
Recorded 11-15 December 1978, ed.
Nowak: 1866
Issue: EMI 127-749417-1, 10 digital ste-
reo LPs, 2 ss, ca. 1987
Timing: 46.48 (12.21, 12.31, 21.56 [III
and IV])
With Bruckner: Symphonies Nos. 2-9
Other issues: Angel EAC 80562, set
EAC 87045/55

4101.KH0   Karajan, Herbert von
Berlin Philharmonic Orchestra
Recorded 26-27 January 1981, ed.
Nowak: Linz, 1866
Issue: DG 2532 062, 1 digital stereo LP,
2 ss [CFB], p. 1982
Timing: 50.37 (12.54, 14.20, 8.54, 14.29)
Notes: Stefan Kunze, Richard Osborne
Other issues: DG 2740 264, 330 2062
(cassette), 415 985-2 (2 CDs, with
Bruckner: Symphony No. 5), F66
G50397/8 (CD), OOMG 0401/11,
28 MG 0479

4101.MK0   Masur, Kurt
Leipzig Gewandhaus Orchestra
Recorded 28 November and 1 Decem-
ber 1977
Issue: Nippon Columbia OX 1113, 1
stereo LP, 2 ss [MG], ca. 1978
Timing: 50.30 (14.30, 11.40, 9.05, 15.25)

4101.NV0 Neumann, Vaclav
Leipzig Gewandhaus Orchestra
Recorded p. 1966, ed. n/a 1866
Issue: Teldec 6.43318, 1 stereo LP, 2 ss
[CFB], © 1986
Timing: 51.25 (13.50, 12.55, 8.55, 15.45)
Other issues: Eterna 825621, Decca SXL
20087, 4.43318 CH (cassette)

4101.SW0 Sawallisch, Wolfgang
Bavarian State Orchestra
Recorded in Aula of the University of
Munich: 25-28 October 1984, ed.
n/a Linz, 1866
Issue: Orfeo S 145 851 A, 1 digital stereo
LP, 2 ss [CFB], p. 1985
Timing: 47.42 (13.02, 12.49, 7.53, 13.46)
Notes: Ekkehart Kroher
Other issues: Orfeo A 145 851 (cas-
sette), C 145 851 (CD), 32CD-10055
(CD)

4101.WG0 Wand, Günter
Cologne Radio Symphony Orchestra
Recorded in WDR, Cologne: 11 July
1981, ed. n/a Vienna, 1891
Issue: EMI CDC 7 47742 2, 1 stereo CD,
1 s [CFB], p. 1982
Timing: 47.45 (12.15, 11.09, 9.08, 15.13)
Notes: Rolf-A. Dimpfel
Other issues: EMI 065-99 937, 127-154
463-3, 567-747 742-2 (CD), Harmo-
nia mundi VLS 3284

4101.ZF0 Zaun, Fritz
[Scherzo only]
Berlin Symphony Orchestra
Recorded < 1948
Issue: Victor 11939, 1 mono 78, 1 s
With Bruckner: Symphony No. 2
Other issues: Victor C 2685, EH 865

Symphony No. 2 in c minor (WAB 102, G/A 94)

*I. Moderato, II. Andante, III. Scherzo: Mäßig schnell, Trio: Gleiches Tempo,
IV. Finale: Mehr schnell. Composed in Vienna in 1872 and revised in 1876 and
1877 at the suggestion and possibly with the help of Johann Herbeck. Deryck
Cooke recommends the score of the 1872 version edited by Haas on the grounds
that Nowak's edition contains elements of Herbeck's excessive influence.*

4102.AV0 Andreae, Volkmar
Vienna Symphony Orchestra
Recorded W. 1953, ed. n/a
Issue: Amadeo AVRS 5041, LP, W.
1965
Other issues: Philips GL 5846, Amadeo
12084

4102.AX0 Asahina, Takashi
Osaka Philharmonic
Recorded live: 11 September 1986, ed.
Haas 1872
Issue: Victor VDC 1211, 1 stereo LP,
2 ss [MG], ca. 1987
Timing: 1.04.51 (19.14, 16.04, 9.11, 20.22)

4102.BD0 · Barenboim, Daniel
Chicago Symphony Orchestra
Recorded p. 1981, ed. Haas 1872
Issue: DG 2740 253, 12 digital stereo
LPs, 2 ss [CFB], p. 1981
Timing: 1.05.47 (19.04, 17.01, 10.14,
19.28)
Notes: Hans-Günter Klein
With Bruckner: nine other symphonies

4102.GC0 Giulini, Carlo Maria
Vienna Symphony Orchestra
Recorded 8-10 December 1974, ed.
Nowak 1877
Issue: Odeon 1C 063 02633Q, LP,
W. 1977
Other issues: Odeon ASD 3146, Angel
EAC 80139

4102.HB0 Haitink, Bernard
Concertgebouw Orchestra, Amsterdam
Recorded 14-16 May 1969, ed. Haas
1872
Issue: Philips 802 912 LY, 1 stereo LP,
2 ss [CFB], W. 1970
Timing: 58.18 (17.39, 15.12, 8.09, 17.18)
Notes: Deryck Cooke
Other issues: Philips SAL 3785, 6717
002, 7311183 (cassette), Sequenza
6527183

4102.HE0 Horn, Erwin
[Scherzo only]
Recorded on the organ of the Basilica,
Waldsassen: ca. 1986, ed. n/a
Issue: Mitra 16 170, 1 digital stereo LP,
1 s, ca. 1986
With Bruckner: String Quintet [Adagio only] and Guilmant: Sonata
No. 1 for organ

4102.IE0 Inbal, Eliahu
Frankfurt Radio Symphony Orchestra
Recorded Alte Oper, Frankfurt/Main:
June 1988, ed. Haas 1872
Issue: Teldec 8.44144 ZK, 1 digital stereo CD, 1 s [CFB], p. 1988
Timing: 1.01.34 (20.01, 16.11, 7.13, 17.51)
Notes: Knut Franke

4102.JE0 Jochum, Eugen
Bavarian Radio Symphony Orchestra
Recorded 27-29 December 1966, ed.
Nowak 1877
Issue: DG SKL 929-939, 11 stereo LPs,
2 ss [CFB], W. 1968
Timing: 51.11 (17.41, 13.52, 6.29, 13.09)
Notes: Leopold Nowak, Eugen Jochum, Constantin Floros
With Bruckner: Symphonies 1-9
Other issues: DG 139132, 2721 010,
2720 047, 2740 136, MGX 7057, MG
9813/24

4102.JE1 Jochum, Eugen
Staatskapelle Dresden
Recorded 11-15 December 1975, ed.
n/a 1872
Issue: EMI 127-749417-1, 10 digital
stereo LPs, 2 ss, ca. 1987
Timing: 52.06 (17.53, 14.35, 6.54, 12.44)
With Bruckner: Symphonies Nos. 1-9
Other issues: EAC 87045/55, EAC
90070

4102.JG0 Jochum, Georg Ludwig
Linz Bruckner Symphony Orchestra
Recorded ca. 1943, ed. Haas 1872
Issue: Urania UR 243-2, 2 mono LPs,
4 ss [CFB], W. 1951
Timing: 59.42 (17.12, 17.11, 9.27, 15.52)
Other issues: Urania URLP 402, UR
5243, Saga XID 5102-3

4102.KH0   Karajan, Herbert von
Berlin Philharmonic Orchestra
Recorded December 1980 - January
1981, ed. Nowak 1877
Issue: DG 2532 063, 1 digital stereo LP,
2 ss [CFB], p. 1982
Timing: 1.00.16 (18.16, 17.40, 6.13, 18.07)
Notes: Stefan Kunze, Richard Osborne
Other issues: DG 415 988-2 (CD), 3302
063 (cassette), 2740 264, 28MG 0480,
00MG 0401/11, F35G 50399 (CD)

4102.KO0   Konwitschny, Franz
Berlin Radio Symphony Orchestra
Recorded ca. 1955, ed. n/a
Issue: Eterna 820 528-9, LP

4102.MC0   Mandeal, Christian
Cluj-Napoca Symphony Orchestra
Recorded ca. 1980, ed. n/a 1872
Issue: Electrecord Stecez 02731/3,
3 stereo LPs, 3? ss
With Bruckner: Symphony No. 3

4102.MK0   Masur, Kurt
Leipzig Gewandhaus Orchestra
Recorded January 1978, ed. n/a
Issue: Nippon Columbia/Denon OB
7352/3, 1 stereo LP, 2 ss
Timing: 1.04.49 (19.44, 15.15, 11.20,
18.30)

4102.RH0   Reichert, Hubert
Westphalian Symphony Orchestra,
Recklinghausen
Recorded ca. 1971, ed. Haas 1872
Issue: Turnabout TV-S 34415, 1 stereo
LP, 2 ss [CFB], W. 1971
Timing: 1.00.55 (18.55, 16.30, 9.15, 16.15)
Notes: Joseph Braunstein

4102.SH0   Stein, Horst
Vienna Philharmonic Orchestra
Recorded Sofiensaal, Vienna: 26-29
November 1973, ed. Haas 1872
Issue: London CS 6879, 1 stereo LP, 2 ss
[CFB], p. 1975
Timing: 57.00 (17.55, 16.20, 6.10, 16.35)
Notes: Joseph Brand
Other issues: London L00C 1326/38,
SLC 2444/K156-9019, SXL 6681,
6.35256

4102.SW0   Swarowsky, Hans
South German Philharmonic Orchestra
Recorded ca. 1970, ed. n/a 1872
Issue: Ampex AMP X 56016, 1 stereo
cassette tape, 2 ss [CFB], ca. 1970
Timing: 59.35 (17.33, 14.13, 10.43, 17.06)

4102.WG0   Wand, Günter
Cologne Radio Symphony Orchestra
Recorded in WDR, Cologne: 1-5 De-
cember 1981, ed. Haas 1872
Issue: EMI CDC 7 47743 2, 1 stereo CD,
1 s [CFB], p. 1982
Timing: 58.30 (19.08, 15.43, 7.33, 16.06)
Notes: Rolf-A. Dimpfel
Other issues: EMI 065-199 938-1, 127-
154 463-3, 567-747 743-2 (CD), Har-
monia Mundi VLS 3285

4102.ZF0   Zaun, Fritz
[Scherzo only]
Berlin Symphony Orchestra
Recorded < 1948
Issue: Victor 11939, 1 mono 78, 1 s
With Bruckner: Symphony No. 1 Other
issues: Victor C 2685, EH 865

Symphony No. 3 in d minor (WAB 103, G/A 95)

I. Gemäßigt, misterioso, II. Adagio, Feierlich, III. Scherzo: Ziemlich schnell, Trio: Gleiches Zeitmaß, IV. Finale: Allegro (version of 1873). Composed in Vienna in 1873 and revised in 1874, 1877, and 1889. The earliest published score was of the 1877 version. This was followed by Franz Schalk's edition of 1889, the Fritz Oeser edition of the 1877 version, and by Hans Redlich's edition of the 1889 version. Nowak edited versions dated 1873, 1877 and 1889 as well as an alternate form of the Adagio dated 1876. Deryck Cooke cites the *deleterious influence of Franz Schalk on the later revisions. Significant differences exist among these editions, a discussion of which can be found in Richard Osborne's article in* Gramophone *(August 1991), Deryck Cooke's* The Bruckner Problem Simplified, *and in the prefaces to the Bruckner Edition scores by Leopold Nowak.*

4103.AF0   Adler, F. Charles
Vienna Philharmonia
Recorded ca. 1953, ed. Schalk 1890
Issue: S.P.A. 30-31, 2 mono LPs, 3 ss, W. 1953
With a work by Mahler

4103.AV0   Andreae, Volkmar
Vienna Symphony Orchestra
Recorded 11-13 January 1955, ed. Schalk 1890
Issue: Epic LC 3218, LP, W. 1956
Other issues: Philips A 00273 L, GL 5697

4103.AY0   Asahina, Takashi
Tokyo Metropolitan Symphony Orchestra
Recorded live: 26 July 1984, ed. Nowak 1877 [MG]
Issue: Victor VDC 1047
Timing: 1.00.02 (19.58, 15.09, 7.40, 17.15)

4103.BD0   Barenboim, Daniel
Chicago Symphony Orchestra
Recorded p. 1981, ed. Oeser 1877

Issue: DG 2740 253, 12 digital stereo LPs, 2 ss [CFB], p. 1981
Timing: 1.00.10 (20.37, 16.41, 7.31, 15.21)
Notes: Hans-Günter Klein
With Bruckner: nine other symphonies

4103.BK0   Böhm, Karl
Vienna Philharmonic Orchestra
Recorded in Sofiensaal, Vienna: September 1970, ed. Nowak 1889
Issue: London CS 6717, 1 stereo LP, 2 ss [CFB], © 1971
Timing: 56.14 (21.56, 14.44, 6.53, 12.41)
Notes: Leopold Nowak
Other issues: Decca 6.48 286 DM, SXL 6505, L25 C-3143, London SOL 9017/8, 15DC 9068/9, SLC 8039, SLC 6102, King SOL 1014/26, LOOC 1326/38, L25C 3143, L15C 2210, F28C 28048 (CD) K18C-5010

4103.CR0   Chailly, Riccardo
Berlin Radio Symphony Orchestra
Recorded in Jesus-Christus-Kirche, Berlin: May 1985, ed. Nowak 1890

Issue: London 417 093, 1 digital stereo LP, 2 ss [CFB], p. 1986
Timing: 55.51 (20.41, 15.49, 7.01, 12.20)
Notes: Michael Kennedy
Other issues: London 417 093-4 (cassette), 417 093-2 (CD), L28C-1982, F35C-50333 (CD), Decca 6.43 357 AZ (LP and cassette)

4103.FZ0   Fekete, Zoltan
Salzburg Mozarteum Orchestra
Recorded W. 1950, ed. Schalk 1889
Issue: Remington 199-138, 1 mono LP, 2 ss [UCB], p. 1953
Timing: 47.55 (18.28, 12.24, 6.20, 10.43)
Notes: Max de Schauensee
Other issues: Concert CHS 1065, Concert Hall CHC 65, Qualiton LPX 1047, Concert Artist LPA 1018, Eurochord LPG 602, Concerteum CR 223

4103.GW0   Goehr, Walter
Netherlands Philharmonic
Recorded ca. 1954, ed. Schalk 1890
Issue: Concert Hall CHS 1195, 1 mono LP, 2 ss, W. 1954
Other issues: Musical Masterpiece Society 2018

4103.HB0   Haitink, Bernard
Concertgebouw Orchestra, Amsterdam
Recorded 27 September-2 October 1963, ed. Oeser 1877
Issue: Philips 835 217 AY, 1 stereo LP, 2 ss [CFB], W. 1965
Timing: 56.24 (19.20, 14.10, 6.53, 15.31)
Notes: Conrad Wilson
Other issues: Philips PHM 500068/PHS 900068, AL/SAL 3506, 6717 002, A 02339 L/835217 AY

4103.IE0   Inbal, Eliahu
Frankfurt Radio Symphony Orchestra
Recorded 14-15 September 1982, ed. Nowak 1873
Issue: Teldec 6.42922, 1 digital stereo LP, 2 ss [CFB], p. 1983
Timing: 1.07.12 (24.00, 18.50, 6.07, 16.15)
Notes: Manfred Wagner
Other issues: Teldec 8.42922 ZK (CD), K38Y-86 (CD), K33Y-10134 (CD), K28C-340, K20C-396/8

4103.JE0   Jochum, Eugen
Bavarian Radio Symphony Orchestra
Recorded 30 December 1966 and 7-8 January 1967, ed. Nowak 1889
Issue: DG SKL 929-939, 11 stereo LPs, 3 ss [CFB], W. 1967
Timing: 52.32 (19.51, 15.04, 7.08, 10.29)
Notes: Leopold Nowak, Eugen Jochum, Constantin Floros
With Bruckner: Symphonies Nos. 1-9
Other issues: DG 139133, 2740 136, 2721 010, 2720 047, 2535 265 (LP and cassette), MGX 7035, MG 9813/24

4103.JE1   Jochum, Eugen
Staatskapelle Dresden
Recorded 22-27 January 1977, ed. n/a 1889
Issue: EMI 127-749417-1, 10 digital stereo LPs, 2 ss, ca. 1987
Timing: 54.37 (20.38, 15.31, 7.30, 10.58)
With Bruckner: Symphonies Nos. 1-9
Other issues: Angel EAC 80536, EAC 87045/55

4103.KH0   Karajan, Herbert von
Berlin Philharmonic Orchestra
Recorded 20-21 September 1980, ed. Nowak 1889

Issue: DG 2532 007, 1 digital stereo LP, 2 ss [CFB], p. 1981
Timing: 56.50 (21.58, 16.21, 6.51, 11.40)
Notes: Stefan Kunze, Richard Osborne
Other issues: DG 2740 264, 413 362-2 (CD), 330 2007 (cassette), 28MG 0118, 00MG 0401/11

4103.KN0   Knappertsbusch, Hans
Bavarian State Orchestra
Recorded live in Munich: October 1954, ed. Schalk 1889
Issue: Music and Arts CD-257, 1 mono CD, 1 s [CFB], p. 1987
Timing: 51.06 (18.05, 12.37, 7.12, 13.12)
Notes: David Breckbill
With Wagner: Rhine Journey and Funeral Music from *Götterdämmerung*

4103.KN1   Knappertsbusch, Hans
Vienna Philharmonic Orchestra
Recorded April 1954, ed. Schalk 1890
Issue: London LL 1044, LP, ss, W. 1955
Timing: 53.46 (19.06, 14.04, 7.19, 13.17)
Other issues: London CM 9107, Everest 3300, LXT 2967, ECS 553, BLK 21020, SMB 25039, King K15 C-5026, London K35Y-1013 (CD), K30Y-1030 (CD), MX 9020

4103.KN2   Knappertsbusch, Hans
North German Radio Orchestra
Recorded live: 15 January 1962, ed. n/a
Issue: Discocorp RR-496, 1 mono LP, 2 ss [CFB], © 1982
Timing: 1.00.32 (22.26, 14.40, 7.41, 15.45)
Notes: Peter Burkhardt
With Wolf: Italian Serenade
Other issues: Seven Seas K30Y-263 (CD)

4103.KO0   Konrath, Anton
[Scherzo only]
Vienna Symphony Orchestra
Recorded ca. 1935, ed. n/a
Issue: Victor 11726, 1 mono 78, 1 s [CST],
Timing: 4.12
With Bruckner: Symphony No. 3 [Scherzo only]
Other issues: Victor C 2659, EH 844, AN 192

4103.KR0   Kubelik, Rafael
Bavarian Radio Symphony Orchestra
Recorded 13-14 October 1980, ed. Oeser 1877
Issue: CBS MK 39033, 1 digital stereo CD, 1 s [CFB], p. 1985
Timing: 57.54 (21.15, 14.40, 7.15, 14.44)
Notes: Anonymous
Other issues: CBS 39033 (LP and cassette), CBS Sony 32CD-549 (CD)

4103.ML0   Maazel, Lorin
Berlin Radio Symphony Orchestra
Recorded ca. 1974, ed. Nowak 1889
Issue: Concert Hall SMS-2567, 1 stereo LP, 2 ss [CFB], ca. 1974
Timing: 51.26 (19.11, 13.21, 6.39, 12.15)
Notes: Willi Reich
Other issues: Concert Hall M 2018, Guilde Int. du Disque SMS 2567

4103.ML5   Mandeal, Christian
Cluj-Napoca Symphony Orchestra
Recorded ca. 1980, ed. n/a 1873
Issue: Electrecord Stecez 02731/3, 3 stereo LPs, 3? ss
With Bruckner: Symphony No. 2

4103.MS0   Masur, Kurt
Leipzig Gewandhaus Orchestra
Recorded 5-7 December 1977
Issue: Denon OX 1128, 1 stereo LP (?),
2 ss [MG], ca. 1980

4103.RG0   Rozhdestvensky, Gennady
Moscow Radio Large Symphony Or-
chestra
Recorded p. 1976, ed. n/a
Issue: Westminster WGS-8327, 1 ste-
reo LP, 2 ss [CFB], p. 1976
Timing: 54.19 (19.45, 14.52, 7.42, 12.00)
Notes: Katherine Calkin
Other issues: Melodiya CM-03579/80,
Melodiya Eurodisc 86612

4103.RG1   Rubahn, Gerd
Berlin Symphony Orchestra
Recorded ca. 1950, ed. Oeser 1877
Issue: Royale 1579, LP
NB: Weber suggests Rubahn is a
pseudonym for Horenstein

4103.SA0   Sanderling, Kurt
Leipzig Gewandhaus Orchestra
Recorded ca. 1970, ed. Nowak 1889
Issue: Electrola E/STE 91357-8, LP, 3 ss
Other issues: Eterna 820 425-6

4103.SC0   Schuricht, Carl
Vienna Philharmonic Orchestra
Recorded < 1966, ed. Schalk 1889
Issue: Seraphim S-60090, 1 stereo LP, 2
ss [CFB], W. 1969
Timing: 54.38 (18.51, 14.30, 7.19, 13.42)

Notes: Bryan Fairfax
Other issues: ALP/ASD 2284, World
Record Club ST 1089, SME 91500

4103.SG0   Szell, George
Cleveland Orchestra
Recorded 28-29 January 1966, ed.
Schalk 1889
Issue: Columbia MS 6897, 1 stereo LP,
2 ss [CFB], W. 1966
Timing: 55.13 (20.04, 15.31, 7.18, 12.20)
Notes: Jack Diether
Other issues: CBS 61 072 [CFB], 32CD
487, Columbia ML 6297, SAX 5294,
Epic BC 1362

4103.SG0a Szell, George
Cleveland Orchestra
Recorded 28-29 January 1966, ed.
Schalk 1889
Issue: CBS 61 072, 1 stereo LP, 2 ss
[CFB], 1974
Timing: 55.13 (20.04, 15.31, 7.18, 12.20)
Notes: Knut Franke
Other issues: Columbia MS 6897 [CFB]
Identical to 4103.SG0

4103.WG0   Wand, Günter
Cologne Radio Symphony Orchestra
Recorded WDR, Cologne: 17 January
1981, ed. Nowak 1889
Issue: EMI CDC 7 47744 2, 1 stereo CD,
1 s [CFB], p. 1981
Timing: 54.28 (21.27, 13.43, 6.42, 12.36)
Notes: Rolf-A. Dimpfel
Other issues: EMI 127-154 463-3, 065-
99 923, 567-747 744-2 (CD), ULS
3269

Symphony No. 4 in E flat Major (WAB 104, G/A 96)

I. Bewegt, nicht zu schnell, II. Andante, quasi Allegretto, III. Scherzo: Bewegt, Trio: Nicht zu schnell, keinesfalls schleppend, IV. Finale: Bewegt, doch nicht zu schnell (1880 version). Composed in Vienna in 1874, revised 1877-78 with a new Scherzo and again in 1880 with a new Finale. Bruckner issued a performing version in 1886. The first published edition was completed by Franz Schalk and Ferdinand Löwe in 1887, was reprinted several times, and is generally discredited. Hans Redlich edited the Schalk and Löwe score for a new printing in 1954. The edition by Robert Haas is based on the 1880 version, while Leopold Nowak edited the versions of 1874 and 1877-78 (with the Finale of 1880) and published the 1878 Finale separately.

4104.AH0   Abendroth, Hermann
Leipzig Symphony Orchestra
Recorded 16 November 1949, ed. Haas 1880
Issue: Urania URLP 401, 2 mono LPs, 4 ss [UCB], W. 1951
Timing: 1.03.02 (16.33, 16.29, 11.00, 19.00)
Notes: Veit Rosskopf
Other issues: Classics Club X 1075-6, Deutsche Schallplatten ET 1518, ET-1023

4104.BD0   Barenboim, Daniel
Chicago Symphony Orchestra
Recorded in Medinah Temple, Chicago: November 1972, ed. Nowak 1880
Issue: DG 410 835-1, 1 stereo LP, 2 ss [CFB], ca. 1984
Timing: 1.03.10 (17.52, 15.36, 9.22, 20.20)
Notes: Uwe Kraemer
Other issues: DG 2740 253 [CFB], 2530 336, 415 616-4 (cassette)

4104.BH0   Blomstedt, Herbert
Staatskapelle Dresden
Recorded in Lukaskirche, Dresden: 7-11 September 1981, ed. Nowak 1878/80
Issue: Denon 38C37-7126, 1 digital stereo CD, 1 s [CFB], p. 1984
Timing: 1.06.50 (18.23, 16.30, 10.51, 21.06)
Notes: Akira Hirano
Other issues: Denon OB-7382 3-ND, 33C-37-7959, 38C-7126

4104.BK0   Böhm, Karl
Vienna Philharmonic Orchestra
Recorded in Sofiensaal, Vienna: 14-19 November 1973, ed. Nowak 1880
Issue: London JL 41039, 1 stereo LP, 2 ss [CFB], p. 1982
Timing: 1.07.45 (20.05, 15.30, 11.05, 21.05)
Notes: Robert Simpson
Other issues: London CSA 2240, Decca 6BB 171.2, 6.35256, 6.48286, 6.35384, 411 581-2 (CD), London 411 581-2 (CD), Teldec JB 120 AV, London SOL 1003/4, L20C 2036, SLC 8010, K15C 9068/9, LOOC 1326/38, L35L-

3002/3, L18C 5011, SOL 9017/8, King SOL 1014/26, London F35L-50049/F35L-26013 (CD)

4104.BK1   Böhm, Karl
Saxon State Orchestra
Recorded W. 1936, ed. Haas 1880
Issue: Victor M 331, 8 mono 78s, 16 ss [CST]
Timing: 58.26 (17.27, 15.56, 5.40, 19.13)
Other issues: Electrola DB 4450-7, Odeon C 053 28924 M, DB 20403 [Scherzo only]

4104.CR0   Chailly, Riccardo
Concertgebouw Orchestra
Recorded in Concertgebouw, Amsterdam: December 1988, ed. Nowak 1880
Issue: London 425 613-2, 1 digital stereo CD, 1 s [CFB], p. 1990
Timing: 1.06.14 (18.43, 15.05, 10.20, 21.56)
Notes: Robert Simpson

4104.CS0   Celibidache, Sergiu
Unidentified orchestra
Recorded ca. 1970, ed. n/a
Issue: Rococo OW 7202/3, 1 stereo LP (?), 2 ss [MG], ca. 1970
Timing: 1.13.26 (19.50, 17.15, 10.40, 25.41)

4104.FW0   Furtwängler, Wilhelm
Vienna Philharmonic Orchestra
Recorded in Stuttgart: 22 October 1951, ed. Loewe 1890
Issue: DG 2740 201, 5 mono LPs, 3 ss [CFB], p. 1979
Timing: 1.05.50 (17.40, 18.25, 10.25, 19.20)
Notes: Günter Birkner

With Bruckner: Symphonies Nos. 7, 8, and 9
Other issues: DG 415 664-2 [CFB], Price King K15 C-5037, DG F35G-50282 (CD), MG 8868/72, Teldec Sat 1, London MX 9012

4104.FW1   Furtwängler, Wilhelm
Vienna Philharmonic Orchestra
Recorded in Congress Hall, Munich: October 1951, ed. Loewe 1890
Issue: Price-Less D14228, 1 mono CD, 1 s [CFB], p. 1987
Timing: 1.01.40 (17.07, 17.31, 9.55, 17.07)
Notes: Charles Stanley
Other issues: Decca KD 11030, Eclipse ECM 685, London SLC 2334, King K15C-5037, Pallate PAL 1074 (CD)

4104.HB0   Haitink, Bernard
Concertgebouw Orchestra, Amsterdam
Recorded 10-12 May 1965, ed. Haas 1880
Issue: Philips 835 385 LY, 1 stereo LP, 2 ss [CFB], W. 1968
Timing: 1.03.26 (18.11, 15.51, 9.42, 19.42)
Notes: Ekkehart Kroher
Other issues: Philips SEL-100 130, PHS 900171, SPS 4 905, SAL 3617, 6717, 835325-6, 6833 029, FG 324, 25CD 5078 (CD), Sequenza 652 7101, 731 1101 (cassette)

4104.HB1   Haitink, Bernard
Vienna Philharmonic Orchestra
Recorded in Musikvereinssaal, Vienna: 20-21 February 1985, ed. Haas 1880
Issue: Philips 412 735-1, 1 digital stereo LP, 2 ss [CFB], p. 1986
Timing: 1.08.13 (20.35, 15.23, 10.35, 21.40)

Notes: Karl Schumann
Other issues: Philips 412 735-2 (CD),
412 735-4 (cassette), 25P-5281, 32CD-
411 (CD)

4104.HH0 Hollreiser, Heinrich
Bamberg Symphony Orchestra
Recorded ca. 1961, ed. Nowak 1880
Issue: Turnabout TV 34107S, 1 stereo
LP, 2 ss [CFB], W. 1967
Timing: 1.04.33 (17.05, 16.40, 10.48,
19.40)
Notes: Charles Stanley
Other issues: Vox VBX 117/SVBX 5117

4104.IE0 Inbal, Eliahu
Frankfurt Radio Symphony Orchestra
Recorded 16-18 September 1982, ed.
Nowak 1874
Issue: Teldec 8.42921, 1 digital stereo
CD, 1 s [CFB], p. 1983
Timing: 1.08.04 (18.53, 18.42, 13.11,
17.18)
Notes: Manfred Wagner
Other issues: Teldec 6.42921 AZ, K28C-
327, K20C-396/8, K38Y-64 (CD),
K33Y-10124 (CD)

4104.JE0 Jochum, Eugen
Berlin Philharmonic Orchestra
Recorded June-July 1965, ed. Nowak
1878/80
Issue: DG SKL 929-939, 11 stereo LPs,
2+ ss [CFB], W. 1968
Timing: 1.00.52 (17.25, 16.35, 9.55, 16.57)
Notes: Leopold Nowak, Eugen Joch-
um, Constantin Floros
With Bruckner: Symphonies Nos. 1-9

Other issues: DG 39134-5/139134-5,
2740 136, 2707 025, 2721 010, 2720
047, 2535 111 (LP and cassette), 2740
363, MG 9813/24, MGX 7036, MG
1435, 20MG 0369

4104.JE1 Jochum, Eugen
Hamburg Philharmonic Orchestra
Recorded W. ca. 1940, ed. Haas 1880
Issue: Telefunken SK 3032-9, 8 mono
78s, 16 ss

4104.JE1 Jochum, Eugen
Bavarian Radio Symphony Orchestra
Recorded ca. 1958, ed. Nowak 1880
Issue: Decca DXE 146, LP, 3 ss, W. 1958
Other issues: DG 19057-8, 19055-6

4104.JE3 Jochum, Eugen
Staatskapelle Dresden
Recorded 1-7 December 1975, ed. n/a
1874
Issue: EMI 127-749417-1, 10 digital ste-
reo LPs, 2 ss, ca. 1987
Timing: 1.04.44 (17.45, 16.39, 10.00,
20.20)
With Bruckner: Symphonies Nos. 1-9
Other issues: EAC 90104, set EAC
87045/55

4104.JM0 Janowski, Marek
Radio France Philharmonic Orchestra
Recorded in Radio France, Studio 104,
Paris: June 1990, ed. Nowak 1880
Issue: Virgin Classics VC 7 91206-2,
1 digital CD, 1 s [CFB], p. 1991
Timing: 1.02.41 (18.44, 15.16, 10.17,
18.24)
Notes: Jonathan Freeman-Attwood
With Bruckner: Overture in g minor

4104.KA0   Karajan, Herbert von
Berlin Philharmonic Orchestra
Recorded 25 September/16 October
1970, ed. Haas 1880
Issue: Angel SC-3779, 3 stereo LPs, 3 ss
[CFB], W. 1972
Timing: 1.10.09 (20.54, 15.30, 10.40,
23.05)
Notes: William Mann, Karl Schumann
With Bruckner: Symphony No. 7
Other issues: Angel SLS 811, C 195
02189-91, AM-34735 (cassette),
CDM-69006 (CD), EMI 055-290 566-
1 (LP and cassette), EMI 555-769
006-2 (CD), Angel EAC 85002, EAC
55017, CC28-3803 (CD)

4104.KA1   Karajan, Herbert von
Berlin Philharmonic Orchestra
Recorded ca. 1976, ed. Nowak 1880
Issue: DG 2530 674, 1 stereo LP, 2 ss
[CFB], 21 April 1975
Timing: 1.03.56 (18.17, 14.29, 10.43,
20.27)
Notes: Constantin Floros
Other issues: DG 415 277-2 (CD), 2740
264, 2530 674 (cassette), MF 1034,
00MG 0401/11, F35G50125 (CD)

4104.KE0   Kempe, Rudolf
Munich Philharmonic Orchestra
Recorded 18-20 January 1976, ed. n/a
1878/80
Issue: Acanta 40.22.739, 2 stereo LPs, 3
ss [CFB], ca. 1977
Timing: 1.24.15 (19.30, 14.27, 10.18,
20.50)
Notes: Knut Franke
Other issues: BASF EB 22739 1, UPS
3130, ULS 3386, 35 CT3 (CD)

4104.KE5   Kempen, Paul van
Hilversum Radio Orchestra (Nether-
lands Radio)
Recorded ca. 1955, ed. Haas 1880
Issue: Telefunken LGX 66026-7, LP,
3 ss, W. 1955
With Sibelius: Symphony No. 7
Other issues: Telefunken SK 3806-13
(78), E 1065-72 (78)

4104.KI0   Kertesz, Istvan
London Symphony Orchestra
Recorded 20-25 October 1965, ed.
Nowak 1886
Issue: London STS 15289, 1 stereo LP,
2 ss [CFB], © 1975
Timing: 1.00.55 (16.35, 15.05, 10.15,
19.00)
Notes: Anonymous
Other issues: London CM 9480/CS
6480, LXT/SXL 6227, GT 9067,
K15C-8057

4104.KO0   Klemperer, Otto
Philharmonia Orchestra
Recorded 18-26 September 1963, ed.
Nowak 1878/80
Issue: Angel RL-32059, 1 stereo LP, 2 ss
[CFB], ca. 1984
Timing: 1.00.48 (16.04, 13.59, 11.43,
19.02)
Notes: Anonymous
Other issues: Time-Life Records STL
142 [CFB], Angel S 36245, EMI CX
1928/SAX 2569, SMC 91356, C 063
00593, 037-00593, FCX/SAXF, CCA
1039, Angel 4AE-34456 (cassette),
CDM-69126 (CD), EAC 50040/AA
8101, CE28-5154 (CD)

4104.KO1   Klemperer, Otto
Vienna Symphony Orchestra
Recorded 18-23 March 1951, ed. Haas
  1880
Issue: Vox PL 11.200, 1 mono LP, 2 ss
  [CFB] © 1959
Timing: 51.15 (13.20, 11.54, 9.37, 16.24)
Notes: Charles Stanley
Other issues: Vox VSPS 14 [CFB], VSPS
  5, PL 6930

4104.KP0   Knappertsbusch, Hans
Berlin Philharmonic Orchestra
Recorded live ca. 1943/44, ed. Schalk/
  Loewe 1890
Issue: Music and Arts CD-249, 1 mono
  CD, 1 s [CFB], manufactured 1986
  (p. 1979)
Timing: 1.00.37 (17.58, 15.12, 9.27, 18.00)
Notes: Jack Diether
Other issues: Bruno Walter Society OW
  7221/2

4104.KP1   Knappertsbusch, Hans
Vienna Philharmonic Orchestra
Recorded in Vienna: April 1955, ed.
  Loewe 1890
Issue: London LL 1250-1, 2 mono LPs,
  3 ss [MG], W. 1956
Timing: 59.39 (17.51, 14.29, 9.57, 17.22)
Other issues: London CMA 7207, LXT
  5065-6, LXT 6279, ECM/ECS 511,
  BLK 12020, SMB 25039, King K15 C-
  5027, MX 9021, K30Y-1029 (CD)

4104.KP2   Knappertsbusch, Hans
Vienna Philharmonic Orchestra
Recorded live in Vienna: 1960, ed. n/a
Issue: Nuova Era 2205, 1 mono CD
  (digitally remastered), 1 s [CFB],
  p. 1988

Timing: 1.09.57 (20.19, 16.59, 11.28,
  20.59)

4104.KQ0   Konwitschny, Franz
Czech Philharmonic Orchestra
Recorded MG. 1952, ed. Haas 1880
Issue: Supraphon SLPV 122-3, 2 mono
  LPs, 4 ss
Timing: 1.09.42 (18.50, 18.44, 10.59,
  21.09)
Other issues: Supraphon SUA 10227-
  8, OS 7086, Ultraphon 5096-7, SLPV
  122-3

4104.KQ1   Konwitschny, Franz
Vienna Symphony Orchestra
Recorded W. 1962, ed. n/a 1880
Issue: World Record Club CM/SCM
  52, LP
Other issues: Eurodisc 70002/3 KK,
  Eterna 820 504-5, Japan Columbia
  OS 3398

4104.KQ3   Konwitschny, Franz
Leipzig Gewandhaus Orchestra
Recorded September 1963, ed. n/a
Issue: Eurodisc 86367 XHK, LP
Other issues: Nippon Columbia OQ
  7018, OW 7776, Eurodisc 15KC-9110

4104.KQ5   Krauss, Clemens
[Scherzo only]
Vienna Philharmonic Orchestra
Recorded < 1948, ed. n/a
Issue: His Master's Voice C 1789, 78
Other issues: His Master's Voice EH
  392

4104.KR0   Kubelik, Rafael
Bavarian Radio Symphony Orchestra
Recorded 18-21 November 1979, ed.
  n/a 1880

Issue: CBS D2 35915, 2 digital stereo LPs, 3 ss [CFB], © 1981
Timing: 1.06.49 (19.19, 15.06, 10.58, 21.26)
Notes: Peter Eliot Stone
With Wagner: *Siegfried Idyll*
Other issues: CBS 52 AC 1168/9, 40 AC 1163/4, 20 AC 1536, CBS Sony 38 CD-6 (CD), 30DC-74 (CD)

4104.LE0   Leinsdorf, Erich
Boston Symphony Orchestra
Recorded 10-11 January 1966, ed. Nowak 1880
Issue: Victor LM/LSC 2915, LP, W. 1967
Timing: 1.09.57 (17.08, 13.51, 10.30, 18.28)
Other issues: Victor RB/SB 6697, RCA RGC 1063, RCL 1016

4104.LJ0   López-Cobos, Jesús
Cincinnati Symphony Orchestra
Recorded in Music Hall, Cincinnati: 10-11 February 1990, ed. Nowak 1874
Issue: Telarc CD-80244, 1 digital stereo CD, 1 s [CFB] ,© 1990
Timing: 1.10.02 (20.02, 20.06, 11.28, 18.26)
Notes: William C. Baxter

4104.MC0   Macal, Zdenek
Hallé Orchestra
Recorded in Free Trade Hall, Manchester: April 1984, ed. n/a
Issue: Classics for Pleasure CFP 41 4471 1, 1 digital stereo LP, 2 ss [CFB], © 1984
Timing: 1.06.54 (19.28, 16.39, 10.04, 20.43)
Notes: Hans-Hubert Schönzeler

4104.MK0   Masur, Kurt
Leipzig Gewandhaus Orchestra
Recorded June-July 1975, ed. Haas (1944) 1880
Issue: RCA RL 25106, 1 stereo LP, 2 ss [CFB], © 1977
Timing: 1.03.33 (18.13, 13.52, 10.32, 20.56)
Notes: Hans-Hubert Schönzeler
Other issues: Ariola XG 27913 K, Eterna 27913, Denon 28C37-12 (CD), Columbia OX 1128

4104.ML0   Matacic, Lovro von
Philharmonia Orchestra
Recorded 12-13 October and 11, 14 December 1954, ed. Löwe 1890
Issue: Angel 35359-60, 2 mono LPs, 3 ss [UCB], W. 1956
Notes: Michael Rose, Mosco Carner
With Bruckner: Overture in g minor, Symphony No. 0 [Scherzo only]
Other issues: Angel 3548 B, CX 1274-5, C 90443-4

4104.MN0   Mehta, Zubin
Los Angeles Philharmonic Orchestra
Recorded in Royce Hall, Los Angeles: 13-14 April 1970, ed. Nowak 1880
Issue: London CS 6695, 1 stereo LP, 2 ss [CFB], W. 1971
Timing: 1.04.35 (16.55, 15.45, 10.55, 21.00)
Notes: Anonymous
Other issues: London SXL 6489, SLA 1034/L18C 5138

4104.MR0   Muti, Riccardo
Berlin Philharmonic Orchestra
Recorded in Dahlem Kirche, Berlin: 4-7 September 1985, ed. Nowak 1878/80

Issue: EMI CDC 747352 2, 1 digital stereo CD, 1 s [CFB], p. 1986
Timing: 1.09.30 (20.04, 15.55, 10.37, 22.54)
Notes: Peter Branscombe, Wolfgang Schultze
Other issues: Angel DS-38311, 747352 2 (cassette), EAC 90310, CC33-3463, EMI 067-270379-1 (LP and cassette), EMI 567-747 352-2 (CD)

4104.OE0   Ormandy, Eugene
Philadelphia Orchestra
Recorded 9 October 1967, ed. n/a
Issue: Columbia M 31920, LP, W. 1973

4104.OW0   Otterloo, Willem van
Hague Residentie Orchestra
Recorded ca. 1953, ed. Haas 1880
Issue: Epic SC 6001, 2 mono LPs, 3 ss, W. 1954
With Mahler: Kindertotenlieder
Other issues: Philips A 00658-9 R

4104.RG0   Rozhdestvensky, Gennadi
USSR Ministry of Culture Symphony
Recorded p. 1978, ed. n/a
Issue: MCA MLD-32115, 1 stereo CD, 1 s [CFB], © 1989
Timing: 1.16.08 (20.15, 18.54, 15.16, 21.43)
Notes: Victor Ledin
Originally a Melodiya release

4104.RH0   Rögner, Heinz
Berlin Radio Symphony Orchestra
Recorded July 1983 and January 1984, ed. n/a
Issue: Deutsche Schallplatten ET-5195, 1 stereo LP, 2 ss [MG], ca. 1985
Timing: 57.56 (15.10, 13.33, 10.50, 18.23)

4104.SE0   Sinopoli, Giuseppe
Staatskapelle Dresden
Recorded in Lukaskirche, Dresden: September 1987, ed. Nowak 1880
Issue: DG 423 677-2, 1 digital stereo CD, 1 s [CFB], p. 1988
Timing: 1.06.58 (18.47, 16.00, 11.01, 20.56)
Notes: Wolfram Steinbeck, Andrew Clements, Jean-Jacques Velly

4104.SG0   Solti, Georg
Chicago Symphony Orchestra
Recorded in Orchestra Hall, Chicago: 26-27 January 1981, ed. Nowak 1880
Issue: London LDR 71038, 1 digital stereo LP, 2 ss [CFB], p. 1981
Timing: 1.03.37 (17.55, 14.41, 10.01, 21.00)
Notes: Anonymous
Other issues: London 410 550-2 LH (CD), Decca 6.42 709 AZ, K 28C-130, 410 550-2 ZK (CD)

4104.SW0   Steinberg, William
Pittsburgh Symphony Orchestra
Recorded 19 April 1956, ed. Löwe 1867
Issue: Capitol P8352, 1 mono LP, 2 ss [CFB], W. 1956
Timing: 1.05.05 (16.30, 12.49, 8.49, 16.57)
Notes: Anonymous
Other issues: Capitol K 80322

4104.TE0   Tchakarov, Emil
Leningrad Philharmonic Symphonic Orchestra
Recorded © 1978, ed. n/a
Issue: Melodiya C10-09477-80, 2 stereo LPs, 4 ss [CFB], © 1978
Timing: 1.03.36 (18.50, 14.18, 10.00, 20.28)
Notes: Anonymous

4104.TK0   Tennstedt, Klaus
Berlin Philharmonic Orchestra
Recorded 13-16 December 1981, ed.
Haas 1880
Issue: Angel DSB-3935, 2 digital stereo
LPs, 4 ss [CFB], p. 1982
Timing: 1.10.12 (20.35, 17.04, 10.11,
22.22)
Notes: Derek Watson
Other issues: Angel EAC-50114/5, CC
38-3124 (CD), CC 30-9025

4104.TU0   Tubbs, Jan
Hastings Symphony
Recorded ca. 1954, ed. Haas 1880
Issue: Allegro 3106-7, 2 mono LPs, 3 ss,
W. 1954
With Rameau: work(s)
Weber identifies Tubbs as pseudonym
for unknown conductor.

4104.UK0   Uno, Koho
Shinsei Nihon Orchestra
Recorded 16 January 1986, ed. n/a
Issue: Art Union 3009, 1 stereo LP(?),
2 ss [MG], ca. 1987
Timing: 1.07.26 (19.53, 13.07, 11.52,
22.34)

4104.WA5   Wallberg, Heinz
Vienna National Orchestra
Recorded W. ca. 1967, ed. n/a
Issue: Concert Hall SMS 2489, LP
Other issues: Guilde Int. du Disque
SMS 2489

4104.WB0   Walter, Bruno
Columbia Symphony Orchestra
Recorded in American Legion Hall,
Hollywood: 13-25 February 1960,
ed. Haas 1880

Issue: Columbia Y 32981, 1 stereo LP,
2 ss [CFB], © 1974
Timing: 1.05.59 (18.40, 15.38, 10.58,
20.43)
Notes: Anonymous
Other issues: Columbia M2L 273/M2S
622, D4L 342/D4S 742, BRG/SBRG
72011-2, 61137, 77401, 23AC 614,
30AC 1277/9, 40AC 182516, MP-
42035 (CD), MPT-39026 (cassette),
CBS 42035 (CD), CBS Sony 35CD117
(CD), 28CD 5049 (CD), 60 297 (LP
and cassette)

4104.WG0   Wand, Günter
Cologne Radio Symphony Orchestra
Recorded in West German Radio Studios, Cologne: 10 February 1976,
ed. n/a 1878/80
Issue: Pro Arte PAL-1044, 1 stereo LP,
2 ss [CFB], p. 1982
Timing: 1.03.33 (17.17, 15.36, 10.30,
20.10)
Notes: Bill Parker
Other issues: EMI 127-154 463-3, 065-
199 738-1 (LP and cassette), 567-747
745-2 (CD), ULS 3270

4104.ZD0   Zsoltay, Denis
South German Philharmonic
Recorded ca. 1977, ed. n/a
Issue: Mace MAV-3609, 5 stereo LPs,
2 ss [CFB], p. 1978
Timing: 1.03.14 (18.41, 14.10, 10.00,
20.24)
With Bruckner: Symphony No. 6 and
Mahler: Symphonies Nos. 6 and 9
Other issues: Intercord 185812, 120872,
Concerto INT 820.717 (CD)

Symphony No. 5 in B flat Major (WAB 105, G/A 97)

I. Introduction: Adagio, Allegro, II. Adagio, Sehr langsam, III. Scherzo: Molto vivace (Schnell), Trio: Im gleichen Tempo, IV. Finale: Adagio, Allegro. Composed in Vienna in 1876 and slightly revised in 1878. Franz Schalk edited the first published score in 1893 with significant alterations. Robert Haas published two slightly different versions of the 1876 score in 1936 and in 1944. The Nowak edition of the 1878 score appeared in 1951.

4105.A_0   Anonymous
[Scherzo only]
Dol Dauber Orchestra
Recorded < 1948, ed. n/a
Issue: Electrola AN 189, 78

4105.AH0   Abendroth, Hermann
Leipzig Radio Orchestra
Recorded 27 May 1949, ed. Haas 1876
Issue: Eterna 1519-20, LP
Other issues: Deutsche Schallplatten
LPi, ET 1024/5

4105.AW0   Albert, Werner Andreas
Bavarian State Youth Orchestra, Augsburg
Recorded ca. 1986, ed. n/a 1876
Issue: Calig CAL 30 838/39, 2 digital stereo LPs, 3 ss, ca. 1986
With Lutoslawski: Concerto for Orchestra

4105.BD0   Barenboim, Daniel
Chicago Symphony Orchestra
Recorded 5, 13 December 1977, ed. Nowak 1878
Issue: DG 2707 113, 2 stereo LPs, 4 ss [CFB], p. 1979
Timing: 1.14.51 (21.15, 17.12, 13.14, 23.10)
Notes: Thomas Kohlhase
Other issues: DG 2740 253 [CFB], MG 8388/9

4105.BE0   Beinum, Eduard van
Concertgebouw Orchestra, Amsterdam
Recorded 12 March 1959, ed. Haas 1876
Issue: Philips 6768 023, 8 mono LPs, 3 ss [CFB], p. 1978
Timing: 1.11.43 (19.50, 15.25, 14.33, 21.55)
Notes: Wouter Paap
With one work each of fifteen other composers
Other issues: Philips 13PC-176/7
Collection titled "The Art of Eduard van Beinum"

4105.BK0   Böhm, Karl
Saxon State Orchestra
Recorded W. 1936, ed. Haas 1876
Issue: Victor M 770-1, 9 mono 78s, 18 ss
Other issues: Grammophone DB 4486-94 (78), EAC 40213/4

4105.FW0   Furtwängler, Wilhelm
Berlin Philharmonic Orchestra
Recorded live in Berlin: 25 and 28 October 1942, ed. n/a 1876
Issue: Bruno Walter Society CD-538, 1 mono CD, 1 s [CFB], p. 1982
Timing: 1.08.18 (19.04, 15.25, 11.57, 21.52)
Notes: Neville Cardus

Other issues: Teldec MA 538 WP (CD), Walter Society OS 7089/90, OZ 7600, 35637-7297 (CD)

4105.FW1   Furtwängler, Wilhelm
Berlin Philharmonic Orchestra
Recorded live in Philharmonie, Berlin: 28 October 1942, ed. Haas 1876
Issue: DG 427 774-2 GDO, 1 mono CD, 1 s [CFB], p. 1989
Timing: 1.07.55 (18.56, 15.17, 11.49, 21.40)
Notes: Yehudi Menuhin, Klaus Lang, Karla Höcker

4105.FW2   Furtwängler, Wilhelm
Vienna Philharmonic Orchestra
Recorded in Festspielhaus, Salzburg: August 1951, ed. n/a
Issue: Rococo 2034, LP, 3 ss, W. 1973
Other issues: Rococo OP 7518/9

4105.HB0   Haitink, Bernard
Concertgebouw Orchestra, Amsterdam
Recorded ca. 1971, ed. n/a 1876
Issue: Philips 6700 055, 2 stereo LPs, 4 ss [CFB], W. 1972
Timing: 1.12.42 (18.54, 18.35, 12.19, 22.54)
Notes: Deryck Cooke

4105.HB1   Haitink, Bernard
Vienna Philharmonic Orchestra
Recorded in Musikverein, Vienna: March 1988, ed. 1878
Issue: Philips 422 342-2 PH2, 2 digital stereo CDs, 2 ss [CFB], p. 1989
Timing: 1.16.59 (21.10, 16.47, 13.36, 25.26)

Notes: Michael Kennedy, Hans Christoph Worbs
With Bruckner: Te Deum

4105.IE0   Inbal, Eliahu
Frankfurt Radio Symphony Orchestra
Recorded in Alte Oper, Frankfurt/Main: October 1987, ed. n/a 1876
Issue: Teldec 6.35785, 2 digital stereo LPs, 3 ss [CFB], p. 1988
Timing: 1.10.31 (19.43, 14.41, 13.45, 22.22)
Notes: Manfred Wagner
With Bruckner: Symphony No. 9 [Finale only]
Other issues: Teldec 4.35785 (cassette), 8.35785 (CD), K30Y-10211/2

4105.JE0   Jochum, Eugen
Bavarian Radio Symphony Orchestra
Recorded February 1958, ed. n/a 1876
Issue: DG 2707 020, 2 stereo LPs, 4 ss [CFB], ca. 1968
Timing: 1.16.08 (20.34, 19.16, 12.25, 23.53)
Notes: Constantin Floros
Other issues: DG SKL 929-939 [CFB], DGMA 300/DGSA 7300, LPM 18500-1/SLPM 1138004-5, LPM 18967-8/SLPM 138967-8, 2721 010, 2720 047, 2740 136, MG 9813/24, SLGM 1147/8, MGX 9915/6, Opus Musicum OM 210/12 [Adagio only]

4105.JE1   Jochum, Eugen
Hamburg Philharmonic Orchestra
Recorded ca. 1937, ed. Haas 1876
Issue: Capitol P 8049-50, 2 mono LPs, 4 ss [UCB], W. 1950
Timing: (IV. = 24.01)
Notes: Anonymous "A.L."
Other issues: Telefunken E 2672-80 (78)

4105.JE2   Jochum, Eugen
Staatskapelle Dresden
Recorded ca. 1986, ed. n/a 1876
Issue: EMI 127-749417-1, 10 digital stereo LPs, 3 ss, February-March 1980
With Bruckner: Symphonies Nos. 1-9
Other issues: EAC 870066/7, set EAC 87045/55

4105.JE2   Jochum, Eugen
Concertgebouw Orchestra, Amsterdam
Recorded live in Ottobeuron Abbey: 30-31 May 1964, ed. n/a 1876
Issue: Philips 426 107-2 PLC, 1 CD (digitally reprocessed), 1 s [CFB], p. 1989
Timing: 1.15.54 (20.54, 18.55, 12.41, 23.04)
Notes: Hans Christoph Worbs
Other issues: Philips PHM 2 591/PHS 2 991, AL/SAL 3532-3, 6700 028, A 02347-8 L/835225-6 AY, 13PC 119/20, PC 5520/1

4105.KH0   Karajan, Herbert von
Berlin Philharmonic Orchestra
Recorded 6-11 December 1976, ed. n/a 1876
Issue: DG 2707 101, 2 stereo LPs, 4 ss [CFB], p. 1977
Timing: 1.20.48 (20.42, 21.34, 13.44, 24.48)
Notes: Hanspeter Krellmann, Richard Osborne
Other issues: DG 415 985-2 (CD), 2740 264, 00MG 0401/11, MG 8313/4, F66G 50347/8

4105.KM0   Kempe, Rudolf
Munich Philharmonic Orchestra
Recorded 25-27 May 1975, ed. n/a 1876
Issue: Columbia Y2 35243, 2 stereo LPs, 4 ss [CFB], p. 1976
Timing: 1.15.10 (20.54, 17.15, 12.43, 24.18)
Notes: Jack Diether
Other issues: BASF 39 22526 7, Bellaphon HA 225267, 22526, Columbia ULS 3387/8, ULS 3131/2, UPS 3131/2

4105.KO0   Klemperer, Otto
New Philharmonia Orchestra
Recorded 9-11, 14-15 March 1967, ed. n/a 1876
Issue: Angel SB-3709, 2 stereo LPs, 4 ss [CFB], © 1967
Timing: 1.19.33 (21.15, 16.39, 14.46, 26.53)
Notes: Bryan Fairfax
Other issues: Angel SAX 5288-9, SMC 91663-4, C 163 00621-2, CVB 2064-5, EAC 85003/4, EAC 50041/2

4105.KO1   Klemperer, Otto
Vienna Philharmonic Orchestra
Recorded live in Vienna: 2 June 1968, ed. n/a
Issue: Hunt HUNTCD 569, 1 stereo CD, 1 s [CFB], p. 1989
Timing: 1.16.17
Notes: Michele Selvini

4105.KP0   Knappertsbusch, Hans
Vienna Philharmonic Orchestra
Recorded in Sofiensaal, Vienna: June 1956, ed. Schalk 1893
Issue: Decca ECS 530, 1 stereo LP, 2 ss [CFB], © 1969
Timing: 1.00.38 (18.32, 13.50, 9.32, 18.44)

Notes: Anonymous

Other issues: London LL 1527-8, CMA 7208/CSA 2205, STS 15121-2, LXT 5255-6, ECM 530, BLK 21020, SMB 25039, King K15 C-7037, London GT 9035, K15C-8011/K15C 9023/4, K33 C70024/5 (CD), K30Y 1028 (CD)

4105.KP1   Knappertsbusch, Hans
Munich Philharmonic Orchestra
Recorded 1961, ed. n/a
Issue: Seven Seas K30Y-264, 1 CD, 1 s [MG], ca. 1980
Timing: 1.03.01 (19.13, 14.15, 10.50, 18.43)

4105.KZ0   Konwitschny, Franz
Leipzig Gewandhaus Orchestra
Recorded 26-30 June 1961, ed. n/a
Issue: Electrola E 91322-3, LP, ca. 1962
Timing: 1.20.30 (21.32, 18.58, 14.02, 26.28)
Other issues: Eterna 820 275-6, Eurodisc 86367 XHK, K15C-9111/2, Nippon Columbia OP 7085/5

4105.MA0   Maazel, Lorin
Vienna Philharmonic Orchestra
Recorded 25-28 March 1974, ed. Nowak 1876
Issue: London CSA 2238, 2 stereo LPs, 4 ss [CFB], © 1974
Timing: 1.15.36 (20.25, 18.06, 12.35, 24.30)
Notes: Joseph Brand
Other issues: Decca SXL 6686-7, 6.35256, London LOOC 1326/38, SLA 1090/1, F60L-28055/6 (CD), King set SOL 1014/26

4105.MK0   Masur, Kurt
Leipzig Gewandhaus Orchestra
Recorded 29 November and 3 December 1976, ed. n/a 1876
Issue: Vanguard VSD 71239/40, 2 stereo LPs, 4 ss [CFB], p. 1978
Timing: 1.18.45 (21.12, 17.07, 14.26, 26.00)
Notes: Joseph Braunstein
Other issues: Denon OQ 7438/9

4105.ML0   Matacic, Lovro von
Czech Philharmonic Orchestra
Recorded 1973, ed. Schalk (with cuts) 1876
Issue: Supraphon 32C37-7418, 1 stereo CD, 1 s [CFB], ca. 1985
Timing: 1.10.03 (19.25, 18.18, 11.50, 20.30)
Notes: Akira Hirano
Other issues: Supraphon SM 1211-2, 1 10 1211-2, XK 85397, Nippon Columbia OQ 7019/20, 32C37-7418 (CD)

4105.OE0   Ormandy, Eugene
Philadelphia Orchestra
Recorded 13 April 1965, ed. Nowak 1876
Issue: Columbia M2S 768, 2 stereo LPs, 3 ss [CFB], W. 1968
Timing: 1.12.24 (20.01, 16.53, 12.30, 23.00)
Notes: Jack Diether
With with Bruckner: Te Deum
Other issues: Columbia CM2S 768, 77222

4105.PG0   Pflügler, Gerhard
Leipzig Philharmonic Orchestra
Recorded © 1955, ed. Haas 1893

Issue: Urania URLP 239, 2 mono LPs, 3 ss [CFB], W. 1955
Timing: 1.13.15 (20.09, 15.36, 13.28, 24.02)
Notes: Richard C. Burns
With Weber: Symphony No. 1

4105.RH0   Rögner, Heinz
Berlin Symphony Orchestra
Recorded September 1983 and January 1984, ed. n/a
Issue: Deutsche Schallplatten 32TC-98, 1 CD, 1 s [MG], ca. 1985
Timing: 1.08.02 (19.38, 14.38, 13.47, 19.59)
Other issues: Deutsche Schallplatten ET 4047/8

4105.SG0   Solti, Georg
Chicago Symphony Orchestra
Recorded in Medinah Temple, Chicago: January 1980, ed. Nowak 1876

Issue: London LDR 10031, 2 digital stereo LPs, 4 ss [CFB], p. 1980
Timing: 1.19.03 (20.13, 21.31, 13.24, 23.55)
Notes: Joseph Brand, R. W. Bayliff
Other issues: London LSOC 8028/9, L45C 3131/2, K25C 16/9

4105.WG0   Wand, Günter
Cologne Radio Symphony Orchestra
Recorded in WDR, Cologne: 7 July 1974, ed. n/a 1876
Issue: EMI CDC 7 47746 2, 1 stereo CD, 1 s [CFB], p. 1977
Timing: 1.14.20 (20.10, 15.49, 14.13, 24.08)
Notes: Anonymous
Other issues: EMI 127-154 463-3, 153-199 670-3, 567-747 746-2 (CD), ULS 3271/2

Symphony No. 6 in A Major (WAB 106, G/A 106)

I. Majestoso, II. Adagio, Sehr feierlich, III. Scherzo: Nicht schnell, Trio: Langsam, IV. Finale: Bewegt, doch nicht zu schnell. Composed in Vienna in 1881. Cyril Hynais edited the first publication of this score in 1899. The later editions by Robert Haas and Leopold Nowak are considered authentic and differ in only minor details.

4106.BD0   Barenboim, Daniel
Chicago Symphony Orchestra
Recorded 13 December 1977, ed. Nowak 1882
Issue: DG 2531 043, 1 stereo LP, 2 ss [CFB], © 1978
Timing: 59.05 (17.35, 18.10, 8.45, 14.35)
Notes: Arnold Werner-Jensen, Richard Osborne

Other issues: DG 2740 253 [CFB], MG1165

4106.BH0   Bongartz, Heinz
Leipzig Gewandhaus Orchestra
Recorded ca. 1967, ed. n/a 1881
Issue: Philips W.S. PHC 9048, LP, W. 1967
Other issues: Philips 835388 LY, Eterna 820 540-1

4106.EC0   Eschenbach, Christoph
Schleswig-Holstein Music Festival
Recorded live in Deutsches Haus,
Flensburg: July 1988, ed. n/a 1881
Issue: BMG 69010-2-RG, 1 digital ste-
reo CD, 1 s [CFB], p. 1989
Timing: 59.21 (16.14, 19.08, 8.37, 15.21)
Notes: Anonymous

4106.HB0   Haitink, Bernard
Concertgebouw Orchestra, Amster-
dam
Recorded W. 1970, ed. Haas 1881
Issue: Philips 6500 164, 1 stereo LP, 2 ss
[CFB], W. 1971
Timing: 54.00 (15.16, 17.25, 7.51, 13.28)
Notes: Deryck Cooke

4106.HE0   Horn, Erwin
[Adagio only]
Recorded on the Klais organ of the
Frauenkirche, Nuremburg: April
1990, ed. Horn
Issue: Novalis 150 071-2, 1 digital ste-
reo CD, 1 s [CFB], p. 1990
Timing: 17.21
Notes: Erwin Horn
With Bruckner: organ works

4106.IE0   Inbal, Eliahu
Radio Symphony Orchestra Frankfurt
Recorded in Alte Oper, Frankfurt: Sep-
tember 1988, ed. n/a 1881
Issue: Teldec 8.44251, 1 digital stereo
CD, 1 s [CFB], p. 1989
Timing: 58.56 (17.51, 17.03, 8.32, 15.02)
Notes: Knut Franke

4106.JE0   Jochum, Eugen
Bavarian Radio Symphony Orchestra
Recorded 1-3 July 1966, ed. Nowak
1881

Issue: DG SKL 929-939, 11 stereo LPs,
2 ss [CFB], W. 1968
Timing: 54.33 (16.23, 17.05, 7.51, 13.14)
Notes: Leopold Nowak, Eugen Joch-
um, Constantin Floros
With Bruckner: Symphonies Nos. 1-9
Other issues: DG 39136/139136, 2740
136, 2721 010, 2720 047, MGX 7058,
MG 9813/24

4106.JE1   Jochum, Eugen
Staatskapelle Dresden
Recorded 9-13 June 1978, ed. n/a 1881
Issue: Angel SZ-37695, 1 stereo LP, 2 ss
[CFB], p. 1981
Timing: 55.41 (15.59, 18.37, 7.55, 13.30)
Notes: Peter Branscombe, Bryan
Fairfax
Other issues: EMI 127-749417-1, EAC
900009, EAC 87045/55

4106.JG0   Jochum, Georg Ludwig
Linz Bruckner Symphony Orchestra
Recorded ca. 1943, ed. n/a 1881
Issue: Urania URLP 7041, LP, W. 1952
Other issues: Classics Club X 141

4106.KH0   Karajan, Herbert von
Berlin Philharmonic Orchestra
Recorded 25-26 September 1979, ed.
n/a 1881
Issue: DG 2531 295, 1 stereo LP, 2 ss
[CFB], p. 1980
Timing: 57.16 (15.14, 18.59, 7.50, 15.13)
Notes: Thomas Kohlhase, Richard
Osborne
Other issues: DG 419 194-2 (CD), 2740
264, OOMG 040/11, 28MG 0028,
F35G50400 (CD)

4106.KJ0   Keilberth, Joseph
Berlin Philharmonic Orchestra

Recorded p. 1963, ed. n/a 1881
Issue: Teldec 8.43194 ZK, 1 stereo CD,
1 s [CFB], © 1985
Timing: 55.33 (17.02, 14.35, 8.43, 15.13)
Notes: Anonymous
Other issues: Telefunken GMS/SMA
83, SLT 43076, SNA 25029, SMT
1272, GT 9179/K17C 8331, K35Y
159 (CD)

4106.KO0   Klemperer, Otto
Concertgebouw Orchestra, Amster-
dam
Recorded live in Amsterdam: 22 June
1961, ed. n/a 1881
Issue: Music and Arts CD-247, 1 mono
CD, 1 s [CFB], p. 1987
Timing: 54.03 (17.27, 12.40, 8.36, 15.20)
Notes: David Breckbill
With Brahms: Variations on a Theme
by Haydn
Other issues: Teldec MA 247 WP,
Movimento musica 01.056

4106.KO1   Klemperer, Otto
New Philharmonia Orchestra
Recorded November 1964, ed. Haas
1881
Issue: Angel 36271, 1 stereo LP, 2 ss
[CFB], W. 1965
Timing: 54.18 (16.45, 14.35, 9.17, 13.41)
Notes: Bryan Fairfax
Other issues: Angel CX 1943/SAX 2582,
SMC 91437, C 06300599, FCX/SAXF
1051, EAC 85023, 50043

4106.MK0 Masur, Kurt
Leipzig Gewandhaus Orchestra
Recorded in Paul-Gerhardt-Kirche
Leipzig: 10-14 September 1978, ed.
Haas 1881

Issue: Eurodisc 300 639-440, 3 quadra-
phonic LPs, 2 ss [CFB], ca. 1979
Timing: 53.39 (14.45, 15.10, 8.32, 15.12)
Notes: Alfred Beaujean
With Bruckner: Symphony No. 8
Other issues: Denon OX 1171

4106.MR0   Muti, Riccardo
Berlin Philharmonic Orchestra
Recorded in Philharmonie, Berlin: Janu-
ary 1988, ed. Nowak 1881
Issue: EMI CDC 7 49408 2, 1 digital
stereo CD, 1 s [CFB], p. 1988
Timing: 56.55 (17.09, 17.21, 7.49, 14.21)
Notes: Peter Branscombe, Knut Franke

4106.RH0   Reichert, Hubert
Westphalian Symphony Orchestra
Recorded ca. 1963, ed. n/a 1881
Issue: Vox STPL 512.540, 1 stereo LP, 2
ss [CFB], W. 1963
Timing: 58.58 (16.53, 16.18, 9.41, 16.06)
Notes: Harry Halbreich
Other issues: Vox PL 12540, Turnabout
TV S 34226

4106.RH5   Rögner, Heinz
Berlin Symphony Orchestra
Recorded 17-19 June 1980, ed. n/a 1881
Issue: Deutsche Schallplatten 32TC52,
1 CD, 1 s [MG], ca. 1981
Timing: 51.54 (13.45, 15.36, 8.02, 14.31)
Other issues: Deutsche Schallplatten
ET-5121

4106.SA0   Sawallisch, Wolfgang
Bavarian State Orchestra
Recorded in Aula of the University
of Munich: 13-14 October 1981, ed.
n/a 1881
Issue: Orfeo S 024821 A, 1 digital stereo
LP, 2 ss [CFB], p. 1982

Timing: 54.54 (14.17, 17.35, 8.26, 14.33)
Notes: Knut Franke
Other issues: Orfeo C-024821 (CD),
28PC 10009, 36CD 10002 (CD)

4106.SG0   Solti, Georg
Chicago Symphony Orchestra
Recorded in Medinah Temple, Chi-
cago: January/June 1979, ed. n/a
1881
Issue: London CS 7173, 1 stereo LP, 2 ss
[CFB], © 1980
Timing: 1.00.01 (16.51, 19.14, 8.48, 15.08)
Notes: George Hall
Other issues: London 417389-2 (CD),
Decca 417 389-2 ZK (CD), King Lon-
don K28C59, London K28C-59,
L25C-8050, F35L-20088 (CD)

4106.SH0   Stein, Horst
Vienna Philharmonic Orchestra
Recorded 14-15 November 1972, ed.
n/a 1881
Issue: London CS 6880, LP, W. 1975
Timing: 53.55 (16.34, 16.03, 8.02, 13.16)
Other issues: Decca SXL 6682, 6.35256,
London SLA 6001, K15C-9020, King
set SOL 1014/26

4106.SS0   Swarowsky, Hans
Vienna Festival Orchestra
Recorded 1960, ed. Haas 1881
Issue: Preludio PHC 3145, 1 stereo CD
(digitally remastered), 1 s [CFB], p.
1989
Timing: 50.45 (13.09, 15.36, 8.06, 13.50)
Notes: Christian Colombeau

4106.ST0   Steinberg, William
Boston Symphony Orchestra
Recorded W. 1969, ed. n/a 1881

Issue: RCA LSC-3177, 1 stereo LP, 2 ss
[CFB], W. 1972
Timing: 52.15 (14.53, 16.15, 8.02, 13.05)
Notes: Winthrop Sargeant

4106.SW0   Swoboda, Henry
Vienna Symphony Orchestra
Recorded © 1950, ed. Haas 1881
Issue: Westminster 5055-6, 2 mono LPs,
3 ss [CFB], W. 1951
Timing: 1.00.02 (15.01, 21.08, 10.01,
13.52)
Notes: Gabriel Engel
With Bruckner: Psalms 112 and 150
Other issues: Westminster W-9700
[CFB], WAL 201, XWN 18074, Nixa
WLP 6201, Véga C30S230

4106.WG0   Wand, Günter
Cologne Radio Symphony Orchestra
Recorded in West German Radio stu-
dios, Cologne: 16-25 August 1976,
ed. n/a 1881
Issue: EMI CDC 7 47747 2, 1 stereo CD,
1 s [CFB], ca. 1987
Timing: 53.03 (15.36, 15.04, 8.45, 13.38)
Notes: Anonymous
Other issues: EMI 127-154 463-3, 065-
99 672, 567-747 747-2 (CD), Harmo-
nia mundi ULS-3273

4106.WG1   Wand, Günter
North German Radio Symphony Or-
chestra
Recorded in Musikhalle, Hamburg:
December 4-5 1988, ed. Nowak 1881
Issue: RCA Victor 60061-2-RC, 1 digi-
tal stereo CD, 1 s [CFB], p. 1989
Timing: 54.55 (16.06, 15.47, 8.57, 13.27)
Notes: Eckhardt van den Hoogen

4106.ZD0   Zsoltay, Denis
South German Philharmonic
Recorded ca. 1977, ed. n/a 1881
Issue: Mace MAV-3609, 5 stereo LPs,
2 ss [CFB], p. 1978

Timing: 50.42 (13.06, 15.37, 8.04, 13.55)
With Bruckner: Symphony No. 4 and
Mahler: Symphonies Nos. 6 and 9
Other issues: Intercord 185812, 120873

Symphony No. 7 in E Major (WAB 107, G/A 110)

I. Allegro moderato, II. Adagio: Sehr feierlich und sehr langsam, III. Scherzo: Nicht schnell, Trio: Langsam, IV. Finale: Bewegt, doch nicht zu schnell. Composed in Vienna in 1883 and revised later that year with the assistance of Josef Schalk and Ferdinand Loewe This latter version appeared as the first edition in 1885 but was superseded by editions of the first version by Robert Haas and Leopold Nowak, both of which differ only slightly from each other.

4107.AT0   Asahina, Takashi
Osaka Philharmonic Orchestra
Recorded 13 September 1983, ed. n/a
Issue: Victor VDC 1067, 1 CD, 1 s [MG],
ca. 1984
Other issues: Victor VDC 511 (CD)

4107.AT1   Asahina, Takashi
Osaka Philharmonic Orchestra
Recorded 12 October 1975, ed. n/a
Issue: Victor VDC 1214, 1 CD, 1 s [MG],
ca. 1976
Timing: 1.12.57 (22.49, 25.01, 9.34, 15.23)
Other issues: Victor KVX 5501/2

4107.BD0   Barenboim, Daniel
Chicago Symphony Orchestra
Recorded March 1979, ed. Nowak 1883
Issue: DG 2707 116, 2 stereo LPs, 3 ss
[CFB], p. 1980
Timing: 1.05.45 (20.25, 22.28, 10.20, 12.32)
Notes: Siegfried Kross, Robert Simpson
With Bruckner: Helgoland and Psalm 150

Other issues: DG 2740 253 [CFB], MG 8430/1

4107.BE0   Beinum, Eduard van
Concertgebouw Orchestra, Amsterdam
Recorded May 1953, ed. n/a 1883
Issue: Decca ECS 571, 1 reprocessed
stereo LP, 2 ss [CFB], p. 1970
Timing: 57.40 (18.16, 18.52, 9.01, 11.31)
Notes: Anonymous
Other issues: London LL 852-3, CMA 7204, LXT 2829-30

4107.BE1   Beinum, Eduard van
Concertgebouw Orchestra, Amsterdam
Recorded 9-10 September 1947, ed. n/a
Issue: London LA 94, 16 mono 78s, 15 ss
With Tchaikovsky: Serenade, Waltz
Other issues: Decca K 1916-23, London T.5108-9, MX HAR 1/15

4107.BH0   Blomstedt, Herbert
Staatskapelle Dresden
Recorded in Lukaskirche, Dresden: June-July 1980, ed. Haas 1883
Issue: Denon 38C37-7286, 1 digital stereo CD, 1 s [CFB], p. 1984
Timing: 1.07.47 (21.03, 24.30, 9.36, 12.23)
Notes: Akira Hirano
Other issues: Denon 33C37-7960 (CD), OB 7375/6

4107.BK0   Böhm, Karl
Vienna State Opera Orchestra
Recorded W. 1944, ed. n/a 1883
Issue: Vox VSPS 14, 5 mono LPs, 3 ss [CFB], p. 1973
Timing: 1.07.26 (19.00, 27.26, 10.05, 10.55)
Notes: Hans F. Redlich
With Bruckner: Symphonies 4, 8 and 9
Other issues: Vox PL 7190, PL 7192, VSPS 5

4107.BK1   Böhm, Karl
Vienna Philharmonic Orchestra
Recorded in Großer Musikvereinssaal, Vienna: 27-29 September 1976, ed. n/a 1883
Issue: DG 2709 068, 3 stereo LPs, 3 ss [CFB], W. 1977
Timing: 1.05.58 (19.30, 23.59, 10.29, 12.00)
Notes: Constantin Floros
With Bruckner: Symphony No. 8
Other issues: DG 2740 179, 413 978-1, 419 858-1 (LP and cassette), 40MG 0583/4, 18MG-4564, DG 3111-20 (CD), F28G-22064 (CD)

4107.CR0   Chailly, Riccardo
Berlin Radio Symphony Orchestra
Recorded in Jesus Christ Church, Berlin: June 1984, ed. n/a 1883
Issue: London 414 290-1, 1 digital stereo LP, 2 ss [CFB], ca. 1986
Timing: 1.08.41 (22.41, 22.46, 9.56, 13.18)
Notes: Duncan Chisholm
Other issues: London 414 290-2 (CD), 414 290-4 (cassette), Decca 6.43 125 AZ (LP and cassette), 414 290-2 ZK (CD), C28C1880, F35L S0064 (CD)

4107.DC0   Davis, Colin
Bavarian Radio Symphony Orchestra
Recorded live in Philharmonie in Münchner Gesteig: 1 May 1987, ed. n/a
Issue: Orfeo C 208 891 A, 1 digital stereo CD, 1 s [CFB], p. 1989
Timing: 1.07.55 (21.18, 10.23, 23.59, 12.15)
Notes: Irmelin Bürgers, Karl Schumann

4107.FO0   Fried, Oskar
Berlin State Opera Orchestra
Recorded W. ca. 1924, ed. n/a
Issue: Grammophon 69753-9, 7 acoustic 78s, 14 ss
Other issues: Polydor 66318-24, Bruno Walter Society BWS 719 (1973)

4107.FW0   Furtwängler, Wilhelm
Berlin Philharmonic Orchestra
Recorded in Berlin-Dahlem: 18 October 1949, ed. Löwe 1883
Issue: Volksplatte SMVP 8055/56, 2 reprocessed stereo LPs, 3 ss [CFB], W. 1965
Timing: 1.01.55 (19.23, 20.58, 9.40, 11.54)
With Wagner: two excerpts from *Parsifal*

Other issues: Odeon STE 91375-6, C 177 29229-30, HQM 1169, FALP 852-3, ASDW 9148-51, C 153 28229-30, AA 8320-1, Angel WF 70036/7, WF 60024/5

4107.FW1   Furtwängler, Wilhelm
Berlin Philharmonic Orchestra
Recorded in Radio Cairo: 23 April 1951, ed. prob. Löwe 1883
Issue: DG 2535 161, 1 mono LP, 2 ss [CFB], p. 1976
Timing: 1.02.07 (18.59, 21.58, 9.32, 11.38)
Notes: Werner Bollert
Other issues: DG 2740 201 [CFB], 2721 202, Rococo 2032, MG 8868/72, MG 6001

4107.FW2   Furtwängler, Wilhelm
Berlin Philharmonic Orchestra
Recorded in Rome: 1 May 1951, ed. n/a 1883
Issue: Discocorp RR 416, LP
Timing: 1.02.55 (19.54, 13.50, 7.40, 21.31)
Other issues: Rococo 2105, Bruno Walter Society OW 7924, OZ 7510, OZ 7601, OW 7824

4107.FW3   Furtwängler, Wilhelm
[Adagio only]
Berlin Philharmonic Orchestra
Recorded 7 April 1942, ed. n/a
Issue: Telefunken SK 3230-2, 3 mono 78s, 6 ss
Other issues: Ultraphone G 22264-6, Rococo 2014, Nippon Columbia OP 7518/9

4107.GC0   Giulini, Carlo Maria
Vienna Philharmonic Orchestra
Recorded in Großer Musikvereinssaal, Vienna: June 1986, ed. n/a 1883

Issue: DG 419 627-2, 1 digital stereo CD, 1 s [CFB], p. 1987
Timing: 1.07.36 (20.22, 24.08, 10.35, 12.31)
Notes: Wolfram Steinbeck, Peter Branscombe, Jean-Jacques Velly
Other issues: DG 419 627-1 (LP and cassette), F35G 20139 (CD)

4107.HB0   Haitink, Bernard
Concertgebouw Orchestra, Amsterdam
Recorded 6-10 October 1966, ed. n/a 1883
Issue: Philips 802 759/60 AY, 2 stereo LPs, 3 ss [CFB], W. 1967
Timing: 1.00.28 (18.14, 21.05, 9.20, 11.49)
Notes: Conrad Wilson
With Bruckner: Te Deum
Other issues: Philips PHM 2 598/PHS 2 998, SAL 3624-5, 6700 038

4107.HB1   Haitink, Bernard
Concertgebouw Orchestra, Amsterdam
Recorded in Amsterdam: 9-10 October 1978, ed. Novak 1883
Issue: Philips 420 805-2, 1 stereo CD, 1 s [CFB], p. 1979
Timing: 1.05.07 (20.51, 22.21, 9.50, 12.05)
Notes: Hans Christoph Worbs
Other issues: Philips 676 9028, 769 9113 (cassette), 25PC-23/4, 18PC-131/2

4107.HJ0   Horenstein, Jascha
Berlin Philharmonic Orchestra
Recorded p. 1928, ed. Löwe/Schalk 1883
Issue: Unicorn UN1-72004, 1 mono LP, 2 ss [CFB], p. 1975
Timing: 56.11 (17.37, 21.36, 8.59, 9.59)
Notes: Anthony Hodgson

Other issues: Polydor 66802-8 (78),
Brunswick 90305-11 (78)

4107.HW0 Horn, Erwin
[Adagio only]
Recorded on the Klais organ of St.
Maria Magdalena Church, Münner-
stadt: ca. 1986, ed. n/a
Issue: Mitra 16 180, 1 digital stereo LP,
1 s, ca. 1986
With Bruckner: Symphony No. 0
[Scherzo only] and four other organ
works by various composers

4107.IE0   Inbal, Eliahu
Frankfurt Radio Symphony Orchestra
Recorded 9-10 September 1985, ed.
Nowak 1883
Issue: Teldec 6.43259, 1 digital stereo
LP, 2 ss [CFB], p. 1986
Timing: 53.27 (19.24, 23.30, 9.39, 10.54)
Notes: Hans Christoph Worbs
Other issues: Teldec 8.43259 ZK (CD),
4.43259 CY (cassette), K28 Y9115-8,
K35Y-10038 (CD), K28C-10010

4107.JE0   Jochum, Eugen
Berlin Philharmonic Orchestra
Recorded 6-10 October 1964, ed. Nowak
1883
Issue: DG SKL 929-939, 11 stereo LPs,
3 ss [CFB], W. 1968
Timing: 1.07.04 (20.21, 24.48, 9.33, 12.22)
Notes: Leopold Nowak, Eugen
Jochum, Constantin Floros
With Bruckner: Symphonies Nos. 1-9
Other issues: DG 39137-8/139137-8,
2740 136, 2707 026, 2721 010, 2720
047, 419391-4 GW (cassette)

4107.JE1   Jochum, Eugen
Staatskapelle Dresden
Recorded 11-14 December 1976, ed.
n/a 1883
Issue: Angel SZB-3892, 2 stereo LPs,
4 ss [CFB], p.. 1980
Timing: 1.09.15 (20.59, 25.52, 9.56, 12.27)
Notes: Peter Branscombe
Other issues: EMI 127-749417-1, EAC
80582/3, EAC set 870 45155

4107.JE2   Jochum, Eugen
Vienna Philharmonic Orchestra
Recorded W. ca. 1940, ed. n/a
Issue: Telefunken SK 3000-7, 8 mono
78s, 16 ss
Other issues: Capitol P 8067-8

4107.JE3   Jochum, Eugen
Berlin Philharmonic Orchestra
Recorded 28-31 March and 2 April
1952, ed. n/a
Issue: Decca DXE 146, LP, 3 ss, W. 1958
Other issues: DG 18033-4, 18112-3

4107.KA0 Kabasta, Oswald
Munich Philharmonic Orchestra
Recorded W.ca. 1943, ed. n/a
Issue: Electrola DB 7684-91, 8 mono
78s, 16 ss

4107.KH0 Karajan, Herbert von
Berlin Philharmonic Orchestra
Recorded 19 October 1970, 3-4 Febru-
ary 1971, ed. Haas 1883
Issue: Angel SC-3779, 3 stereo LPs, 3 ss
[CFB], W. 1972
Timing: 1.17.34 (21.36, 22.47, 10.25,
12.46)
Notes: William Mann, Karl Schumann
With Bruckner: Symphony No. 4

Other issues: Angel SLS 811, EMI C 195 02189-91, EAC 55041/2, AA 965/7

4107.KH1 Karajan, Herbert von
Berlin Philharmonic Orchestra
Recorded 14-15 May 1975, ed. Nowak 1883
Issue: DG 2107 102, 2 stereo LPs, 3 ss [CFB], W. 1977
Timing: 1.04.22 (20.08, 22.04, 9.52, 12.28)
Notes: Hanspeter Krellmann, Richard Osborne
With Wagner: Siegfried Idyll
Other issues: DG 419 195-2 (CD), 2707 102, 2740 264, OOMG 0401/11, MG 8261/2, F35G-50386 (CD)

4107.KO0 Klemperer, Otto
Philharmonia Orchestra
Recorded 1-5 November 1960, ed. n/a 1883
Issue: Angel AE-34420, 1 stereo LP, 2 ss [CFB], p. 1985
Timing: 1.05.47 (19.51, 21.51, 14.31, 9.34)
Notes: William Mann
Other issues: Angel S 3626 B, CX 1808-9/SAX 2455-6, C/STC 91210-1, FCX/SAXF CCA 945-6, 4AE-34420 (cassette), CDM-69127 (CD), EMI 037-290 004-1 (LP and cassette), 555-769 126-2 (CD), EAC 50044/5, CE 28-5155 (CD)

4107.KO1 Klemperer, Otto
Berlin Philharmonic Orchestra
Recorded in Lucerne: 3 September 1958, ed. Schalk/Löwe 1885
Issue: Frequenz CMD 1, 1 stereo CD, 1 s [CFB], p. 1985
Timing: 1.00.00 (18.57, 19.04, 9.29, 12.30)
Notes: Anonymous
Other issues: Movimento Musica 01.057

4107.KP0 Knappertsbusch, Hans
Vienna Philharmonic Orchestra
Recorded in Salzburg: 30 August 1949, ed. n/a 1896
Issue: Music and Arts CD-209, 1 mono CD, 1 s [CFB], p. 1983
Timing: 1.02.19 (20.02, 20.31, 9.23, 12.23)
Notes: Peter Burkhardt, John Rockwell
Other issues: Discocorp RR-209, Bruno Walter Society OS 7154, 30C37-7921 (CD)

4107.KP1 Knappertsbusch, Hans
Cologne Radio Symphony Orchestra
Recorded 5 May 1963, ed. 1887
Issue: Cavier K19C-18/19, 1 LP (?), 2 ss [MG], ca. 1980
Timing: 1.07.33 (20.29, 20.16, 12.03, 14.45)
Other issues: Seven Seas K17C9479/80

4107.KW0 Konwitschny, Franz
Gewandhaus Orchestra, Leipzig
Recorded 20-22 June 1958, ed. n/a 1883
Issue: Eterna 820 060-1, LP
Other issues: Eurodisc K15C-9113/4, Nippon Columbia OC 7112

4107.LJ0 López-Cobos, Jesús
Cincinnati Symphony Orchestra
Recorded in Music Hall, Cincinnati: 22-23 January 1989, ed. Nowak 1883
Issue: Telarc CD-80188, 1 digital stereo CD, 1 s [CFB], p. 1989
Timing: 1.06.19 (21.10, 22.47, 10.10, 12.12)
Notes: William C. Baxter

4107.MA0 Maazel, Lorin
Berlin Philharmonic Orchestra
Recorded in Philharmonie, Berlin: February 1988, ed. Nowak 1883
Issue: EMI CDC 7 49584 2, 1 digital stereo CD, 1 s [CFB], p. 1989
Timing: 1.13.47 (23.15, 26.44, 10.23, 13.08)
Notes: Hans-Hubert Schönzeler, Ulrich Tank

4107.MK0 Masur, Kurt
Leipzig Gewandhaus Orchestra
Recorded 10-12 June 1974, ed. n/a 1883
Issue: Eterna 8 26 759-760, 2 stereo LPs, 4 ss [CFB], ca. 1976
Timing: 1.05.00 (19.55, 21.55, 10.00, 13.10)
Notes: Walther Siegmund-Schultze
Other issues: Ariola XG 27913 K, Denon OB 7787/8, 28C 37-13 (CD)

4107.ML0 Matacic, Lovro von
Czech Philharmonic Orchestra
Recorded p. 1968, ed. n/a 1883
Issue: Supraphon SUA ST 50809/10, 2 stereo LPs, 3 ss [CFB], p. 1968
Timing: 1.08.35 (21.27, 23.49, 10.37, 12.42)
Notes: Kamil Slapak
With Wagner: *Götterdämmerung* Suite
Other issues: Supraphon SUA 10809/10, Eurodisc XK 85397, Aris 880 194-911 (CD), Supraphon OQ 7124/5, OZ 7104/5, OQ 7021/2

4107.ML1 Matacic, Lovro von
Slovene Philharmonic Orchestra
Recorded in Great Concert Hall, Cankarjev, Yugoslavia: June 1984, ed. n/a 1887

Issue: Denon 32CO-2035, 1 stereo CD, 1 s [CFB], 19-22 June 1984
Timing: 1.05.46 (20.04, 22.00, 10.42, 13.00)
Notes: Ivo Petric
This was Matacic's last recording.

4107.OE0 Ormandy, Eugene
Philadelphia Orchestra
Recorded in Academy of Music, Philadelphia: 3 October 1968, ed. n/a 1883
Issue: RCA LSC-3059, 1 stereo LP, 2 ss [CFB], p. 1969
Timing: 55.35 (17.59, 18.46, 9.12, 10.11)
Notes: Winthrop Sargeant
Other issues: Victor SB 6803

4107.OE1 Ormandy, Eugene
Minneapolis Symphony Orchestra
Recorded in Northrup Auditorium: W. 1935, ed. Löwe/Schalk 1883
Issue: Victor M 276, 7 mono 78s, 14 ss [CST],
Timing: 51.51 (17.36, 25.00, 9.06, 10.09)
Notes: Anonymous
Other issues: Grammophone DB 2626-33, 8770/7

4107.OW0 Otterloo, Willem van
Vienna Symphony Orchestra
Recorded W. 1954, ed. Haas 1883
Issue: Epic SC 6006, 2 mono LPs, 3 ss, W. 1955
With Bruckner: Overture in g minor
Other issues: Philips A 00249-50

4107.PL0 Pesek, Libor
Czech Philharmonic Orchestra
Recorded in Dvorak Hall, Prague: January-November 1986, ed. n/a 1883

Issue: Supraphon CO-72647, 1 digital stereo CD, 1 s [CFB], p. 1988
Timing: 1.00.12 (19.27, 18.37, 9.33, 12.35)
Notes: Jiri Vyslouzil
With Bruckner: Overture in g minor

4107.RE0   Rögner, Heinz
Berlin Radio Symphony Orchestra
Recorded May-August 1983, ed. n/a
Issue: Deutsche Schallplatten 32TC-96, 1 CD, 1 s [MG], ca. 1984
Timing: 59.52 (18.49, 18.47, 9.14, 13.02)
Other issues: Deutsche Schallplatten ET-4035/6

4107.RH0   Rosbaud, Hans
Southwest German Radio Orchestra, Baden-Baden
Recorded ca. 1958, ed. Haas 1883
Issue: Turnabout TV 34083S, 1 stereo LP, 2 ss [CFB], W. 1966
Timing: 1.03.03 (19.00, 21.35, 10.45, 11.43)
Notes: Hans F. Redlich
Other issues: Turnabout CT-4083 (cassette), Vox PL 10750, STPL 10752, VBX 117/SVBX 5117, Eurodisc 70508-9 XK

4107.RM0   Rudolf, Max
Cincinnati Symphony Orchestra
Recorded 6 December 1966, ed. n/a 1883
Issue: Westminster MCA-1412, 1 stereo LP, 2 ss [CFB], p. 1980
Timing: 55.12 (17.02, 18.11, 8.29, 11.30)
Notes: Joseph Sagmaster
Other issues: Decca DL 710139

4107.SA0   Sanderling, Kurt
Danish Radio Symphony Orchestra
Recorded in Denmark Radio Concert Hall, Copenhagen: January 1977, ed. Haas 1883
Issue: Unicorn UKC 356, 1 stereo cassette tape, 2 ss [CFB], p. 1979
Timing: 1.03.45 (20.25, 21.36, 9.38, 12.16)
Notes: Anthony Hodgson

4107.SC0   Schuricht, Carl
Berlin Philharmonic Orchestra
Recorded W.ca. 1939, ed. n/a
Issue: Polydor 67195-202, 8 mono 78s, 15 ss
With Reger: Toccata in d minor

4107.SC1   Schuricht, Carl
The Hague Philharmonic Orchestra [The Hague Residentie Orchestra]
Recorded September 1964, ed.n/a 1883
Issue: Preludio PHC 1126, 1 stereo CD, 1 s [CFB], p. 1987
Timing: 1.00.31 (20.16, 10.56, 16.31, 12.48)
Notes: Anonymous
Other issues: Nonesuch H 71139, Guilde Int. du Disque SMS 2394, Concert Hall SMSC 2394, Columbia OC 7259, Denon 3OCO-1339

4107.SG0   Solti, Georg
Vienna Philharmonic Orchestra
Recorded in Sofiensaal, Vienna: 19-27 October 1965, ed. n/a 1883
Issue: London CMA 7216, 2 mono LPs, 3 ss [CFB], W. 1966
Timing: 1.04.50 (20.05, 22.55, 9.40, 12.10)
Notes: Robin Golding
With Wagner: Siegfried Idyll
Other issues: London CSA 2216, MET/SET 323-4, 417631-2 (CD), King SOL 1014/26, LOOC 1366/38, London SLC 1758/9, K15C 9028/9, F28L 28047 (CD)

Timing: 1.08.31 (21.27, 25.11, 10.09, 11.44)

Notes: William Mann

Other issues: London 417 631-1, 417 631-4 (cassette), F35C20153 (CD)

4107.SG2   Solti, Georg

Chicago Symphony Orchestra

Recorded in Royal Albert Hall, London: © 1978, ed. n/a

Issue: London 071 205-1 LH, 1 stereo CD Video, 2 ss [CFB], p. 1988

Timing: 1.33.18 (22.03, 24.14, 10.31, 16.30)

Notes: Duncan Chisholm

With introductory comments by Sir Georg Solti (6.00).

4107.SW0   Steinberg, William

Pittsburgh Symphony Orchestra

Recorded in Soldiers and Sailors Memorial Hall, Pittsburgh: April 1968, ed. n/a 1883

Issue: Command 12002 S, 2 stereo LPs, 3+ ss [CFB], W. 1970

Timing: 1.00.15 (17.57, 21.22, 8.36, 12.20)

Notes: F.B. Weille

With Bruckner: Overture in g minor

4107.SZ0   Szell, George

Vienna Philharmonic Orchestra

Recorded ca. 1960, ed. n/a 1883

Issue: Rococo 2081, LP, 3 ss

4107.WB0   Walter, Bruno

Columbia Symphony Orchestra

Recorded in American Legion Hall, Hollywood: 11-27 March 1961, ed. Haas 1883

Issue: Columbia Y2 35238, 2 stereo LPs, 3 ss [CFB], p.. 1979

Timing: 54.55 (20.50, 19.20, 10.25, 13.50)

Notes: Anonymous

With Bruckner: Te Deum

Other issues: Columbia M2L 290/M2S 690, D4L 342/D4S 742, BRG/SBRG 72139-40, 61128-9, 77401, CBS M2K-42036 (CD), 23 AC 615, 40AC 1827/8, 30AC 1279/80, CBS Sony 56DC 129/30 (CD), 28DC-5050

4107.WG0   Wand, Günter

Cologne Radio Symphony Orchestra

Recorded in WDR, Cologne: 19 January 1980, ed. n/a 1883

Issue: EMI CDC 7 47748 2, 1 stereo CD, 1 s [CFB], p. 1980

Timing: 1.04.22 (19.57, 22.38, 9.45, 12.02)

Notes: Ekkehart Kroher

Other issues: EMI 127-154 463-3, 153-99 877/78, 567-747 748-2 (CD), Harmonia mundi ULS 3274/5

Symphony No. 8 in c minor (WAB 108, G/A 118)

I. Allegro moderato, II. Scherzo: Allegro moderato, Trio: Allegro moderato, III. Adagio: Feierlich langsam, doch nicht schleppend, IV. Finale: Feierlich, nicht schnell [1887 version]. The first version was composed in Vienna in 1887 and was revised with the aid of Josef Schalk in 1890. This revision was published in 1892 with further editing by Schalk. Both the 1887 and the 1890 versions are available in editions by Leopold Nowak, while Robert Haas edited a score which drew upon both versions, in an effort to discern and to synthesize Bruckner's original intentions.

4108.AT0   Asahina, Takashi
Osaka Philharmonic Orchestra
Recorded ca. 1988, ed. Haas 1890
Issue: Bellaphon JVC 5013/14, 2 stereo
    CDs, 2 ss, 14 September 1983
Timing: 1.25.15 (15.59, 16.32, 27.52,
    24.52)
Other issues: Victor VDC 5013/2 (CD),
    VIC 2401/2

4108.AT1   Asahina, Takashi
Osaka Philharmonic Orchestra
Recorded 24 October 1980, ed. Haas
Issue: Victor KVX 5529/30, 1 stereo
    LP(?), 2 ss [MG], ca. 1981
Timing: 1.28.04 (16.46, 17.08, 29.13,
    24.57)

4108.BD0   Barenboim, Daniel
Chicago Symphony Orchestra
Recorded 6, 9 December 1980, ed. Haas
    1887/90
Issue: DG 2741 007, 2 digital stereo LPs,
    3 ss [CFB], p. 1981
Timing: 1.18.53 (15.11, 15.01, 25.51,
    22.50)
Notes: Stefan Kunze, Robert Simpson
With Bruckner: Te Deum
Other issues: DG 2740 253 [CFB], 52MG
    0214/5

4108.BE0   Beinum, Eduard van
Concertgebouw Orchestra, Amsterdam
Recorded 6-9 June 1955, ed. Haas 1887
Issue: Epic SC 6011, 2 mono LPs, 3 ss,
    W. 1956
With Schubert: one work
Other issues: Philips ABL 3086-7,
    13PC-178/9, A 00294-5 L, Eterna
    820 198-9

4108.BK0   Böhm, Karl
Vienna Philharmonic Orchestra
Recorded in Großer Musikvereinssaal,
    Vienna: 2, 5 February 1976, ed. Haas
    1887/90
Issue: DG 2709 068, 3 stereo LPs, 3 ss
    [CFB], W. 1977
Timing: 1.19.38 (14.46, 14.19, 27.42,
    22.51)
Notes: Constantin Floros
With Bruckner: Symphony No. 7
Other issues: DG 2740 179, 2727 011,
    40MG 0585/6, MG 8235/7

4108.CS0   Celibidache, Sergiu
Unidentified orchestra
Recorded ca. 1970, ed. n/a
Issue: Rococo OW 7204/5, 1 stereo
    LP(?), 2 ss [MG], ca. 1970

Timing: 1.25.35 (16.15, 14.05, 28.30, 26.45)

4108.FW0 Furtwängler, Wilhelm
Vienna Philharmonic Orchestra
Recorded in Großer Musikvereinssaal, Vienna: 17 October 1944, ed. Haas 1887/90
Issue: DG 2740 201, 5 mono LPs, 3 ss [CFB], p. 1979
Timing: 1.16.48 (15.13, 14.07, 25.08, 22.20)
Notes: Günter Birkner
With Bruckner: Symphonies Nos. 4, 7 and 9
Other issues: Unicorn UNI 109-10, MG 8868/72, Angel WF 70012/3, WF 60054/5

4108.FW1 Furtwängler, Wilhelm
Berlin Philharmonic Orchestra
Recorded in Berlin-Dahlem: 14 March 1949, ed. Haas 1887/90
Issue: Vox VSPS 14, 5 mono LPs, 3 ss [CFB], p. 1973
Timing: 1.17.40 (15.18, 14.17, 25.30, 22.45)
Notes: Joseph Braunstein
With Bruckner: Symphonies Nos. 4, 7 and 9
Other issues: Odeon STE 91377-8, SMVP 8057-8, C 177 29231-2, FALP 850-1, ASDW 9148-51, C 053 28231-2, AA 8322-3, Angel WF 70038/9, WF 60054/5
Possibly identical to 4108.FW2

4108.FW2 Furtwängler, Wilhelm
Berlin Philharmonic Orchestra
Recorded live in Titania Palast: 15 March 1949, ed. Haas 1887/90

Issue: Rococo 2032, 2 mono LPs, 4 ss [CFB],
Timing: 1.15.30 (15.20, 13.34, 24.41, 21.45)
Other issues: Discocorp RR 457, Rococo OP 75147, OS 7091/2, OC 7139/40

4108.FW3 Furtwängler, Wilhelm
Vienna Philharmonic Orchestra
Recorded live in Großer Musikvereinssaal, Vienna: 10 April 1954, ed. Nowak 1890
Issue: Hunt CDWFE 355, 1 mono CD, 1 s [CFB], p. 1989
Timing: 1.21.20 (16.18, 14.22, 28.52, 21.48)
Notes: Michele Selvini
With Seven Seas K20C 191/2

4108.GC0 Giulini, Carlo Maria
Vienna Philharmonic Orchestra
Recorded in Großer Musikvereinssaal, Vienna: 23-30 May 1984, ed. Nowak 1890
Issue: DG 415 124-1, 2 digital stereo LPs, 4 ss [CFB], p. 1985
Timing: 1.27.20 (17.00, 15.25, 29.15, 24.40)
Notes: Mosco Carner, Manfred Wagner, Pierre Vidal
Other issues: DG 415-124-2 (CD), 415-124-4 (cassette), F66G 50119/20 (CD), 52MG 856/7

4108.HB0 Haitink, Bernard
Concertgebouw Orchestra, Amsterdam
Recorded W. 1969, ed. Haas 1887/90
Issue: Philips 6700 020, 2 stereo LPs, 4 ss [CFB], W. 1971

Timing: 1.10.28 (13.55, 13.33, 25.17, 20.43)
Notes: Deryck Cooke

4108.HB1   Haitink, Bernard
Concertgebouw Orchestra, Amsterdam
Recorded 25-26 May 1981, ed. Haas 1887/90
Issue: Philips 6769 080, 2 digital stereo LPs, 4 ss [CFB], p. 1981
Timing: 1.24.56 (15.59, 16.00, 29.08, 23.49)
Notes: Karl Schumann
Other issues: Philips 412 465-2 (CD), 6725 014, 28PC 28/9, 35CD 94/5

4108.HH0   Hoof, Harry van
[Excerpt from Adagio only]
Unidentified studio orchestra
Recorded p. 1980, ed. van Hoof 1980
Issue: Mercury SRM 1-3817, 1 stereo LP, 1 s [CFB], p. 1980
Timing: 2.57
With eleven popular pieces for pan flute and orchestra.
This selection titled "Adagio 8."

4108.HJ0   Horenstein, Jascha
Vienna Symphony Orchestra
Recorded ca. 1955, ed. Nowak 1890
Issue: Turnabout THS 65090/91, 2 mono LPs, 4 ss [CFB], ca. 1970
Timing: 1.16.03 (13.34, 14.50, 25.15, 22.24)
Notes: Joseph Braunstein
Other issues: Vox PL 9682 "Vienna Pro Musica Orchestra", VUX 2016, VSPS 5, Turnabout TV S 34357-8, CT-2180 (cassette)

4108.IE0   Inbal, Eliahu
Frankfurt Radio Symphony Orchestra
Recorded in Old Opera House, Frankfurt/Main: 24-25 August 1982, ed. Nowak 1887
Issue: Teldec 6.48218.DY, 2 digital stereo LPs, 4 ss [CFB], p. 1983
Timing: 1.15.23 (14.00, 13.26, 26.47, 21.11)
Notes: Anonymous
This is the first recording of this version.
Other issues: Teldec 8.48218 (CD), 4.48218 (cassette), K28Y-9115/8, K20C-396/8, K25C-280/1, K30Y-128/9 (CD), K28Y-10135/6

4108.JA0   Järvi, Neeme
London Philharmonic Orchestra
Recorded in All Saints Church, Tooting, London: 17-19 November 1986, ed. Haas 1890
Issue: Chandos CHAN 8843/4, 2 digital stereo CDs, 2 ss [CFB], p. 1990
Timing: 1.00.27 (16.50, 15.16, 28.12, 23.51)
Notes: Noël Goodwin
With Reger: Variations and Fugue on a Theme of Beethoven

4108.JE0   Jochum, Eugen
Hamburg Philharmonic State Orchestra
Recorded ca. 1948, ed. Haas 1890
Issue: Decca DX-109, 3 mono LPs, 5 ss [CFB], W.ca. 1948
Timing: 1.20.31 (14.43, 13.43, 29.28, 22.37)
Notes: Irving Kolodin
With Bruckner: Te Deum

Other issues: Polydor 68338-48 (78),
DGS 17 (78), DG 18051-2, 18124-5,
Heliodor 478430-1, DG 69548-55 (78)

4108.JE1   Jochum, Eugen
Berlin Philharmonic Orchestra
Recorded W. 1964, ed. Nowak 1890
Issue: DG 2707 017, 2 stereo LPs, 4 ss
[CFB], W. 1965
Timing: 1.13.12 (13.26, 13.47, 26.20,
19.39)
Notes: Constantin Floros
Other issues: DG SKL 929-39 [CFB],
18918-9/138918-9, 2721 010, 2720
047, 2740 136

4108.JE2   Jochum, Eugen
Staatskapelle Dresden
Recorded 3-7 November 1976, ed.
Nowak 1887
Issue: Angel SB-3893, 2 stereo LPs, 4 ss
[CFB], p. 1979
Timing: 1.15.59 (13.51, 13.59, 27.23,
20.46)
Notes: Eugen Jochum, James Durant
Other issues: EMI 127-749417-1, EAC
80517/8, EAC SCL 87045/55

4108.KH0   Karajan, Herbert von
Berlin Philharmonic Orchestra
Recorded 23-25 May 1957, ed. Haas
1887/90
Issue: Classics for Pleasure CFPD 4434,
2 stereo LPs, 4 ss [CFB], ca. 1983
Timing: 1.26.37 (16.57, 15.57, 27.31,
26.12)
Notes: Michael Rose
Other issues: Angel S 3576 B, CX 1586-
7, STC 90972-3, World Record Club
T/ST 772-3, EMI C 063 00763-4, C
187 00763-4

4108.KH1   Karajan, Herbert von
Berlin Philharmonic Orchestra
Recorded 20, 23 January, 22 April 1975,
ed. Haas 1887/90
Issue: DG 2707 085, 2 stereo LPs, 4 ss
[CFB], W. 1976
Timing: 1.22.40 (16.57, 15.11, 26.22,
24.10)
Notes: Hanspeter Krellmann, Richard
Osborne
Other issues: DG 419 196-2 (CD), 2740
264, OOMG 0401/11, MG 8198/9

4108.KH2   Karajan, Herbert von
Vienna Philharmonic Orchestra
Recorded live in London: 1965, ed.
Nowak 1887
Issue: Nuova Era 2251/52, 2 digitally
remastered stereo CDs, 2 ss [CFB],
p. 1989
Timing: 1.24.51 (16.26, 15.07, 26.45,
25.49)
Notes: Alessandro Nava (?)
With R. Strauss: Four Last Songs

4108.KH3   Karajan, Herbert von
Vienna Philharmonic Orchestra
Recorded in Musikverein, Vienna:
November 1988, ed. Haas 1890
Issue: DG 427 611-2GH2, 2 digial ste-
reo CDs, 2 ss [CFB], p. 1989
Timing: 1.22.33 (16.56, 16.25, 25.13,
23.59)
Notes: John Warrack

4108.KH7   Kegel, Herbert
Leipzig Radio Symphony Orchestra
Recorded p. 1990, ed. n/a 1890
Issue: Pilz Magma 442063-2, 1 stereo
CD, 1 s [CFB], p. 1990
Timing: 1.18.52 (15.54, 14.49, 24.03,
23.50)

4108.KM0 Kempe, Rudolf
Zurich Tonhalle Orchestra
Recorded W. 1975, ed. n/a
Issue: Tudor 74 0 03/04 Q, 2 quadra-
phonic LPs, 4 ss, ca. 1975

4108.KO0 Klemperer, Otto
New Philharmonia Orchestra
Recorded October-November 1970, ed.
Nowak 1890
Issue: Angel SB-3799, 2 stereo LPs, 4 ss
[CFB], W. 1973
Timing: 1.23.55 (17.50, 19.48, 26.55,
19.22)
Notes: Hans Keller, Peter Andry
Other issues: Angel SLS 872, EMI C191
02259, EAC 85012/3, EAC 50046/7

4108.KO1 Klemperer, Otto
[Adagio only]
Berlin State Opera Orchestra
Recorded W.ca. 1924, ed. n/a
Issue: Polydor 66325-8, acoustic 78,
7 ss
Other issues: Polydor 69764/7

4108.KP0 Knappertsbusch, Hans
Munich Philharmonic Orchestra
Recorded Bavaria Studios, Munich:
January 1963, ed. Schalk 1892
Issue: Music Guild MS-6208, 2 stereo
LPs, 4 ss [CFB], W. 1969
Timing: 1.24.50 (15.42, 15.52, 27.22,
25.54)
Other issues: Westminster WAL 2235/
WST 235, VIC 5201/2, 64XK 10/11
(CD), G10562/3, World Record Club
CM/SCM 71-2, Véga C 30 A 441-2,
CBS 72486-7

4108.KP1 Knappertsbusch, Hans
Bavarian State Orchestra

Recorded Munich: December 1955, ed.
Schalk 1892
Issue: Music and Arts CD-266, 1 mono
CD, 1 s [CFB], p. 1987
Timing: 1.09.41 (12.44, 13.16, 22.14,
21.27)
Notes: David Breckbill

4108.KP2 Knappertsbusch, Hans
Berlin Philharmonic Orchestra
Recorded live in Berlin: 29 January
1952, ed. n/a
Issue: Hunt HUNTCD 711, 1 mono
CD, 1 s [CFB], p. 1990
Timing: 1.20.43 (15.00, 15.58, 27.01,
22.44)

4108.KP5 Knappertsbusch, Hans
Vienna Philharmonic Orchestra
Recorded 28-29 October 1961, ed. n/a
Issue: BWS OW 7216/7, 1 LP(?), 2 ss
[MG], ca. 1970
Timing: 1.18.20 (13.00, 14.25, 25.45,
25.10)

4108.KR0 Kubelik, Rafael
Bavarian Radio Symphony Orchestra
Recorded live in Herkulessaal der
Münchner Residenz, Munich: 8
November 1963, ed. n/a
Issue: Orfeo C 203 891 A, 1 digitally
reprocessed mono CD, 1 s [CFB],
p. 1989
Timing: 1.13.53 (14.39, 14.24, 22.36,
22.14)
Notes: Karl Schumann

4108.MK0 Masur, Kurt
Leipzig Gewandhaus Orchestra
Recorded in Paul-Gerhardt-Kirche
Leipzig: 19-23 June 1978, ed. Haas
1887/90

Issue: Eurodisc 300 639-440, 3 quadra-
phonic LPs, 4 ss [CFB], ca. 1979
Timing: 1.21.50 (16.55, 14.20, 26.20,
24.15)
Notes: Alfred Beaujean
With Bruckner: Symphony No. 6
Other issues: Denon OQ 7452/3

4108.ML0 Matacic, Lovro von
Japan Broadcasting Corporation Sym-
phony Orchestra
Recorded in NHK Hall, Tokyo: 7 March
1984, ed. Nowak 1890
Issue: Denon 35CO-1001, 1 digital ste-
reo CD, 1 s [CFB], p. 1986
Timing: 1.14.13 (13.55, 14.38, 25.18,
20.12)
Notes: Isao Uno

4108.ML5
[Finale: selected bass Wagner tuba parts
only]
Boston Symphony Orchestra, bass
Wagner tuba in F solo
Recorded in Symphony Hall, Boston:
p. 1956, ed. n/a
Issue: Vox DL 300, 1 mono LP, 1 s
[CSUS], p. 1956
Timing: 0.43
Notes: R.D. Darrell
With excerpts from thirteen other
works by various composers

4108.MZ0 Mehta, Zubin
Los Angeles Philharmonic Orchestra
Recorded in Royce Hall, UCLA, Los
Angeles: April 1974, ed. Nowak
1890
Issue: London CSA 2237, 2 stereo LPs,
4 ss [CFB], W. 1974
Timing: 1.18.51 (14.57, 14.27, 27.54,
21.33)

Notes: Deryck Cooke
Other issues: Decca SXL 6671-2, 6.48063
FA, SLA 1138/9, L36C 5139/Y-0

4108.MZ7 Mravinsky, Eugene
Leningrad Philharmonic Orchestra
Recorded W. ca. 1958, ed. Haas 1887
Issue: Artia MK 210 B, LP, W. 1961
Other issues: Melodiya D 06187-90,
Shinsekai SMK 7590-1

4108.NA0 Nanut, Anton
Ljubljana Symphony Orchestra
Recorded p. 1989, ed. Nowak 1890
Issue: Stradivari SCD-6059, 1 digital
stereo CD, 1 s [CFB], © 1989
Timing: 1.16.02 (15.30, 14.24, 25.27,
20.31)
Notes: Anonymous

4108.PC0 Paita, Carlos
Philharmonic Symphony Orchestra
Recorded in Kingsway Hall, London:
May 1982, ed. Haas 1887/90
Issue: Lodia LO-CD 783/4, 2 digital
stereo CDs, 1+ ss [CFB], ca. 1984
Timing: 1.13.41 (13.08, 13.36, 25.55,
21.02)
Notes: Paul-Gilbert Langevin
With Wagner: Prelude and Liebestod
from *Tristan und Isolde*

4108.RH0 Rögner, Heinz
Berlin Radio Symphony Orchestra
Recorded ca. 1980, ed. n/a
Issue: Deutsche Schallplatten ET-4059/
60, 1 stereo LP, 2 ss [MG], ca. 1980
Timing: 1.14.34 (12.28, 13.12, 26.14,
22.40)
Other issues: Deutsche Schallplatten
32TC-100 (CD)

4108.SC0   Schuricht, Carl
Vienna Philharmonic Orchestra
Recorded ca. 1963, ed. Nowak 1890
Issue: Angel SB 3656, LP, ss, W. 1965
Timing: 1.10.59 (15.34, 13.59, 21.44,
    19.42)
Other issues: Angel ALP 2053-4/ASD
    602-3, SME 91272-3, FALP/ASDF
    825-6, EAC 550434, EAC 80179/80

4108.SG0   Solti, Georg
Vienna Philharmonic Orchestra
Recorded in Sofiensaal, Vienna: Octo-
    ber and December 1966, ed. Nowak
    1890
Issue: London CSA 2219, 2 stereo LPs,
    4 ss [CFB], W. 1968
Timing: 1.14.35 (14.50, 14.30, 24.50,
    20.25)
Notes: Deryck Cooke
Other issues: Decca MET/SET 335-6,
    King SOL 1014/26, London SLC
    1791/2, LOOC 1326/38, K15C-
    9030/1, F50L-28053/4 (CD)

4108.SO0   Suitner, Otmar
Berlin Radio Symphony Orchestra
Recorded 22-29 August 1986, ed. Haas
Issue: Deutsche Schallplatten 27TC-
    159/60, 2 stereo CDs, 1 s [MG], ca.
    1987
Timing: 1.20.51 (15.31, 14.54, 26.27,
    23.59)

4108.SV0   Svetlanov, Yevgeny
U.S.S.R. Academic Symphony Orches-
    tra
Recorded in U.S.S.R.: 1981, ed. Haas
    1896
Issue: Melodiya MCD 238, 1 stereo CD,
    1 s [CFB], p. 1989

Timing: 1.18.40 (18.05, 14.14, 23.49,
    22.26)
Notes: Julian Haylock

4108.SZ0   Szell, George
Cleveland Orchestra
Recorded ca. 1970, ed. Nowak 1890
Issue: Columbia M2 30070, 2 stereo
    LPs, 4 ss [CFB], October 1966
Timing: 1.21.22 (14.22, 16.10, 28.55,
    21.55)
Notes: Jack Diether
Other issues: Columbia 77235, CBS
    26AC 795/6, 52DC 207/8 (CD),
    40AC 2045/6

4108.TK0   Tennstedt, Klaus
London Philharmonic Orchestra
Recorded 24-26 September 1982, ed.
    Nowak 1890
Issue: Angel DSB-3936, 2 digital stereo
    LPs, 4 ss [CFB], p. 1983
Timing: 1.15.25 (14.15, 14.06, 26.02,
    21.02)
Notes: Derek Watson
Other issues: Angel CC38-3106/7 (CD),
    CC30-9086/7 (CD), EAC 90156/7

4108.WA5   Wallberg, Heinz
Vienna National Orchestra
Recorded ca. 1968, ed. n/a
Issue: Concert Hall SMS 2604, LP, 3 ss
Other issues: Guilde Int. du Disque
    SMS 2604

4108.WG0   Wand, Günter
Cologne Radio Symphony Orchestra
Recorded in West German Radio, Co-
    logne: 28 May 1979, ed. Haas 1887/
    90
Issue: EMI CDS 7 47749 8, 2 stereo CDs,
    2 ss [CFB], p. 1979

Timing: 1.21.26 (15.48, 15.04, 26.10, 24.24)

Notes: Wolf-Eberhard von Lewinski

Other issues: EMI 127-154 463-3, 153-99 853/54, 667-747 749-8 (CD), ULS 3276/7

4108.WG1 Wand, Günter

Cologne Gürzenich Orchestra

Recorded W. 1976, ed. n/a

Issue: BASF 22 22158 3, 2 stereo LPs, 4 ss

Other issues: BASF DE 221583

4108.WG2 Wand, Günter

North German Radio Symphony Orchestra

Recorded live in Lübeck Cathedral: 24-26 June 1988, ed. Haas 1890

Issue: EMI CDCB 49718, 2 digital stereo CDs, 2 ss [CFB], p. 1987

Timing: 1.26.11 (16.50, 15.37, 28.29, 25.15)

Notes: Eckhardt van den Hoogen

Other issues: EMI CDS 7 49718 2 (CD), RCA Victor 60364-2-RC [4108.WG3] This issue and 4108.WG3 are identical. The notes to the former give recording dates of 22-23 August 1987.

4108.WG3 Wand, Günter

North German Radio Symphony Orchestra

Recorded live in Lübeck Cathedral, Lübeck: 24-26 June 1988, ed. Haas 1890

Issue: RCA Victor 60364-2-RC, 2 digital stereo CDs, 2 ss [CFB], © 1989

Timing: 1.26.21 (16.50, 15.37, 28.29, 25.15)

Notes: Eckhardt van den Hoogen

Other issues: EMI CDCB 49718 (CD), EMI CDS 7 49718 (CD), RCA Victor 60364-4-RC (cassette)

See comments to 4108.WG2.

Symphony No. 9 in d minor (WAB 109, G/A 124)

I. Feierlich, misterioso, II. Scherzo: Bewegt, lebhaft, Trio: Schnell, III. Adagio: Langsam, feierlich. Composed in Vienna in 1894 and left with the Finale unfinished at Bruckner's death in 1896. There are two recorded completions of the Finale, but most performances conclude with the Adagio. The symphony was never revised by Bruckner, however Ferdinand Löwe edited the first published score in 1903, which contained significant alterations. Later editions by Alfred Orel and Leopold Nowak are accurate and nearly identical.

4109.AH0   Abendroth, Hermann
Leipzig Radio Orchestra
Recorded 29 October 1951, ed. n/a
1894
Issue: Eterna ET 1521, LP [MG]
Timing: 53.29 (23.27, 8.57, 21.35)
Other issues: Deutsche Schallplatten
ET-1026

4109.AL0   Adler, F. Charles
Vienna Philharmonia Orchestra
Recorded ca. 1952, ed. Löwe 1903
Issue: S.P.A. 24-25, 2 mono LPs, 3 ss
[UCB], W. 1952
Timing: 50.18 (13.31, 10.22, 25.55)
Notes: Edward Lawton
With Bruckner: Overture in g minor

4109.AT0   Asahina, Takashi
Nomiuri Nippon Philharmonic Or-
chestra
Recorded 4 June 1980, ed. n/a
Issue: Victor KVX-5531/2, 1 stereo
LP(?), 2 ss [MG], ca. 1980
Timing: 1.06.08 (27.18, 10.40, 28.10)
Other issues: Victor SJX 1151/9

4109.BD0   Barenboim, Daniel
Chicago Symphony Orchestra
Recorded May 1975, ed. Nowak 1894
Issue: DG 2530 639, 1 stereo LP, 2 ss
[CFB], W. 1976

Timing: 1.00.19 (23.57, 10.57, 25.25)
Notes: Hanspeter Krellmann, Richard
Osborne
Other issues: DG 2740 253 [CFB], MG
1008

4109.BE0   Beinum, Eduard van
Concertgebouw Orchestra, Amster-
dam
Recorded 17-19 September 1956, ed.
n/a 1894
Issue: Epic LC 3401, 1 mono LP, 2 ss
[CFB], W. 1957
Timing: 59.01 (22.24, 10.15, 26.22)
Notes: Anonymous
Other issues: Philips 6540 008, A 00390
L, L 09011 L, 836937 DSY, 894050
ZKY, FCM34/PC 5512, Eterna 820
189

4109.BL0   Bernstein, Leonard
New York Philharmonic
Recorded 4 February 1962, ed. n/a
1894
Issue: Columbia M 30828, 1 stereo LP,
2 ss [CFB], W. 1971
Timing: 1.00.45 (24.57, 11.18, 24.30)
Notes: Jack Diether
Other issues: CBS-Sony SOCN10299/
SOCL 163

4109.CS0   Celibidache, Sergiu
Turin RAI Symphonic Orchestra
Recorded in Turin: 2 May 1969, ed.
n/a
Issue: Hunt CDLSMH 34045, 1 digi-
tally reprocessed stereo (?) CD, 1 s
[CFB], p. 1989
With Brahms: Variations on a Theme
of Haydn

4109.CS0   Celibidache, Sergiu
Stuttgart Radio Symphony Orchestra
Recorded ca. 1970, ed. n/a
Issue: Rococo OZ 7556, 1 LP (?), 2 ss
[MG], ca. 1970
Timing: 1.03.33 (24.15, 11.00, 28.18)

4109.DC0   Dohnányi, Christoph von
Cleveland Orchestra
Recorded in Masonic Auditorium,
Cleveland: October 1988, ed. n/a
Issue: London 425 405-2 LH, 1 digital
stereo CD, 1 s [CFB], p. 1989
Timing: 57.57 (22.06, 9.46, 25.59)
Notes: Misha Donat

4109.FW0 Furtwängler, Wilhelm
Berlin Philharmonic Orchestra
Recorded Berlin: 7 October 1944, ed.
Haas 1894
Issue: DG 2740 201, 5 mono LPs, 2 ss
[CFB], p. 1979
Timing: 57.40 (23.20, 9.15, 25.05)
Notes: Günter Birkner
With Bruckner: Symphonies Nos. 4, 7,
and 8
Other issues: DG LPM 18854, KL 27-
31, 2730 005, Heliodor 2548 701,
88019, Eterna 820 380, MG 1450/
SMG 9020, MG 8868/74

4109.GC0   Giulini, Carlo Maria
Chicago Symphony Orchestra
Recorded 1-2 December 1976, ed.
Nowak 1894
Issue: Angel S-37287, 1 quadraphonic
LP, 2 ss [CFB], W. 1977
Timing: 1.03.09 (25.10, 11.09, 26.50)
Notes: Rory Guy
Other issues: Angel ASD 3382, 1C 063
02885Q, CDC-47637 (CD), EAC
80385

4109.GC1   Giulini, Carlo Maria
Vienna Philharmonic Orchestra
Recorded live in Musikverein, Vienna:
June 1988, ed. Nowak 1894
Issue: DG 427 345-2 GH, 1 digital ste-
reo CD, 1 s [CFB], p. 1989
Timing: 1.08.30 (28.02, 10.39, 29.30)
Notes: Peter Branscombe

4109.HB0   Haitink, Bernard
Concertgebouw Orchestra, Amster-
dam
Recorded W. 1964, ed. n/a 1894
Issue: Philips 835 381 LY, 1 stereo LP,
2 ss [CFB], W. 1971
Timing: 59.30 (23.16, 11.16, 24.58)
Notes: Anonymous
Other issues: Philips PHS 900162, SAL
3575

4109.HB1   Haitink, Bernard
Concertgebouw Orchestra, Amster-
dam
Recorded 11-12 November 1981, ed.
n/a 1894
Issue: Philips 6514 191, 1 digital stereo
LP, 2 ss [CFB], p. 1982
Timing: 1.00.02 (24.16, 10.19, 25.27)
Notes: Karl Schumann

Other issues: Philips 410 039-2 (CD),
6725 014, 28PC 61

4109.HG0   Hausegger, Siegmund von
Munich Philharmonic Orchestra
Recorded 1938, ed. Orel 1894
Issue: Past Masters PM-13, 1 mono LP,
2 ss [CFB], ca. 1978
Timing: 54.52 (23.30, 8.49, 22.33)
Notes: Abraham Veinus
Other issues: Victor M 627, DB 4515-
21, Victor 15972-7 (78), 15784-90

4109.HJ0   Horenstein, Jascha
Vienna Symphony Orchestra [prob-
ably = Vienna Pro Musica Orches-
tra]
Recorded ca. 1953, ed. n/a 1894
Issue: Vox VSPS 14, 5 mono LPs, 2 ss
[CFB], p. 1973
Timing: 52.13 (21.30, 9.52, 20.51)
Notes: Kurt Stone
With Bruckner: Symphonies Nos. 4, 7,
and 8
Other issues: Vox VSPS 5, Turnabout
TV S 34356, CT-2228 (cassette), Vox
PL 8040, Orb BL 703

4109.IE0   Inbal, Eliahu
Frankfurt Radio Symphony Orchestra
Recorded p. 1987, ed. n/a 1894
Issue: Teldec 8.43302 ZK, 1 digital ste-
reo CD, 1 s [CFB], p. 1987
Timing: 57.10 (23.05, 10.24, 23.41)
Notes: Hans Christoph Worbs
Other issues: Teldec 6.43302, 4.43302AZ
(cassette)

4109.IE1   Inbal, Eliahu
[Finale only]
Frankfurt Radio Symphony Orchestra
Recorded in Alte Oper, Frankfurt am
Main: 11-13 September 1986, ed.
Nicola Samale and Giuseppe
Mazzuca 1985
Issue: Teldec 6.35785, 2 digital stereo
LPs, 1 s [CFB], p. 1988
Timing: 20.44
Notes: Manfred Wagner
With Bruckner: Symphony No. 5
Other issues: Teldec 4.35785 (cassette),
8.35785 (CD), K25Y 10032/3, K28Y
9115/8, K28C 10028, K33Y 10133
(CD)

4109.JE0   Jochum, Eugen
Bavarian Radio Symphony Orchestra
Recorded ca. 1956, ed. n/a 1894
Issue: Decca DX-139, 2 mono LPs, 3 ss
[CFB], W. 1956
Timing: 58.25 (21.55, 9.33, 26.57)
Notes: Joseph Braunstein
With Beethoven: Choral Fantasy
Other issues: Heliodor H 25007 [CFB],
DG LPM 18247-8, 29333, 89551

4109.JE1   Jochum, Eugen
Berlin Philharmonic Orchestra
Recorded 1-5 December 1964, ed.
Nowak 1894
Issue: DG 2707 024, 2 stereo LPs, 3 ss
[CFB], W. 1966
Timing: 59.49 (23.01, 9.37, 27.11)
Notes: Constantin Floros
With Bruckner: Te Deum
Other issues: DG SKL 929-39 (q.v.),
39117-8/139117-8, 2721 010, 2720
047, MGX 7037, MG 2043

4109.JE2   Jochum, Eugen
Staatskapelle Dresden
Recorded in Lukaskirche, Dresden: 13-16 January 1978, ed. Nowak 1894
Issue: Angel AM-34736, 1 remastered digital stereo LP, 2 ss [CFB], p. 1985
Timing: 1.00.28 (23.06, 9.47, 27.35)
Notes: Peter Branscombe
Other issues: Angel AM-34736 (cassette), EMI 127-749417-1, EMI 055-290 492-1 (LP and cassette), EAC 90086, EAC 87045155

4109.KH0   Karajan, Herbert von
Berlin Philharmonic Orchestra
Recorded 15-19 March 1966, ed. n/a 1894
Issue: DG 139 011, 1 stereo LP, 2 ss [CFB], W. 1968
Timing: 58.45 (23.45, 9.58, 25.12)
Notes: Karl Schumann
Other issues: DG MG 4012/20, MG 0395

4109.KH1   Karajan, Herbert von
Berlin Philharmonic Orchestra
Recorded 13-16 September 1975, ed. n/a 1894
Issue: DG 2530 828, 1 stereo LP, 2 ss [CFB], W. 1977
Timing: 1.01.02 (24.42, 10.34, 25.46)
Notes: Hanspeter Krellmann
Other issues: DG 419 083-2 (CD), 2740 264, 2530 828 (cassette), 2535 342 (LP and cassette), MG 1057, OOMG 0401/11, F35G-50369 (CD)

4109.KJ0   Keilberth, Joseph
Hamburg State Philharmonic Orchestra
Recorded 31 October and 3 November 1956, ed. n/a 1894

Issue: Telefunken TCS 18043, 1 stereo LP, 2 ss [CFB], W. 1961
Timing: 56.28 (23.16, 10.44, 22.28)
Other issues: Telefunken TC 8043, LGX 66072, GMA/SMA 104, LSK 7034, LT/SLT 43043, SMT 1138, GT 1116, GT 9180, K17C 8332, Teldec 8.44068 (CD)[CFB]

4109.KL0   Klemperer, Otto
New Philharmonia Orchestra
Recorded 7-21 February 1970, ed. n/a 1894
Issue: Angel S 36873, LP, 2 ss, W. 1972
Other issues: Decca ASD 2719, SHZE 360, C 069 02158, EAC 70173, EAC 81037

4109.KN0   Knappertsbusch, Hans
Berlin Philharmonic Orchestra
Recorded 29 January 1950, ed. Löwe 1894
Issue: Music and Arts CD-219, 1 mono CD, 1 s [CFB], p. 1986
Timing: 58.51 (23.42, 11.30, 23.39)
Notes: Jack Diether, Peter Burkhardt, John Rockwell
Other issues: RCA RCL 7312, Legends of Music R32C 1095 (CD), Bruno Walter Society OS 7155

4109.KN1   Knappertsbusch, Hans
Berlin Philharmonic Orchestra
Recorded live in Berlin: February 1950, ed. Löwe 1894
Issue: Suite CDS 1-6004, 1 mono CD, 1 s [CFB], p. 1987
Timing: 54.32 (22.04, 10.53, 21.35)

4109.KN2   Knappertsbusch, Hans
Bavarian State Orchestra
Recorded live in Monaco: 1958, ed.
1894
Issue: Hunt HUNTCD 710, 1 digitally
remastered stereo CD, 1 s [CFB],
p. 1990
Timing: 55.02 (25.35, 9.57, 19.30)
With Mahler: *Kindertotenlieder*

4109.KN3   Knappertsbusch, Hans
Bavarian Radio Symphony Orchestra
Recorded ca. 1950, ed. n/a
Issue: Seven Seas K 20C 52, 1 LP, 2 ss
[MG], ca. 1970
Timing: 50.15 (20.37, 10.03, 19.35)
Other issues: Seven Seas K17C 9481

4109.LL0   Lucas, Leighton
[Trio only]
Leighton Lucas Orchestra
Recorded < 1948, ed. arr. Lucas
Issue: EMI E.P. 24, 1 mono 78, 1 s

4109.MK0   Masur, Kurt
Leipzig Gewandhaus Orchestra
Recorded in Lukaskirche, Dresden: 28,
30 April 1975, ed. Haas 1894
Issue: Eurodisc SQ 27914 KK, 1 quad-
raphonic LP, 2 ss [CFB], ca. 1975
Timing: 54.30 (21.50, 10.30, 21.50)
Notes: Knut Franke
Other issues: Ariola K 27914 K, Eterna
826761, Columbia OX 1021, Denon
OX 1021

4109.ML0   Matacic, Lovro von
Czech Philharmonic Orchestra
Recorded December 1980, ed. n/a 1894
Issue: Supraphon 32C37-7420, 1 stereo
CD, 1 s [CFB], ca. 1985

Timing: 59.50 (23.32, 10.08, 26.10)
Notes: Akira Hirano
Other issues: Supraphon OZ 7106, OX
1209, Aris 880 195-911 (CD)

4109.ML1   Matacic, Lovro von
Vienna Symphony Orchestra
Recorded 12-13 March 1983, ed. n/a
1894
Issue: Polygram Vienna 410 963-2,
1 stereo CD, 1 s, ca. 1988
Timing: 58.59 (24.21, 10.10, 24.28)
Other issues: Amadeo 32CD-3124 (CD)

4109.MN0   Mehta, Zubin
Vienna Philharmonic Orchestra
Recorded p. 1965, ed. Haas 1894
Issue: London CS 6462, 1 stereo LP, 2 ss
[CFB], 3-7 May 1965
Timing: 1.03.40 (25.55, 10.40, 27.05)
Notes: Deryck Cooke
Other issues: London CM 9462, Decca
LXT/SXL 6202, London SLA 6284,
King K15C-9025, SOL 1014/26,
F28L-28050 (CD), London LOOC
1326/38

4109.MY0   Mravinsky, Yevgeny
Leningrad Philharmonic Orchestra
Recorded live in Leningrad: 30 Janu-
ary 1980, ed. n/a 1894
Issue: Turnabout TV 34823, 1 mono
LP, 2 ss [CFB], p. 1984
Timing: 1.00.02 (23.30, 10.05, 26.27)
Notes: Kurt Stone
Other issues: Melodya VIC-1031, VIC-
9043/4, VIC-3101, VDC-1119 (CD),
Turnabout CT-4823 (cassette)

4109.RE0   Rögner, Heinz
Berlin Radio Symphony Orchestra
Recorded 9-12 February 1983, ed. n/a
Issue: Deutsche Schallplatten ET 5172,
    1 stereo LP, 2 ss [MG], ca. 1984
Timing: 53.58 (22.21, 10.13, 21.24)
Other issues: Deutsche Schallplatten
    32TC 36 (CD)

4109.RG0   Rozhdestvensky, Gennady
Moscow Radio Large Symphony Or-
    chestra
Recorded in Moscow: May 1970, ed.
    n/a 1894
Issue: Westminster Gold WG-8347,
    2 mono LPs, 3 ss [CFB], p. 1977
Timing: 57.50 (23.10, 11.51, 22.49)
Notes: Karen Monson
With Bach: thirteen chorale preludes
Other issues: Melodiya CM-02875/76,
    CM-02877/78, Chant du Monde
    Melodiya LDX 78534, Eurodisc
    Melodiya MK 80890, Victor VIC
    9542, VIC 5009

4109.SA0   Sawallisch, Wolfgang
Bavarian State Orchestra
Recorded in Aula der Universität
    München: 23-24 December 1984, ed.
    n/a 1894
Issue: Orfeo M 160851 A, 1 digital ste-
    reo cassette tape, 2 ss [CFB], p. 1987
Timing: 55.43 (22.16, 9.49, 23.31)
Notes: Ekkehart Kroher
Other issues: Orfeo S 160851 A, C 160851
    (CD), 32CD 10113 (CD)

4109.SC0   Schuricht, Carl
Vienna Philharmonic Orchestra
Recorded ca. 1961, ed. n/a 1894
Issue: Seraphim S-60057, 1 stereo LP,
    2 ss [CFB], W. 1967
Timing: 56.10 (25.30, 10.25, 20.15)
Notes: Malcolm Rayment
Other issues: Odeon ALP 1929/ASD
    493, World Record Club 678, CfP
    194, E/STE 91221, C 053 00647,
    FALP 744/ASDF 280, C 053 00647,
    EAC 55018, EAC 85024

4109.SC1   Schuricht, Carl
Berlin Municipal Orchestra
Recorded W. ca. 1943, ed. Orel 1894
Issue: Polydor 68109-16, 8 mono 78s,
    15 ss

4109.SG0   Solti, Georg
Chicago Symphony Orchestra
Recorded in Orchestra Hall, Chicago:
    October 1985, ed. n/a 1894
Issue: London 417 295-2, 1 digital ste-
    reo CD, 1 s [CFB], p. 1986
Timing: 1.00.55 (23.37, 10.22, 26.56)
Notes: Andrew Huth
Other issues: London 417 295-1, 417
    295-4 (cassette), L28C-1999, F35L-
    20045 (CD), Decca 6.43 381 AZ (LP
    and cassette), Decca 417 295-2 ZK
    (CD)

4109.TY0   Talmi, Yoav
Oslo Philharmonic Orchestra
Recorded in Oslo Philharmonic Hall:
    August 1985, ed. and with the Fi-
    nale completed by Carragan 1983
Issue: Chandos CHAN 8468/9, 2 digi-
    tal stereo CDs, 1+ ss [CFB], p. 1986
Timing: 1.22.07 (23.35, 10.53, 25.26,
    21.55)

Notes: Noel Goodwin, William Carragan

With Bruckner: original sketches for Symphony No. 9 [Finale]

Other issues: Chandos DBRD-2010, DBTD-2010 (cassette)

4109.WA5 Wallberg, Heinz
Vienna National Orchestra
Recorded W.ca. 1968, ed. n/a 1894
Issue: Concert Hall SMSC 2541, LP
Other issues: Guilde Int. du Disque SMS 2541

4109.WB0 Walter, Bruno
Vienna Philharmonic Orchestra
Recorded at Salzburg Festival: August 1953, ed. n/a 1894
Issue: Movimento Musica 01.053, 1 mono LP, 2 ss [CFB], p. 1983
Timing: 49.41 (20.56, 9.55, 18.50)
Notes: Anonymous

4109.WB1 Walter, Bruno
Columbia Symphony Orchestra
Recorded in American Legion Hall, Hollywood: 16 and 18 November 1959, ed. n/a 1894
Issue: Columbia Y 35220, 1 stereo LP, 2 ss [CFB], p. 1979
Timing: 58.51 (23.55, 11.36, 23.20)
Notes: Anonymous
Other issues: Columbia ML 5571/MS 6171, D4L 342/D4S 742, Philips ABL 3339/SABL 179, A 01468 L/835561 AY, C.B.S. BRG/SBRG 72095, 61194, 72095, 77401, MP-39129, MK-42037 (CD), MPT-39129 (cassette), CBS Sony 35DC-128, 35DC-IN, 28CD-5051, 23AC573, 20AC1829

4109.WB2 Walter, Bruno
New York Phiharmonic
Recorded live in New York: July 2, 1953, ed. n/a 1894
Issue: Nuova Era 2225, 1 mono CD, 1 s [CFB], p. 1988
Timing: 50.37 (20.32, 10.09, 19.46)

4109.WG0 Wand, Günter
Cologne Radio Symphony Orchestra
Recorded in West German Radio, Cologne: 5-10 June 1978, ed. n/a 1894
Issue: Pro Arte PAL-1058, 1 stereo LP, 2 ss [CFB], p. 1982
Timing: 57.57 (23.55, 10.23, 23.39)
Notes: D.R. Martin
Other issues: EMI 065-99 804, 127-154 463-3, 567-747 751-2 (CD), VLS 3278

4109.WG1 Wand, Günter
North German Radio Symphony Orchestra
Recorded live in Lübeck Cathedral, Lübeck: 22-23 August 1987, ed. n/a
Issue: RCA Victor 60365-2-RC, 1 digital stereo CD, 1 s [CFB], © 1989
Timing: 1.03.05 (26.02, 10.24, 26.08)
Notes: Eckhardt van den Hoogen, Günter Wand
Notes give recording dates of 24-26 June 1988.

Symphony No. 9 in d minor [sketches for the Finale] (WAB 143, G/A without number)

These are the unedited fragments which Bruckner left for the Finale at the time of his death in 1896. For two posthumous completions of this movement see 4109.IE1 and 4109.TY0.

4143.TY0   Talmi, Yoav
 Oslo Philharmonic Orchestra
 Recorded in Oslo Philharmonic Hall:
  August 1985, ed. Wm. Carragan
  1896
 Issue: Chandos CHAN 8468/9: 2 digi-
  tal stereo CDs, 1 s [CFB], p. 1986

Timing: 15.51
Notes: Noel Goodwin, William
 Carragan
Other issues: Chandos DBRD-2010,
 DBTD-2010 (cassette)

Bibliography

Bielefelder Katalog: Klassik. Stuttgart: Vereinigte Motor-Verlag, 1988–1990.

Clark, Sedgwick. "With Fire and Brimstone." *American Record Guide* 41, No. 4 (February 1978): 11–14.

Clough, Francis F., and G. J. Cuming. *The World's Encyclopaedia of Recorded Music*. London: Sidgwick & Jackson, 1952.

Cooke, Deryck. "The Bruckner Problem Simplified." New York: The Musical Newsletter, 1975. (First published in *The Musical Newsletter* 110 (1969): 20–22, 142–144, 362–365, 479–482, 828.)

Göllerich, August, and Max Auer. *Anton Bruckner: Ein Lebens- und Schaffensbild*. Reprint. Regensburg: Gustav Bosse Verlag, 1974.

Grasberger, Renate. *Bruckner-Bibliographie (bis 1974)*. Anton Bruckner Dokumente und Studien, 4. Graz: Akademische Druck- und Verlagsanstalt, 1985.

Grasberger, Renate. *Werkverzeichnis Anton Bruckner*. Tutzing: Hans Schneider, 1977.

Haggin, B. H. *Music on Records*. New York: Alfred A. Knopf, 1945.

Holmes, John L. *Conductors on Record*. Westport, Connecticut: Greenwood Press, 1982.

The Long Player 1, no. 3 (August 1952): 32.

Osborne, Richard. "The Gramophone Collection: Bruckner." *Gramophone* 69, No. 819 (August 1991): 33–36.

Opus [formerly *Schwann Catalog*] (1984–1991).

Slonimsky, Nicholas, ed. *Baker's Biographical Dictionary of Musicians*, 7th ed. New York: Schirmer Books, 1984.

Weber, J.F. *Bruckner*. Discography Series, 10. Utica, New York: J. F. Weber, 1975.

Conductor Index

Abbado, Claudio (b. 1933)
Symphony No. 1 in c minor
Vienna Philharmonic Orchestra
(1969): 4101.AC0
Abendroth, Hermann (b. 1883)
Symphony No. 4 in E flat Major
Leipzig Symphony Orchestra
(1949): 4104.AH0
Symphony No. 5 in B flat Major
Leipzig Radio Orchestra (1949):
4105.AH0
Symphony No. 9 in d minor
Leipzig Radio Orchestra (1951):
4109.AH0
Adler, F. Charles (1889-1959)
Mass No. 1 in d minor
Radio Vienna Chorus and Orches-
tra (1957): 1026.AC0
Overture in g minor
Vienna Philharmonia Orchestra
(1952): 4098.AF0
Symphony No. 1 in c minor
Vienna Orchestral Society (1955):
4101.AF0
Symphony No. 3 in d minor
Vienna Philharmonia (1953):
4103.AF0
Symphony No. 9 in d minor
Vienna Philharmonia Orchestra
(1952): 4109.AL0

Albert, Werner Andreas
Symphony No.   in B flat Major
Bavarian State Youth Orchestra,
Augsburg (1986): 4105.AW0
Alldis, John (b. 1929)
Ave Maria
John Alldis Choir (1967): 1006.AJ0
Christus factus est
John Alldis Choir (1967): 1011.AJ0
Locus iste
John Alldis Choir (1967): 1023.AJ0
Virga Jesse
John Alldis Choir (1967): 1052.AJ0
Andreae, Volkmar (b. 1879)
Symphony No. 1 in c minor
Austrian State Symphony Orches-
tra (1951): 4101.AV0
Symphony No. 2 in c minor
Vienna Symphony Orchestra (1953):
4102.AV0
Symphony No. 3 in d minor
Vienna Symphony Orchestra (1955):
4103.AV0
Anonymous
Locus iste
Vienna Hofmusikkapelle (1909):
1023.AA0
Mass No. 1 in d minor
Basilica Chorus (1935): 1026.AA0

Anonymous
  Um Mitternacht
    Essen Schubertbund (1960): 1090
    .AA0
  Symphony No. 5 in B flat Major
    Dol Dauber Orchestra (1948): 4105.
    AA0
Arndt, Günther (b. 1907)
  Ave Maria
    Berlin Handel Chorus (1962): 1006.
    AR0
  Virga Jesse
    Berlin Motet Choir (1948): 1052.AR0
Asahina, Takashi
  Mass No. 3 in f minor
    Osaka Philharmonic Orchestra
    (1983): 1028.AT0
  Symphony No. 1 in c minor
    Japan Philharmonic Orchestra
    (1983): 4101.AX0
  Symphony No. 2 in c minor
    Osaka Philharmonic Orchestra
    (1986): 4102.AX0
  Symphony No. 3 in d minor
    Tokyo Metropolitan Symphony
    Orchestra (1984): 4103.AY0
  Symphony No. 7 in E Major
    Osaka Philharmonic Orchestra
    (1975): 4107.AT1
    Osaka Philharmonic Orchestra
    (1983): 4107.AT0
  Symphony No. 8 in c minor
    Osaka Philharmonic Orchestra
    (1980): 4108.AT1
    Osaka Philharmonic Orchestra
    (1988): 4108.AT0
  Symphony No. 9 in d minor
    Nomiuri Nippon Philharmonic
    Orchestra (1980): 4109.AT0

Bader, Roland
  Ave Maria
    St. Hedwig's Cathedral Choir, Ber-
    lin (1987): 1006.BA5
Barenboim, Daniel (b. 1942)
  Mass No. 2 in e minor
    English Chamber Orchestra (1974):
    1027.BD0
  Mass No. 3 in f minor
    New Philharmonia Orchestra
    (1972): 1028.BD0
  Psalm 150
    Chicago Symphony Orchestra
    (1979): 1038.BD0
  Te Deum
    New Philharmonia Orchestra
    (1969): 1045.BD0
    Chicago Symphony Orchestra
    (1981): 1045.BD1
  Helgoland
    Chicago Symphony Orchestra
    (1979): 1071.BD0
  Symphony No. 0 in d minor
    Chicago Symphony Orchestra
    (1979): 4100.BD0
  Symphony No. 1 in c minor
    Chicago Symphony Orchestra
    (1981): 4101.BD0
  Symphony No. 2 in c minor
    Chicago Symphony Orchestra
    (1981): 4102.BD0
  Symphony No. 3 in d minor
    Chicago Symphony Orchestra
    (1981): 4103.BD0
  Symphony No. 4 in E flat Major
    Chicago Symphony Orchestra
    (1972): 4104.BD0
  Symphony No. 5 in B flat Major
    Chicago Symphony Orchestra
    (1977): 4105.BD0

Barenboim, Daniel (b. 1942)
  Symphony No. 6 in A Major
    Chicago Symphony Orchestra
    (1977): 4106.BD0
  Symphony No. 7 in E Major
    Chicago Symphony Orchestra
    (1979): 4107.BD0
  Symphony No. 8 in c minor
    Chicago Symphony Orchestra
    (1980): 4108.BD0
  Symphony No. 9 in d minor
    Chicago Symphony Orchestra
    (1975): 4109.BD0
Beinum, Eduard van (1901-1959)
  Symphony No. 5 in B flat Major
    Concertgebouw Orchestra, Amster-
    dam (1959): 4105.BE0
  Symphony No. 7 in E Major
    Concertgebouw Orchestra, Amster-
    dam (1947): 4107.BE1
    Concertgebouw Orchestra, Amster-
    dam (1953): 4107.BE0
  Symphony No. 8 in c minor
    Concertgebouw Orchestra, Amster-
    dam (1955): 4108.BE0
  Symphony No. 9 in d minor
    Concertgebouw Orchestra, Amster-
    dam (1956): 4109.BE0
Berberich, Ludwig
  Ave Maria
    Munich Cathedral Choir (1931):
    1006.BL0
  Locus iste
    Munich Cathedral Choir (1931):
    1023.BE0
  Mass No. 2 in e minor [excerpts]
    Munich Cathedral Choir (1931):
    1027.BL0
  Os justi
    Munich Cathedral Choir (1931):
    1030.BL0

Berberich, Ludwig
  Tantum ergo, D Major
    Munich Cathedral Choir (1931):
    1042.BL0
  Tota pulchra es
    Munich Cathedral Choir (1929):
    1046.BL0
Beringer, Karl-Friedrich
  Christus factus est
    Windsbacher Knabenchor (1986):
    1011.BK0
  Locus iste
    Windsbacher Knabenchor (1986):
    1023.BF0
  Os justi
    Windsbacher Knabenchor (1986):
    1030.BL5
Bernardi, Lorenzo
  Te Deum
    Leipzig Bach Festival Orchestra
    (1970): 1045.BL0
Bernstein, Leonard (1918-1990)
  Symphony No. 9 in d minor
    New York Philharmonic (1962):
    4109.BL0
Bertola, Giulio (b. 1921)
  Afferentur regi
    Coro Polifonico Italiano (1965):
    1001.BG0
  Locus iste
    Coro Polifonico Italiano (1965):
    1023.BG0
  Pange lingua et Tantum ergo
    Coro Polifonico Italiano (1965):
    1033.BG0
  Vexilla regis
    Coro Polifonico Italiano (1965):
    1051.BG0
  Virga Jesse
    Coro Polifonico Italiano (1965):
    1052.BG0

Best, Matthew
  Afferentur regi
    Corydon Singers (1982): 1001.BM0
  Ave Maria
    Corydon Singers (1982): 1006.BM0
  Christus factus es
    Corydon Singers (1982): 1011.BM0
  Ecce sacerdos
    Corydon Singers (1982): 1013.BM0
  Inveni David
    Corydon Singers (1982): 1019.BM0
  Libera me, Domine
    English Chamber Orchestra Wind
    Ensemble (1985): 1022.BM0
  Locus iste
    Corydon Singers (1982): 1023.BM0
  Mass No. 2 in e minor
    English Chamber Orchestra Wind
    Ensemble (1985): 1027.BM0
  Os justi
    Corydon Singers (1982): 1030.BM0
  Pange lingua et Tantum ergo
    Corydon Singers (1982): 1033.BM0
  Psalm 112
    English Chamber Orchestra (1987):
    1035.BM0
  Psalm 114
    Corydon Singers (1987): 1036.BM0
  Requiem in d minor
    English Chamber Orchestra (1987):
    1039.BE0
  Tota pulchra es
    Corydon Singers (1982): 1046.BM0
  Vexilla regis
    Corydon Singers (1982): 1051.BM0
  Virga Jesse
    Corydon Singers (1982): 1052.BM0
Beuerle, Hans Michael (b. 1941)
  Requiem in d minor
    Werner Keltsch Instrumental En-
    semble (1973): 1039.BH0

Blomstedt, Herbert (b. 1927)
  Symphony No. 4 in E flat Major
    Staatskapelle Dresden (1981):
    4104.BH0
  Symphony No. 7 in E Major
    Staatskapelle Dresden (1980):
    4107.BH0
Böck, Herbert (b. 1958)
  Ave Maria
    Concentus Vocalis Wien (1988):
    1006.BM0h
  Christus factus est
    Concentus Vocalis Wien (1988):
    1011.BO0
  Os justi
    Concentus Vocalis Wien (1988):
    1030.BN0
  Tota pulchra es
    Concentus Vocalis Wien (1988):
    1046.BO0
  Virga Jesse
    Concentus Vocalis Wien (1988):
    1052.BM0h
Böhm, Karl (1894-1981)
  Symphony No. 3 in d minor
    Vienna Philharmonic Orchestra
    (1970): 4103.BK0
  Symphony No. 4 in E flat Major
    Saxon State Orchestra (1936):
    4104.BK1
    Vienna Philharmonic Orchestra
    (1973): 4104.BK0
  Symphony No. 5 in B flat Major
    Saxon State Orchestra (1936):
    4105.BK0
  Symphony No. 7 in E Major
    Vienna State Opera Orchestra
    (1944): 4107.BK0 '
    Vienna Philharmonic Orchestra
    (1976): 4107.BK1

Böhm, Karl
  Symphony No. 8 in c minor
    Vienna Philharmonic Orchestra
    (1976): 4108.BK0
Boles, Frank Woodhouse (b. 1955)
  Os justi
    Choir of St. Paul's Episcopal Church
    (1984): 1030.BO0
Bongartz, Heinz
  Symphony No. 6 in A Major
    Leipzig Gewandhaus Orchestra
    (1967): 4106.BH0
Bradshaw, Richard (b. 1944)
  Ave Maria
    Saltarello Choir (1974): 1006.BR0
  Christus factus est
    Saltarello Choir (1974): 1011.BR0
  Locus iste
    Saltarello Choir (1974): 1023.BR0
  Os justi
    Saltarello Choir (1974): 1030.BR0
  Virga Jesse
    Saltarello Choir (1974): 1052.BR0
Brandstetter, Manfred
  Virga Jesse
    Bach Choir Hannover (1970):
    1052.BM1
Breitschaft, Mathias
  Asperges me
    Limburger Domsingknaben (1977):
    1004.BM0
  Ave Maria
    Limburger Domsingknaben (1977):
    1006.BM1
  Christus factus est
    Limburger Domsingknaben (1977):
    1011.BT0
  In S. Angelum custodem
    Limburger Domsingknaben (1977):
    1018.BM0

Breitschaft, Mathias
  Locus iste
    Limburger Domsingknaben (1977):
    1023.BT0
  Os justi
    Limburger Domsingknaben (1977):
    1030.BT0
  Pange lingua et Tantum ergo
    Limburger Domsingknaben (1977):
    1033.BM5
  Tantum ergo, D Major
    Limburger Domsingknaben (1977):
    1042.BM0
  Vexilla regis
    Limburger Domsingknaben (1977):
    1051.BM5
Celibidache, Sergiu (b. 1912)
  Symphony No. 4 in E flat Major
    unidentified orchestra (1970):
    4104.CS0
  Symphony No. 8 in c minor
    unidentified orchestra (1970):
    4108.CS0
  Symphony No. 9 in d minor
    Turin RAI Symphonic Orchestra
    (1969): 4109.CS0
    Stuttgart Radio Symphony Orches-
    tra (1970): 4109.CS0
Chailly, Riccardo (b. 1953)
  Overture in g minor
    Berlin Radio Symphony Orchestra
    (1988): 4098.CR0
  Symphony No. 0 in d minor
    Berlin Radio Symphony Orchestra
    (1988): 4100.CR0
  Symphony No. 1 in c minor
    Berlin Radio Symphony Orchestra
    (1987): 4101.CR0
  Symphony No. 3 in d minor
    Berlin Radio Symphony Orchestra
    (1985): 4103.CR0

Flämig, Martin
  Vexilla regis
    Dresdner Kreuzchor (1985): 1051.FA5
  Virga Jesse
    Dresdner Kreuzchor (1985): 1052.FA5
Forster, Karl (1904-1963)
  Ave Maria
    St. Hedwig's Cathedral Choir (1948): 1006.FE5
  Mass No. 2 in e minor
    Berlin Philharmonic Orchestra (1955): 1027.FK0
  Mass No. 3 in f minor
    Berlin Symphony Orchestra (1962): 1028.FK0
  Os justi
    St. Hedwig's Cathedral Choir (1948): 1030.FK0
  Te Deum
    Berlin Philharmonic Orchestra (1955): 1045.FK0
Fried, Oskar (b. 1871)
  Symphony No. 7 in E Major
    Berlin State Opera Orchestra (1924): 4107.FO0
Fries, Felix
  Ave Maria
    Les Rossignols de Bruxelles (1960): 1006.FF0
Froschauer, Hellmut
  Ave Maria
    Singverein der Gesellschaft der Musikfreunde (1958): 1006.FH0
  Locus iste
    Singverein der Gesellschaft der Musikfreunde (1958): 1023.FH0
Fuchs, Johannes (b. 1903)
  Afferentur regi
    Zurich Chamber Choir (1984): 1001. FJ0

Fuchs, Johannes
  Ave Maria
    Zurich Chamber Choir (1984): 1006. FU0
  Christus factus est
    Zurich Chamber Choir (1984): 1011. FJ0
  Ecce sacerdos
    Zurich Chamber Choir (1984): 1013. FJ0
  Inveni David
    Zurich Chamber Choir (1984): 1019. FJ0
  Locus iste
    Zurich Chamber Choir (1984): 1023. FJ0
  Os justi
    Zurich Chamber Choir (1984): 1030. FU0
  Pange lingua et Tantum ergo
    Zurich Chamber Choir (1984): 1033. FJ0
  Tota pulchra es
    Zurich Chamber Choir (1984): 1046. FJ0
  Vexilla regis
    Zurich Chamber Choir (1984): 1051. FJ0
  Virga Jesse
    Zurich Chamber Choir (1984): 1052. FX0
Furtwängler, Wilhelm (1886-1954)
  Symphony No. 4 in E flat Major
    Vienna Philharmonic Orchestra (1951): 4104.FW1
    Vienna Philharmonic Orchestra (1951): 4104.FW0
  Symphony No. 5 in B flat Major
    Berlin Philharmonic Orchestra (1942): 4105.FW0
    Berlin Philharmonic Orchestra (1942): 4105.FW1

Furtwängler, Wilhelm
  Symphony No. 5 in B flat Major
    Vienna Philharmonic Orchestra
    (1951): 4105.FW2
  Symphony No. 7 in E Major
    Berlin Philharmonic Orchestra
    (1942): 4107.FW3
    Berlin Philharmonic Orchestra
    (1949): 4107.FW0
    Berlin Philharmonic Orchestra
    (1951): 4107.FW1
    Berlin Philharmonic Orchestra
    (1951): 4107.FW2
  Symphony No. 8 in c minor
    Vienna Philharmonic Orchestra
    (1944): 4108.FW0
    Berlin Philharmonic Orchestra
    (1949): 4108.FW1
    Vienna Philharmonic Orchestra
    (1954): 4108.FW3
  Symphony No. 9 in d minor
    Berlin Philharmonic Orchestra
    (1944): 4109.FW0
Garbers, Wilfried
  Ave Maria
    Herrenhäuser Chorgemeinschaft
    (1986): 1006.GA5
  Locus iste
    Herrenhäuser Chorgemeinschaft
    (1986): 1023.GA5
Gatz, Felix Maria (1892-1942)
  Te Deum
    Berlin Staatskapelle (1928):
    1045.GF0
Gelmini, Hortense von
  Symphony No. 0 in d minor
    Nuremburg Symphony Orchestra
    (1975): 4100.GH0
Gillesberger, Hans (b. 1909)
  Ave Maria
    Vienna Academy Chamber Choir
    (1960): 1006.GH1

Gillesberger, Hans
  Ave Maria
    Vienna Kammerchor (1964): 1006
    .GH0
    Vienna Choir Boys (1972): 1006.GH2
  Christus factus est
    Vienna Academy Chamber Choir
    (1960): 1011.GH0
    Vienna Choir Boys (1972): 1011.GH1
  Locus iste
    Vienna Kammerchor (1960): 1023.
    GH1
    Vienna Kammerchor (1964): 1023.
    GH0
    Vienna Choir Boys (1972): 1023.GH2
  Mass No. 2 in e minor
    Vienna State Opera Orchestra
    (1964): 1027.GH0
  Os justi
    Vienna Academy Chamber Choir
    (1960): 1030.GE0
    Vienna Academy Chamber Choir
    (1964): 1030.GE2
    Vienna Choir Boys (1972): 1030.GE3
  Virga Jesse
    Vienna Academy Chamber Choir
    (1960): 1052.GH0
    Vienna Choir Boys (1972): 1052.GH1
Giulini, Carlo Maria (b. 1914)
  Symphony No. 2 in c minor
    Vienna Symphony Orchestra (1974):
    4102.GC0
  Symphony No. 7 in E Major
    Vienna Philharmonic Orchestra
    (1986): 4107.GC0
  Symphony No. 8 in c minor
    Vienna Philharmonic Orchestra
    (1984): 4108.GC0
  Symphony No. 9 in d minor
    Chicago Symphony Orchestra
    (1976): 4109.GC0

Giulini, Carlo Maria (b. 1914)
Symphony No. 9 in d minor
Vienna Philharmonic Orchestra
(1988): 4109.GC1
Goehr, Walter (1903-1960)
Symphony No. 3 in d minor
Netherlands Philharmonic (1954):
4103.GW0
Goldman, Richard Franko (1910-1980)
Apollo March
Goldman Band (1958): 4115.GR0
Gönnenwein, Wolfgang
Christus factus est
Stuttgart Madrigal Choir (1962):
1011.GW0
Locus iste
Stuttgart Madrigal Choir (1962):
1023.GW0
Mass No. 2 in e minor
Southwest German Radio Orches-
tra (1971): 1027.GW0
Os justi
Stuttgart Madrigal Choir (1962):
1030.GO0
Tantum ergo, D Major
Stuttgart Madrigal Choir (1962):
1042.GW0
Gronostay, Uwe (b. 1939)
Afferentur regi
Denmark Radio Choir (1985): 1001.
GE0
Ave Maria
Denmark Radio Choir (1985): 1006.
GH3
Christus factus est
Denmark Radio Choir (1985): 1001.
GU0
Ecce sacerdos
Denmark Radio Choir (1985): 1013.
GE0

Gronostay, Uwe (b. 1939)
Locus iste
Denmark Radio Choir (1985): 1023.
GW3
Os justi
Denmark Radio Choir (1985): 1030.
GO0
Pange lingua et Tantum ergo
Denmark Radio Choir (1985): 1033.
GO0
Tota pulchra es
Denmark Radio Choir (1985): 1046.
GU0
Vexilla regis
Denmark Radio Choir (1985): 1051.
GU0
Virga Jesse
Denmark Radio Choir (1985):
1052.GU0
Grossmann, Ferdinand (1887-1970)
Mass No. 3 in f minor
Vienna State Philharmonia (1953):
1028.GF0
Guest, George (b. 1924)
Afferentur regi
Choir of St. John's College, Cam-
bridge (1973): 1001.GG0
Christus factus est
Berkshire Boy Choir (1967): 1011.
GW1
Ecce sacerdos
Choir of St. John's College, Cam-
bridge (1973): 1013.GG0
Inveni David
Choir of St. John's College, Cam-
bridge (1973): 1019.GG0
Os justi
Choir of St. John's College, Cam-
bridge (1973): 1030.GG0
Pange lingua et Tantum ergo
Choir of St. John's College, Cam-
bridge (1973): 1033.GG0

Günther, Hubert
Ave Maria
Rhenish Choral Society (1976): 1006.GH5
Ecce sacerdos
Rhenish Youth Choir (1976): 1013.GH0
Locus iste
Rheinische Singgemeinschaft (1976): 1023.GW5
Missa Solemnis in B flat Major
BRT Symphony Orchestra, Brussels (1986): 1029.GH0
Os justi
Männergesangverein Concordia Hamm (1976): 1030.GH0
Pange lingua et Tantum ergo
Rheinische Singgemeinschaft (1976): 1033.GH0
Requiem in d minor
Rhenish Symphony Orchestra (1976): 1039.GH0
Tantum ergo, D Major
Rheinische Singgemeinschaft (1976): 1042.GW5
Trösterin Musik
Männergesangverein Concordia Hamm (1976): 1088.GH0
Um Mitternacht
(1976): 1090.GI0
Hostias
Männergesangverein Concordia Hamm (1976): 1999.GH0
Habel, Ferdinand
Pange lingua et Tantum ergo
St. Stephen's Cathedral Choir of Vienna (1931): 1033.HF0
Vexilla regis
St. Stephen's Cathedral Choir of Vienna (1931): 1051.HF0

Habel, Ferdinand
Virga Jesse
St. Stephen's Choir of Vienna (1931): 1052.HA0
Hager, Leopold
Overture in g minor
Southwest German Radio Symphony Orchestra (1988): 4098.HL0
Hahn, Hans Helmut
Christus factus est
St. Jakobschor Rothenburg (1986): 1011.HA5
Locus iste
St. Jakobschor Rothenburg (1986): 1023.HA5
Os justi
St. Jakobschor Rothenburg (1986): 1030.HA5
Tantum ergo, D Major
St. Jakobschor Rothenburg (1986): 1042.HH0
Haitink, Bernard (b. 1929)
Te Deum
Concertgebouw Orchestra, Amsterdam (1966): 1045.HB0
Vienna Philharmonic Orchestra (1988): 1045.HB1
Symphony No. 0 in d minor
Concertgebouw Orchestra, Amsterdam (1966): 4100.HB0
Symphony No. 1 in c minor
Concertgebouw Orchestra, Amsterdam (1972): 4101.HB0
Symphony No. 2 in c minor
Concertgebouw Orchestra, Amsterdam (1969): 4102.HB0
Symphony No. 3 in d minor
Concertgebouw Orchestra, Amsterdam (1963): 4103.HB0

Haitink, Bernard
  Symphony No. 4 in E flat Major
    Concertgebouw Orchestra, Amsterdam (1965): 4104.HB0
    Vienna Philharmonic Orchestra (1985): 4104.HB1
  Symphony No. 5 in B flat Major
    Concertgebouw Orchestra, Amsterdam (1971): 4105.HB0
    Vienna Philharmonic Orchestra (1988): 4105.HB1
  Symphony No. 6 in A Major
    Concertgebouw Orchestra, Amsterdam (1970): 4106.HB0
  Symphony No. 7 in E Major
    Concertgebouw Orchestra, Amsterdam (1966): 4107.HB0
    Concertgebouw Orchestra, Amsterdam (1978): 4107.HB1
  Symphony No. 8 in c minor
    Concertgebouw Orchestra, Amsterdam (1969): 4108.HB0
    Concertgebouw Orchestra, Amsterdam (1981): 4108.HB1
  Symphony No. 9 in d minor
    Concertgebouw Orchestra, Amsterdam (1964): 4109.HB0
    Concertgebouw Orchestra, Amsterdam (1981): 4109.HB1
Harrassowitz, Hermann
  Os justi
    Bach-Chor St. Lorenz Nürnberg (1986): 1030.HA5
Hausegger, Siegmund von (1872-1948)
  Symphony No. 9 in d minor
    Munich Philharmonic Orchestra (1938): 4109.HG0
Hausmann, Elmar
  Ave Maria
    Capella Vocale St. Aposteln, Cologne (1986): 1006.HA5

Hausmann, Elmar
  Missa Solemnis in B flat Major
    Capella Vocale St. Aposteln, Cologne (1986): 1029.HE0
  Os justi
    Capella Vocale St. Aposteln, Cologne (1986): 1030.HA5
  Tota pulchra es
    Capella Vocale St. Aposteln, Cologne (1986): 1046.HE0
  Virga Jesse
    Capella Vocale St. Aposteln, Cologne (1986): 1052.HA5
Helbich, Wolfgang
  Te Deum
    Bremen Bach Orchestra (1986): 1045.HW0
Hellmann, Diethard (b. 1928)
  Ave Maria
    Bach Choir of Mainz (1979): 1006.HD0
  Christus factus est
    Bach Choir of Mainz (1979): 1011.HD0
  Locus iste
    Bach Choir of Mainz (1979): 1023.HD0
  Os justi
    Bach Choir of Mainz (1979): 1030.HD0
  Virga Jesse
    Bach Choir of Mainz (1979): 1052.HD0
Herreweghe, Philippe
  Ave Maria
    La Chapelle Royale (1989): 1006.HA5
  Christus factus est
    La Chapelle Royale (1989): 1011.HP0

Herreweghe, Philippe
  Locus iste
    La Chapelle Royale (1989): 1023.
      HP0
  Mass No. 2 in e minor
    Ensemble Musique Oblique (1989):
      1027.HE0
  Os justi
    La Chapelle Royale (1989): 1030.
      HP0
  Vexilla regis
    La Chapelle Royale (1989): 1051.
      HP0
Herzog, Franz
  Ave Maria
    Göttinger Boys' Choir (1960):
      1006.HE0
Hoch, Alphonse
  Ave Maria
    Strasbourg Cathedral Choir (1940):
      1006.HL0
Holliday, Robert
  Os justi
    Hamline Choir (1948): 1030.HR0
Hollreiser, Heinrich (b. 1913)
  Symphony No. 4 in E flat Major
    Bamberg Symphony Orchestra
      (1961): 4104.HH0
Hömberg, Johannes
  Mass No. 2 in e minor [Kyrie only]
    Pro Musica Köln (1978): 1027.HJ0
Hoof, Harry van
  Symphony No. 8 in c minor [excerpt
    from Adagio]
    Unidentified studio orchestra
      (1980): 4108.HH0
Horenstein, Jascha (1898-1973)
  Symphony No. 7 in E Major
    Berlin Philharmonic Orchestra
      (1928): 4107.HJ0

Horenstein, Jascha (1898-1973)
  Symphony No. 8 in c minor
    Vienna Symphony Orchestra (1955):
      4108.HJ0
  Symphony No. 9 in d minor
    Vienna Symphony Orchestra (1953):
      4109.HJ0
Inbal, Eliahu (b. 1936)
  Symphony No. 1 in c minor
    Frankfurt Radio Symphony Orches-
      tra (1987): 4101.IE0
  Symphony No. 2 in c minor
    Frankfurt Radio Symphony Orches-
      tra (1988): 4102.IE0
  Symphony No. 3 in d minor
    Frankfurt Radio Symphony Orches-
      tra (1982): 4103.IE0
  Symphony No. 4 in E flat Major
    Frankfurt Radio Symphony Orches-
      tra (1982): 4104.IE0
  Symphony No. 5 in B flat Major
    Frankfurt Radio Symphony Orches-
      tra (1987): 4105.IE0
  Symphony No. 6 in A Major
    Radio Symphony Orchestra Frank-
      furt (1988): 4106.IE0
  Symphony No. 7 in E Major
    Frankfurt Radio Symphony Orches-
      tra (1985): 4107.IE0
  Symphony No. 8 in c minor
    Frankfurt Radio Symphony Orches-
      tra (1982): 4108.IE0
  Symphony No. 9 in d minor
    Frankfurt Radio Symphony Orches-
      tra (1987): 4109.IE0
  Symphony No. 9 in d minor [Finale
    only]
    Frankfurt Radio Symphony Orches-
      tra (1986): 4109.IE1

Itai, Avner
Locus iste
Israel Kibbutz Choir (1986):
1023.IA0
Janigro, Antonio (b. 1918)
Te Deum
Angelicum Orchestra of Milan
(1975): 1045.JA0
Janowski, Marek
Overture in g minor
Radio France Philharmonic Orches-
tra (1990): 4098.MJ0
Symphony No. 4 in E flat Major
Radio France Philharmonic Orches-
tra (1990): 4104.MJ0
Järvi, Neeme
Symphony No. 8 in c minor
London Philharmonic Orchestra
(1986): 4108.JA0
Jochum, Eugen (b. 1902)
Afferentur regi
Chorus of the Bavarian Radio (1966):
1001.JE0
Ave Maria
Chorus of the Bavarian Radio (1966):
1006.JE0
Christus factus est
Chorus of the Bavarian Radio (1966):
1011.JE0
Ecce sacerdos
Chorus of the Bavarian Radio (1966):
1013.JE0
Locus iste
Chorus of the Bavarian Radio (1966):
1023.JE0
Mass No. 1 in d minor
Bavarian Radio Symphony Orches-
tra (1973): 1026.JE0
Mass No. 2 in e minor
Bavarian Radio Symphony Orches-
tra (1971): 1027.JE0

Jochum, Eugen
Mass No. 3 in f minor
Bavarian Radio Symphony Orches-
tra (1962): 1028.JE0
Os justi
Chorus of the Bavarian Radio (1966):
1030.JE0
Pange lingua et Tantum ergo
Chorus of the Bavarian Radio (1966):
1033.JE0
Psalm 150
Berlin Philharmonic Orchestra
(1965): 1038.JE0
Te Deum
Munich Radio Symphony Orches-
tra (1948): 1045.JE0
Bavarian Radio Symphony Orches-
tra (1954): 1045.JE2
Berlin Philharmonic Orchestra
(1965): 1045.JE1
Tota pulchra es
Chorus of the Bavarian Radio (1966):
1046.JE0
Vexilla regis
Chorus of the Bavarian Radio (1966):
1051.JE0
Virga Jesse
Chorus of the Bavarian Radio (1966):
1052.JE0
Symphony No. 1 in c minor
Berlin Philharmonic Orchestra
(1965): 4101.JE0
Staatskapelle Dresden (1978):
4101.JE1
Symphony No. 2 in c minor
Bavarian Radio Symphony Orches-
tra (1966): 4102.JE0
Staatskapelle Dresden (1975):
4102.JE1
Symphony No. 3 in d minor
Bavarian Radio Symphony Orches-
tra (1967): 4103.JE0

Jochum, Eugen
  Symphony No. 3 in d minor
    Staatskapelle Dresden (1977):
    4103.JE1
  Symphony No. 4 in E flat Major
    Hamburg Philharmonic Orchestra
    (1940): 4104.JE1
    Bavarian Radio Symphony Orches-
    tra (1958): 4104.JE1
    Berlin Philharmonic Orchestra
    (1965): 4104.JE0
    Staatskapelle Dresden (1975):
    4104.JE3
  Symphony No. 5 in B flat Major
    Hamburg Philharmonic Orchestra
    (1937): 4105.JE1
    Bavarian Radio Symphony Orches-
    tra (1958): 4105.JE0
    Concertgebouw   Orchestra,
    Amsterdam (1964): 4105.JE2
    Staatskapelle Dresden (1986):
    4105.JE2
  Symphony No. 6 in A Major
    Bavarian Radio Symphony Orches-
    tra (1966): 4106.JE0
    Staatskapelle Dresden (1978):
    4106.JE1
  Symphony No. 7 in E Major
    Vienna Philharmonic Orchestra
    (1940): 4107.JE2
    Berlin Philharmonic Orchestra
    (1952): 4107.JE3
    Berlin Philharmonic Orchestra
    (1964): 4107.JE0
    Staatskapelle Dresden (1976):
    4107.JE1
  Symphony No. 8 in c minor
    Hamburg Philharmonic State Or-
    chestra (1948): 4108.JE0
    Berlin Philharmonic Orchestra
    (1964): 4108.JE1

Jochum, Eugen
  Symphony No. 8 in c minor
    Staatskapelle Dresden (1976):
    4108.JE2
  Symphony No. 9 in d minor
    Bavarian Radio Symphony Orches-
    tra (1956): 4109.JE0
    Berlin Philharmonic Orchestra
    (1964): 4109.JE1
    Staatskapelle Dresden (1978):
    4109.JE2
Jochum, Georg Ludwig (1909-1970)
  Symphony No. 2 in c minor
    Linz Bruckner Symphony Orches-
    tra (1943): 4102.JG0
  Symphony No. 6 in A Major
    Linz Bruckner Symphony Orches-
    tra (1943): 4106.JG0
Jürgens, Jürgen (b. 1925)
  In jener letzten der Nächte (1984):
    1017.JJ0
  Magnificat in B flat Major
    Israel Chamber Orchestra (1984):
    1024.JJ0
  Missa Solemnis in B flat Major
    Israel Chamber Orchestra (1984):
    1029.JJ0
  O du liebes Jesu Kind (1984): 1145.JJ0
Kabasta, Oswald (1896-1946)
  Symphony No. 7 in E Major
    Munich Philharmonic Orchestra
    (1943): 4107.KA0
Kalt, Pius
  Ave Maria
    St. Hedwig's Cathedral Choir
    (1925): 1006.KA0
  Mass No. 1 in d minor
    St. Hedwig's Cathedral Choir
    (1925): 1026.KP0

Karajan, Herbert von (b. 1908)
  Te Deum
    Vienna Symphony Orchestra (1952):
    1045.KH2
    Berlin Philharmonic Orchestra
    (1976): 1045.KH0
    Vienna Philharmonic Orchestra
    (1984): 1045.KH1
  Symphony No. 1 in c minor
    Berlin Philharmonic Orchestra
    (1981): 4101.KH0
  Symphony No. 2 in c minor
    Berlin Philharmonic Orchestra
    (1981): 4102.KH0
  Symphony No. 3 in d minor
    Berlin Philharmonic Orchestra
    (1980): 4103.KH0
  Symphony No. 4 in E flat Major
    Berlin Philharmonic Orchestra
    (1970): 4104.KA0
    Berlin Philharmonic Orchestra
    (1976): 4104.KA1
  Symphony No. 5 in B flat Major
    Berlin Philharmonic Orchestra
    (1976): 4105.KH0
  Symphony No. 6 in A Major
    Berlin Philharmonic Orchestra
    (1979): 4106.KH0
  Symphony No. 7 in E Major
    Berlin Philharmonic Orchestra
    (1971): 4107.KH0
    Berlin Philharmonic Orchestra
    (1975): 4107.KH1
  Symphony No. 8 in c minor
    Berlin Philharmonic Orchestra
    (1957): 4108.KH0
    Vienna Philharmonic Orchestra
    (1965): 4108.KH2
    Berlin Philharmonic Orchestra
    (1975): 4108.KH1
    Vienna Philharmonic Orchestra
    (1988): 4108.KH3

Karajan, Herbert von (b. 1908)
  Symphony No. 9 in d minor
    Berlin Philharmonic Orchestra
    (1966): 4109.KH0
    Berlin Philharmonic Orchestra
    (1975): 4109.KH1
Kegel, Herbert (b. 1920)
  Symphony No. 8 in c minor
    Leipzig Radio Symphony Orches-
    tra (1990): 4108.KH7
Keilberth, Joseph (1908-1968)
  Symphony No. 6 in A Major
    Berlin Philharmonic Orchestra
    (1963): 4106.KJ0
  Symphony No. 9 in d minor
    Hamburg State Philharmonic Or-
    chestra (1956): 4109.KJ0
Kempe, Rudolf (1910-1976)
  Symphony No. 4 in E flat Major
    Munich Philharmonic Orchestra
    (1976): 4104.KE0
  Symphony No. 5 in B flat Major
    Munich Philharmonic Orchestra
    (1975): 4105.KM0
  Symphony No. 8 in c minor
    Zurich Tonhalle Orchestra (1975):
    4108.KM0
Kempen, Paul van
  Symphony No. 4 in E flat Major
    Hilversum Radio Orchestra (1955):
    4104.KE5
Kertesz, Istvan (1929-1973)
  Symphony No. 4 in E flat Major
    London Symphony Orchestra
    (1965): 4104.KI0
Klemperer, Otto (1885-1973)
  Symphony No. 4 in E flat Major
    Vienna Symphony Orchestra (1951):
    4104.KO1
    Philharmonia Orchestra (1963):
    4104.KO0

Klemperer, Otto
  Symphony No. 5 in B flat Major
    New Philharmonia Orchestra
    (1967): 4105.KO0
    Vienna Philharmonic Orchestra
    (1968): 4105.KO1
  Symphony No. 6 in A Major
    Concertgebouw Orchestra, Amsterdam (1961): 4106.KO0
    New Philharmonia Orchestra
    (1964): 4106.KO1
  Symphony No. 7 in E Major
    Berlin Philharmonic Orchestra
    (1958): 4107.KO1
    Philharmonia Orchestra (1960):
    4107.KO0
  Symphony No. 8 in c minor [Adagio
  only]
    Berlin State Opera Orchestra (1924):
    4108.KO1
    New Philharmonia Orchestra
    (1970): 4108.KO0
  Symphony No. 9 in d minor
    New Philharmonia Orchestra
    (1970): 4109.KL0
Knappertsbusch, Hans (1888-1965)
  Symphony No. 3 in d minor
    Bavarian State Orchestra (1954):
    4103.KN0
    Vienna Philharmonic Orchestra
    (1954): 4103.KN1
    North German Radio Orchestra
    (1962): 4103.KN2
  Symphony No. 4 in E flat Major
    Berlin Philharmonic Orchestra
    (1943/44): 4104.KP0
    Vienna Philharmonic Orchestra
    (1955): 4104.KP1
    Vienna Philharmonic Orchestra
    (1960): 4104.KP2

Knappertsbusch, Hans (1888-1965)
  Symphony No. 5 in B flat Major
    Vienna Philharmonic Orchestra
    (1956): 4105.KP0
    Munich Philharmonic Orchestra
    (1961): 4105.KP1
  Symphony No. 7 in E Major
    Vienna Philharmonic Orchestra
    (1949): 4107.KP0
    Cologne Radio Symphony Orchestra (1963): 4107.KP1
  Symphony No. 8 in c minor
    Berlin Philharmonic Orchestra
    (1952): 4108.KP2
    Bavarian State Orchestra (1955):
    4108.KP1
    Vienna Philharmonic Orchestra
    (1961): 4108.KP5
    Munich Philharmonic Orchestra
    (1963): 4108.KP0
  Symphony No. 9 in d minor
    Berlin Philharmonic Orchestra
    (1950): 4109.KN0
    Berlin Philharmonic Orchestra
    (1950): 4109.KN1
    Bavarian Radio Symphony Orchestra (1950): 4109.KN3
    Bavarian State Orchestra (1958):
    4109.KN2
Koekelkoeren, Martin
  Inveni David
    Maastreechter Staar (1966): 1019.
    KM0
Konrath, Anton
  Symphony No. 3 in d minor [Scherzo
  only]
    Vienna Symphony Orchestra (1935):
    4103.KO0
Konwitschny, Franz
  Symphony No. 2 in c minor
    Berlin Radio Symphony Orchestra
    (1955): 4102.KO0

Mandeal, Christian
  Symphony No. 3 in d minor
    Cluj-Napoca Symphony Orchestra
    (1980): 4103.ML5
Martini, Joachim
  Afferentur regi
    Junge Kantorei, Darmstadt (1973):
    1001.MJ0
  Ave Maria
    Darmstadt Junge Kantorei (1971):
    1006.MA0
  Christus factus est
    Darmstadt Junge Kantorei (1971):
    1011.MJ0
  Ecce sacerdos·
    Junge Kantorei, Darmstadt (1973):
    1013.MJ0
  Inveni David
    Junge Kantorei, Darmstadt (1973):
    1019.MJ0
  Locus iste
    Junge Kantorei, Darmstadt (1971):
    1023.MJ0
  Mass No. 2 in e minor
    Vienna Symphony (1973):1027.MJ0
  Os justi
    Junge Kantorei, Darmstadt (1971):
    1030.MJ0
  Pange lingua et Tantum ergo
    Junge Kantorei, Darmstadt (1971):
    1033.MJ0
  Tota pulchra es
    Junge Kantorei, Darmstadt (1971):
    1046.MJ0
Märzendorfer, Ernst (b. 1921)
  Symphony No. 0 in d minor
    Austrian Broadcast Symphony Or-
    chestra (1978): 4100.ME0
Masur, Kurt (b. 1927)
  Symphony No. 1 in c minor
    Leipzig Gewandhaus Orchestra
    (1977): 4101.MK0

Masur, Kurt
  Symphony No. 2 in c minor
    Leipzig Gewandhaus Orchestra
    (1978): 4102.MK0
  Symphony No. 3 in d minor
    Leipzig Gewandhaus Orchestra
    (1977): 4103.MS0
  Symphony No. 4 in E flat Major
    Leipzig Gewandhaus Orchestra
    (1975): 4104.MK0
  Symphony No. 5 in B flat Major
    Leipzig Gewandhaus Orchestra
    (1976): 4105.MK0
  Symphony No. 6 in A Major
    Leipzig Gewandhaus Orchestra
    (1978): 4106.MK0
  Symphony No. 7 in E Major
    Leipzig Gewandhaus Orchestra
    (1974): 4107.MK0
  Symphony No. 8 in c minor
    Leipzig Gewandhaus Orchestra
    (1978): 4108.MK0
  Symphony No. 9 in d minor
    Leipzig Gewandhaus Orchestra
    (1975): 4109.MK0
Matacic, Lovro von (1899-1985)
  Overture in g minor
    Philharmonia Orchestra (1954):
    4098.MA0
  Symphony No. 0 in d minor
    Philharmonia Orchestra (1954):
    4100.ML0
  Symphony No. 4 in E flat Major
    Philharmonia Orchestra (1954):
    4104.ML0
  Symphony No. 5 in B flat Major
    Czech Philharmonic Orchestra
    (1973): 4105.ML0
  Symphony No. 7 in E Major
    Czech Philharmonic Orchestra
    (1968): 4107.ML0

Matacic, Lovro von (1899-1985)
  Symphony No. 7 in E Major
    Slovene Philharmonic Orchestra
    (1984): 4107.ML1
  Symphony No. 8 in c minor
    Japan Broadcasting Corporation
    Symphony Orchestra (1984):
    4108.ML0
  Symphony No. 9 in d minor
    Czech Philharmonic Orchestra
    (1980): 4109.ML0
    Vienna Symphony Orchestra (1983):
    4109.ML1
Matkowitz, Wolfgang
  Ave Maria
    Heinrich-Schütz-Kreis Berlin (1986):
    1006.MA2
Mattmann, Erwin
  Locus iste
    Trinity Church Choir, Bern (1986):
    1023.MT0
Mauersberger, Rudolf
  Ave Maria
    Dresden Kreuzchor (1948): 1006.
    MA5
  Os justi
    Dresden Kreuzchor (1948): 1030.
    MR0
  Virga Jesse
    Dresden Kreuzchor (1948): 1052.
    MR0
Mayer, Ludwig Karl
  March in d minor
    Berlin Municipal Orchestra (1948):
    4096.ML0
  Three Orchestral Pieces
    Berlin Municipal Orchestra (1948):
    4097.ML0
  Overture in g minor
    Berlin Municipal Orchestra (1948):
    4098.ML0

Mehta, Zubin (b. 1936)
  Mass No. 2 in e minor
    Vienna Philharmonic Orchestra
    (1976): 1027.MZ0
  Te Deum
    Vienna Philharmonic Orchestra
    (1976): 1045.MZ0
  Symphony No. 4 in E flat Major
    Los Angeles Philharmonic Orches-
    tra (1970): 4104.MN0
  Symphony No. 8 in c minor
    Los Angeles Philharmonic Orches-
    tra (1974): 4108.MZ0
  Symphony No. 9 in d minor
    Vienna Philharmonic Orchestra
    (1965): 4109.MN0
Messner, Josef (b. 1893)
  Te Deum
    Salzburg Festival Orchestra and
    Chorus (1949): 1045.MZ5
  Tota pulchra es
    Salzburg Cathedral Choir (1930):
    1046.MJ0
Meyer, Xaver
  Ave Maria
    Vienna Choir Boys (1958): 1006.ME1
    Vienna Academy Kammerchor
    (1975): 1006.ME0
  Os justi
    Vienna Academy Kammerchor
    (1975): 1030.MX0
Miller, Gary
  Ave Maria
    New York City Gay Men's Chorus
    (1983): 1006.MG0
Mittergradnegger, Günther
  Ave Maria
    Klagenfurt Madrigal Chorus (1975):
    1006.MT0

Möller, Edith
  Ave Maria
    Obernkirchen Children's Choir
    (1965): 1006.MT1
  In jener letzten der Nächte
    Obernkirchen Children's Choir
    (1965): 1017.ME0
Morris, Wyn (b. 1929)
  Helgoland
    Symphonica of London (1977):
    1071.MW0
Mravinsky, Eugene (b. 1903)
  Symphony No. 8 in c minor
    Leningrad Philharmonic Orchestra
    (1958): 4108.MZ7
  Symphony No. 9 in d minor
    Leningrad Philharmonic Orchestra
    (1980): 4109.MY0
Muti, Riccardo (b. 1941)
  Symphony No. 4 in E flat Major
    Berlin Philharmonic Orchestra
    (1985): 4104.MR0
  Symphony No. 6 in A Major
    Berlin Philharmonic Orchestra
    (1988): 4106.MR0
Nanut, Anton
  Symphony No. 8 in c minor
    Ljubljana Symphony Orchestra
    (1989): 4108.NA0
Neumann, Vaclav (b. 1920)
  Symphony No. 1 in c minor
    Leipzig Gewandhaus Orchestra
    (1966): 4101.NV0
Norrington, Roger (b. 1934)
  Mass No. 2 in e minor
    Philip Jones Wind Ensemble (1973):
    1027.NR0
Odermath, Hermann
  Mass No. 2 in e minor
    Gregorius-Chor and Orchestra of
      the Liebfrauenkirche, Zürich
    (1930): 1027.OH0

Ormandy, Eugene (1899-1986)
  Te Deum
    Philadelphia Orchestra (1966):
    1045.OE0
  Symphony No. 4 in E flat Major
    Philadelphia Orchestra (1967):
    4104.OE0
  Symphony No. 5 in B flat Major
    Philadelphia Orchestra (1965):
    4105.OE0
  Symphony No. 7 in E Major
    Minneapolis Symphony Orchestra
    (1935): 4107.OE1
    Philadelphia Orchestra (1968):
    4107.OE0
Otterloo, Willem van (1907-1978)
  Overture in g minor
    Vienna Symphony Orchestra (1955):
    4098.OW0
  Symphony No. 4 in E flat Major
    Hague Residentie Orchestra (1953):
    4104.OW0
  Symphony No. 7 in E Major
    Vienna Symphony Orchestra (1954):
    4107.OW0
Paita, Carlos (b. 1932)
  Symphony No. 8 in c minor
    Philharmonic Symphony Orches-
    tra (1982): 4108.PC0
Peerik, Jan S.
  Mass for Holy Thursday
    Ensemble Vocal Raphael (1987):
    1009.PJ0
  Locus iste
    Ensemble Vocal Raphael (1987):
    1023.PJ0
Peloquin, C. Alexander
  Ave Maria
    Peloquin Chorale (1960): 1006.PC0

Pernoud, Pierre (b. 1930)
  Ave Maria.
    La Psallette de Genève (1970):
    1006.PP0
  Ave regina coelorum
    La Psallette de Genève (1970):
    1008.PP0
  Christus factus est
    La Psallette de Genève (1970):
    1011.PP0
  Os justi
    La Psallette de Genève (1970):
    1030.PP0
  Tota pulchra es
    La Psallette de Genève (1970):
    1046.PP0
Pecek, Libor
  Overture in g minor
    Czech Philharmonic Orchestra
    (1986): 4098.PL0
  Symphony No. 7 in E Major
    Czech Philharmonic Orchestra
    (1986): 4107.PL0
Pflügler, Gerhard
  Symphony No. 5 in B flat Major
    Leipzig Philharmonic Orchestra
    (1955): 4105.PG0
Pitz, Wilhelm (1897-1973)
  Ave Maria
    New Philharmonia Chorus (1966):
    1006.PW0
  Christus factus est
    New Philharmonia Chorus (1966):
    1011.PW0
  Locus iste
    New Philharmonia Chorus (1966):
    1023.PW0
  Os justi
    New Philharmonia Chorus (1966):
    1030.PW0

Pitz, Wilhelm
  Virga Jesse
    New Philharmonia Chorus (1966):
    1052.PW0
Raabe, Gerson
  Locus iste
    Gerson Raabe Brass Ensemble
    (1986): 1023.RG0
Rehmann, Theodor
  Afferentur regi
    Aachen Cathedral Choir (1945):
    1001.RT0
  Ave Maria
    Aachen Cathedral Choir (1955):
    1006.RT0
  Ave regina coelorum
    Aachen Cathedral Choir (1948):
    1008.RT0
  Locus iste
    Aachen Cathedral Choir (1956):
    1023.RT0
  Mass No. 2 in e minor
    Berlin Symphony Orchestra (1938):
    1027.RE0
  Tantum ergo
    Aachen Cathedral Choir (1948):
    1042.RT0
  Herbstlied
    Aachen Cathedral Choir (1955):
    1073.RT0
Reichel, Helmuth
  Afferentur regi
    Zürcher Bach-Kantorei (1981):
    1001.RT5
  Ave Maria
    Zürcher Bach-Kantorei (1981):
    1006.RT5
  Christus factus est
    Zürcher Bach-Kantorei (1981):
    1011.RE5

Reichel, Helmuth
  Ecce sacerdos
    Zürcher Bach-Kantorei (1981):
    1013.RH0
  Locus iste
    Zürcher Bach-Kantorei (1981):
    1023.RT5
  Os justi
    Zürcher Bach-Kantorei (1981):
    1030.RE5
  Pange lingua et Tantum ergo
    Zürcher Bach-Kantorei (1981):
    1033.RH0
  Tota pulchra es
    Zürcher Bach-Kantorei (1981):
    1046.RH0
  Vexilla regis
    Zürcher Bach-Kantorei (1981):
    1051.RH0
  Virga Jesse
    Zürcher Bach-Kantorei (1981):
    1052.RH0
Reichert, Hubert
  Symphony No. 2 in c minor
    Westphalian Symphony Orchestra,
    Recklinghausen (1971): 4102.
    RH0
  Symphony No. 6 in A Major
    Westphalian Symphony Orchestra
    (1963): 4106.RH0
Riedelbauch, Wolfgang
  Mass in C Major
    (1973): 1025.RW0
  Psalm 146
    Nuremberg Symphony Orchestra
    (1973): 1037.RW0
Rilling, Helmut (b. 1933)
  Christus factus est
    Figuralchor Stuttgart (1986):
    1011.RH0

Rilling, Helmut (b. 1933)
  Mass No. 2 in e minor
    Bach-Collegium Stuttgart (1972):
    1027.RH0
  Os justi
    Gächinger Kantorei Stuttgart (1986):
    1030.RH0
Rinscheid, Michael
  Ave Maria
    Singkreis Wehbach (1987): 1006.RT5
  Locus iste
    Singkreis Wehbach (1987): 1023.RT5
Rögner, Heinz
  Mass No. 2 in e minor
    Berlin Radio Symphony Orchestra
    (1988): 1027.RZ0
  Symphony No. 4 in E flat Major
    Berlin Radio Symphony Orchestra
    (1984): 4104.RH0
  Symphony No. 5 in B flat Major
    Berlin Symphony Orchestra (1984):
    4105.RH0
  Symphony No. 6 in A Major
    Berlin Symphony Orchestra (1980):
    4106.RH5
  Symphony No. 7 in E Major
    Berlin Radio Symphony Orchestra
    (1983): 4107.RE0
  Symphony No. 8 in c minor
    Berlin Radio Symphony Orchestra
    (1980): 4108.RH0
  Symphony No. 9 in d minor
    Berlin Radio Symphony Orchestra
    (1983): 4109.RE0
  Te Deum
    Berlin Radio Symphony Orchestra
    (1988): 1045.RH0
Rosbaud, Hans (1895-1962)
  Symphony No. 7 in E Major
    Southwest German Radio Orches-
    tra, Baden-Baden (1958):
    4107.RH0

Rozhdestvensky, Gennadi (b. 1931)
Symphony No. 00 in f minor
USSR Symphony Orchestra (1983):
4099.RG0
Symphony No. 0 in d minor
USSR Symphony Orchestra (1983):
4100.RG0
Symphony No. 3 in d minor
Moscow Radio Large Symphony
Orchestra (1976): 4103.RG0
Symphony No. 4 in E flat Major
USSR Ministry of Culture Sym-
phony (1978): 4104.RG0
Symphony No. 9 in d minor
Moscow Radio Large Symphony
Orchestra (1970): 4109.RG0
Rubahn, Gerd
Symphony No. 3 in d minor
Berlin Symphony Orchestra (1950):
4103.RG1
Rudolf, Max (b. 1902)
Symphony No. 7 in E Major
Cincinnati Symphony Orchestra
(1966): 4107.RM0
Sanderling, Kurt (b. 1912)
Symphony No. 3 in d minor
Leipzig Gewandhaus Orchestra
(1970): 4103.SA0
Symphony No. 7 in E Major
Danish Radio Symphony Orchestra
(1977): 4107.SA0
Sawallisch, Wolfgang (b. 1923)
Symphony No. 1 in c minor
Bavarian State Orchestra (1984):
4101.SW0
Symphony No. 6 in A Major
Bavarian State Orchestra (1981):
4106.SA0
Symphony No. 9 in d minor
Bavarian State Orchestra (1984):
4109.SA0

Schäfer, Wolfgang (b. 1945)
Afferentur regi
Freiburg Vocal Ensemble (1984):
1001.SW0
Ave Maria
Freiburg Vocal Ensemble (1984):
1006.SW0
Christus factus est
Freiburg Vocal Ensemble (1984):
1011.SW0
Ecce sacerdos
Freiburg Vocal Ensemble (1984):
1013.SW0
Locus iste
Freiburg Vocal Ensemble (1984):
1023.SW0
Os justi
Freiburg Vocal Ensemble (1984):
1030.SW0
Pange lingua et Tantum ergo
Freiburg Vocal Ensemble (1984):
1033.SW0
Tota pulchra es
Freiburg Vocal Ensemble (1984):
1046.SW0
Vexilla regis
Freiburg Vocal Ensemble (1984):
1051.SW0
Virga Jesse
Freiburg Vocal Ensemble (1984):
1052.SW0
Schauerte, Gustav
Christus factus est
Paderborn Cathedral Choir (1928):
1011.SW1
Schneider, Walther
Um Mitternacht
Stuttgart Liederkreis (1950):
1090.SW0

Schönzeler, Hans-Hubert (b. 1925)
Requiem in d minor
London Philharmonic Orchestra
(1970): 1039.SH0
March in d minor
London Philharmonic Orchestra
(1970): 4096.SH0
Three Orchestral Pieces
London Philharmonic Orchestra
(1970): 4097.SH0
Schrems, Theobald
Ave Maria
Regensburger Domspatzen (1974):
1006.SW1
Locus iste
Regensburg Cathedral Choir (1948):
1023.SW1
Virga Jesse
Regensburger Domspatzen (1974):
1052.SW1
Herbstlied
Regensburg Cathedral Choir (1948):
1073.ST0
Schuricht, Carl (1880-1967)
Symphony No. 3 in d minor
Vienna Philharmonic Orchestra
(1966): 4103.SC0
Symphony No. 7 in E Major
Berlin Philharmonic Orchestra
(1939): 4107.SC0
The Hague Philharmonic Orches-
tra (1964): 4107.SC1
Symphony No. 8 in c minor
Vienna Philharmonic Orchestra
(1963): 4108.SC0
Symphony No. 9 in d minor
Berlin Municipal Orchestra (1943):
4109.SC1
Vienna Philharmonic Orchestra
(1961): 4109.SC0

Schweizer, Rolf
Ave Maria
Pforzheim Motettenchor (1976):
1006.SW3
Christus factus est
Pforzheim Motettenchor (1976):
1010.SR0
Os justi
Pforzheim Motettenchor (1976):
1030.SZ0
Shapirra, Elyakum (b. 1926)
Overture in g minor
London Symphony Orchestra
(1972): 4098.SE0
Symphony No. 00 in f minor
London Symphony Orchestra
(1972): 4099.SE0
Sinopoli, Giuseppe (b. 1946)
Symphony No. 4 in E flat Major
Staatskapelle Dresden (1987):
4104.SE0
Smith, Jack
Ave Maria
Keighly Vocal Union (1960): 1006.
SW4
Solti, Georg (b. 1912)
Symphony No. 4 in E flat Major
Chicago Symphony Orchestra
(1981): 4104.SG0
Symphony No. 5 in B flat Major
Chicago Symphony Orchestra
(1980): 4105.SG0
Symphony No. 6 in A Major
Chicago Symphony Orchestra
(1979): 4106.SG0
Symphony No. 7 in E Major
Vienna Philharmonic Orchestra
(1965): 4107.SG0
Chicago Symphony Orchestra
(1978): 4107.SG2
Chicago Symphony Orchestra
(1986): 4107.SG1

Talmi, Yoav (b. 1943)
  Symphony No. 9 in d minor
    Oslo Philharmonic Orchestra (1985):
    4109.TY0
  Symphony No. 9 in d minor (sketch of
    Finale only)
    Oslo Philharmonic Orchestra (1985):
    4143.TY0
Tchakarov, Emil (b. 1928)
  Symphony No. 4 in E flat Major
    Leningrad Philharmonic Sym-
    phonic Orchestra (1978):
    4104.TE0
Tennstedt, Klaus (b. 1926)
  Symphony No. 4 in E flat Major
    Berlin Philharmonic Orchestra
    (1981): 4104.TK0
  Symphony No. 8 in c minor
    London Philharmonic Orchestra
    (1982): 4108.TK0
Thomas, Kelvin
  Ave Maria
    Silver Ring Choir of Bath (1969):
    1006.TK0
Thurn, Max
  Mass No. 2 in e minor
    Hamburg State Opera Orchestra
    (1938): 1027.TM0
Tubbs, Jan
  Symphony No. 4 in E flat Major
    Hastings Symphony (1954):
    4104.TU0
Uno, Koho
  Symphony No. 4 in E flat Major
    Shinsei Nihon Orchestra (1986):
    4104.UK0
Valen, Sverre
  Locus iste
    Valen Choir (1988): 1023.VS0

Wallberg, Heinz
  Te Deum
    Vienna National Orchestra (1967):
    1045.WA0
  Symphony No. 4 in E flat Major
    Vienna National Orchestra (1967):
    4104.WA5
  Symphony No. 8 in c minor
    Vienna National Orchestra (1968):
    4108.WA5
  Symphony No. 9 in d minor
    Vienna National Orchestra (1968):
    4109.WA5
Walter, Bruno (1876-1962)
  Te Deum
    New York Philharmonic (1953):
    1045.WB0
    Vienna Philharmonic Orchestra
    (1955): 1045.WB1
  Symphony No. 4 in E flat Major
    Columbia Symphony Orchestra
    (1960): 4104.WB0
  Symphony No. 7 in E Major
    Columbia Symphony Orchestra
    (1961): 4107.WB0
  Symphony No. 9 in d minor
    Vienna Philharmonic Orchestra
    (1953): 4109.WB0
    New York Phiharmonic (1953):
    4109.WB2
    Columbia Symphony Orchestra
    (1959): 4109.WB1
Walter, Friedrich (b. 1907)
  March in d minor
    Hamburg New Symphony Orches-
    tra (1960): 4096.WF0
  Three Orchestral Pieces
    Hamburg New Symphony Orches-
    tra (1960): 4097.WF0

Wand, Günter (b. 1912)
  Symphony No. 1 in c minor
    Cologne Radio Symphony Orchestra (1981): 4101.WG0
  Symphony No. 2 in c minor
    Cologne Radio Symphony Orchestra (1981): 4102.WG0
  Symphony No. 3 in d minor
    Cologne Radio Symphony Orchestra (1981): 4103.WG0
  Symphony No. 4 in E flat Major
    Cologne Radio Symphony Orchestra (1976): 4104.WG0
  Symphony No. 5 in B flat Major
    Cologne Radio Symphony Orchestra (1974): 4105.WG0
  Symphony No. 6 in A Major
    Cologne Radio Symphony Orchestra (1976): 4106.WG0
    North German Radio Symphony Orchestra (1988): 4106.WG1
  Symphony No. 7 in E Major
    Cologne Radio Symphony Orchestra (1980): 4107.WG0
  Symphony No. 8 in c minor
    Cologne Gürzenich Orchestra (1976): 4108.WG1
    Cologne Radio Symphony Orchestra (1979): 4108.WG0
    North German Radio Symphony Orchestra (1987): 4108.WG2
    North German Radio Symphony Orchestra (1988): 4108.WG3
  Symphony No. 9 in d minor
    Cologne Radio Symphony Orchestra (1978): 4109.WG0
    North German Radio Symphony Orchestra (1987): 4109.WG1

Wasner, Franz
  Tota pulchra es
    Trapp Family Singers (1956): 1046.WF0

Wilhelm, Gerhard
  Ave Maria
    Stuttgarter Hymnus-Chorknaben (1986): 1006.WG0
  Tantum ergo, D Major
    Stuttgarter Hymnus-Chorknaben (1986): 1042.WG0

Wollenweider, Hans
  Tantum ergo, D Major
    Haselbach [Choir] (1958): 1042.WH0

Wood, Henry J. (1869-1944)
  Overture in g minor
    Queen's Hall Orchestra (1937): 4098.WH0

Wormsbächer, Hellmut
  Ave Maria
    Bergedorfer Chamber Choir (1960): 1006.WH0
  Mass No. 2 in e minor
    Hamburg State Philharmonic Orchestra (1973): 1027.WH0

Zanotelli, Hans
  Afferentur regi
    Philharmonisches Vocalensemble Stuttgart (1987): 1001.ZH0
  Ave Maria
    Philharmonisches Vocalensemble Stuttgart (1987): 1006.ZH0
  Christus factus est
    Philharmonisches Vocalensemble Stuttgart (1987): 1011.ZH0
  Ecce sacerdos
    Philharmonisches Vocalensemble Stuttgart (1987): 1013.ZH0

Zanotelli, Hans
Inveni David
Philharmonisches Vocalensemble
Stuttgart (1987): 1019.ZH0
Libera me, Domine
Philharmonisches Vocalensemble
Stuttgart (1987): 1022.ZH0
Locus iste
Philharmonisches Vocalensemble
Stuttgart (1987): 1023.ZH0
Os justi
Philharmonisches Vocalensemble
Stuttgart (1987): 1030.ZH0
Pange lingua et Tantum ergo
Philharmonisches Vocalensemble
Stuttgart (1987): 1033.ZH0
Tota pulchra es
Philharmonisches Vocalensemble
Stuttgart (1987): 1046.ZH0
Vexilla regis
Philharmonisches Vocalensemble
Stuttgart (1987): 1051.ZH0
Virga Jesse
Philharmonisches Vocalensemble
Stuttgart (1987): 1052.ZH0

Zapf, Gerd
Inveni David
Bavaria-Blechsolisten München
(1984): 1019.ZG0
Zaun, Fritz
Symphony No. 0 in d minor [Scherzo only]
Berlin State Opera Orchestra (1948): 4100.ZF0
Symphony No. 1 in c minor [Scherzo only]
Berlin Symphony Orchestra (1948): 4101.ZF0
Symphony No. 2 in c minor [Scherzo only]
Berlin Symphony Orchestra (1948): 4102.ZF0
Zsoltay, Denis
Symphony No. 4 in E flat Major
South German Philharmonic (1977): 4104.ZD0
Symphony No. 6 in A Major
South German Philharmonic (1977): 4106.ZD0

Orchestra Index

Berlin Municipal Orchestra
Overture in g minor
Mayer (Polydor, 1948): 4098.ML0
Symphony No. 9 in d minor
Schuricht (Polydor, 1943): 4109.SC1
Berlin Philharmonic Orchestra
Symphony No. 1 in c minor
Jochum (DG, 1965): 4101.JE0
Karajan (DG, 1981): 4101.KH0
Symphony No. 2 in c minor
Karajan (DG, 1981): 4102.KH0
Symphony No. 3 in d minor
Karajan (DG, 1980): 4103.KH0
Symphony No. 4 in E flat Major
Jochum (DG, 1965): 4104.JE0
Karajan (Angel, 1970): 4104.KA0
Karajan (DG, 1976): 4104.KA1
Knappertsbusch (Music & Arts, 1943/44): 4104.KP0
Muti (EMI, 1985): 4104.MR0
Tennstedt (Angel, 1981): 4104.TK0
Symphony No. 5 in B flat Major
Furtwängler (Bruno Walter Society, 1942): 4105.FW0
Furtwängler (DG, 1942): 4105.FW1
Karajan (DG, 1976): 4105.KH0
Symphony No. 6 in A Major
Karajan (DG, 1979): 4106.KH0
Keilberth (Teldec, 1963): 4106.KJ0
Muti (EMI, 1988): 4106.MR0
Symphony No. 7 in E Major
Furtwängler (Telefunken, 1942): 4107.FW3
Furtwängler (Volksplatte, 1949): 4107.FW0
Furtwängler (DG, 1951): 4107.FW1
Furtwängler (Discocorp, 1951): 4107.FW2
Horenstein (Unicorn, 1928): 4107.HJ0
Jochum (Decca, 1952): 4107.JE3

Berlin Philharmonic Orchestra
Symphony No. 7 in E Major
Jochum (DG, 1964): 4107.JE0
Karajan (Angel, 1971): 4107.KH0
Karajan (DG, 1975): 4107.KH1
Klemperer (Frequenz, 1958): 4107.KO1
Maazel (EMI, 1988): 4107.MA0
Schuricht (Polydor, 1939): 4107.SC0
Symphony No. 8 in c minor
Furtwängler (Vox, 1949): 4108.FW1
Furtwängler (Rococo, 1949): 4108.FW2
Jochum (DG, 1964): 4108.JE1
Karajan (Classics for Pleasure, 1957): 4108.KH0
Karajan (DG, 1975): 4108.KH1
Knappertsbusch (Hunt, 1952): 4108.KP2
Symphony No. 9 in d minor
Furtwängler (DG, 1944): 4109.FW0
Jochum (DG, 1964): 4109.JE1
Karajan (DG, 1966): 4109.KH0
Karajan (DG, 1975): 4109.KH1
Knappertsbusch (Music & Arts, 1950): 4109.KN0
Knappertsbusch (Suite, 1950): 4109.KN1
Berlin Radio Symphony Orchestra
Overture in g minor
Chailly (London, 1988): 4098.CR0
Symphony No. 0 in d minor
Chailly (London, 1988): 4100.CR0
Symphony No. 1 in c minor
Chailly (London, 1987): 4101.CR0
Symphony No. 2 in c minor
Konwitschny (Eterna, 1955): 4102.KO0
Symphony No. 3 in d minor
Chailly (London, 1985): 4103.CR0

Berlin Radio Symphony Orchestra
Symphony No. 3 in d minor
Maazel (Concert Hall, 1974): 4103.
ML0
Symphony No. 4 in E flat Major
Rögner (Deutsche Schallplatten,
1984): 4104.RH0
Symphony No. 7 in E Major
Chailly (London, 1984): 4107.CR0
Rögner (Deutsche Schallplatten,
1983): 4107.RE0
Symphony No. 8 in c minor
Rögner (Deutsche Schallplatten,
1980): 4108.RH0
Suitner (Deutsche Schallplatten,
1986): 4108.SO0
Symphony No. 9 in d minor
Rögner (Deutsche Schallplatten,
1983): 4109.RE0
Berlin State Opera Orchestra
Symphony No. 0 in d minor [Scherzo
only]
Zaun (Victor, 1948): 4100.ZF0
Symphony No. 7 in E Major
Fried (Grammophon, 1924): 4107.
FO0
Symphony No. 8 in c minor [Adagio
only]
Klemperer   (Polydor,   1924):
4108.KO1
Berlin Symphony Orchestra
Symphony No. 1 in c minor [Scherzo
only]
Zaun (Victor, 1948): 4101.ZF0
Symphony No. 2 in c minor [Scherzo
only]
Zaun (Victor, 1948): 4102.ZF0
Symphony No. 3 in d minor
Rubahn (Royale, 1950): 4103.RG1
Symphony No. 5 in B flat Major
Rögner (Deutsche Schallplatten,
1984): 4105.RH0

Berlin Symphony Orchestra
Symphony No. 6 in A Major
Rögner (Deutsche Schallplatten,
1980): 4106.RH5
Boston Symphony Orchestra
Symphony No. 4 in E flat Major
Leinsdorf (Victor, 1966): 4104.LE0
Symphony No. 6 in A Major
Steinberg (RCA, 1969): 4106.ST0
Symphony No. 8 in c minor [excerpt
from Finale]
none (Vox, 1956): 4108.ML5
Chicago Symphony Orchestra
Symphony No. 0 in d minor
Barenboim (DG, 1979): 4100.BD0
Symphony No. 1 in c minor
Barenboim (DG, 1981): 4101.BD0
Symphony No. 2 in c minor
Barenboim (DG, 1981): 4102.BD0
Symphony No. 3 in d minor
Barenboim (DG, 1981): 4103.BD0
Symphony No. 4 in E flat Major
Barenboim (DG, 1972): 4104.BD0
Solti (London, 1981): 4104.SG0
Symphony No. 5 in B flat Major
Barenboim (DG, 1977): 4105.BD0
Solti (London, 1980): 4105.SG0
Symphony No. 6 in A Major
Barenboim (DG, 1977): 4106.BD0
Solti (London, 1979): 4106.SG0
Symphony No. 7 in E Major
Barenboim (DG, 1979): 4107.BD0
Solti (London, 1978): 4107.SG2
Solti (London, 1986): 4107.SG1
Symphony No. 8 in c minor
Barenboim (DG, 1980): 4108.BD0
Symphony No. 9 in d minor
Barenboim (DG, 1975): 4109.BD0
Giulini (Angel, 1976): 4109.GC0
Solti (London, 1985): 4109.SG0

Concertgebouw Orchestra, Amsterdam
Symphony No. 7 in E Major
Beinum (London, 1947): 4107.BE1
Beinum (Decca, 1953): 4107.BE0
Haitink (Philips, 1966): 4107.HB0
Haitink (Philips, 1978): 4107.HB1
Symphony No. 8 in c minor
Beinum (Epic, 1955): 4108.BE0
Haitink (Philips, 1969): 4108.HB0
Haitink (Philips, 1981): 4108.HB1
Symphony No. 9 in d minor
Beinum (Epic, 1956): 4109.BE0
Haitink (Philips, 1964): 4109.HB0
Haitink (Philips, 1981): 4109.HB1
Czech Philharmonic Orchestra
Overture in g minor
Pesek (Supraphon, 1986): 4098.PL0
Symphony No. 4 in E flat Major
Konwitschny (Supraphon, 1952):
4104.KQ0
Symphony No. 5 in B flat Major
Matacic (Supraphon, 1973): 4105.
ML0
Symphony No. 7 in E Major
Matacic (Supraphon, 1968): 4107.
ML0
Pesek (Supraphon, 1986): 4107.PL0
Symphony No. 9 in d minor
Matacic (Supraphon, 1980): 4109.
ML0
Danish Radio Symphony Orchestra
Symphony No. 7 in E Major
Sanderling (Unicorn, 1977):
4107.SA0
Dol Dauber Orchestra
Symphony No. 5 in B flat Major
Anonymous (Electrola, 1948): 4105.
AA0
Frankfurt Radio Symphony Orchestra
Symphony No. 1 in c minor
Inbal (Teldec, 1987): 4101.IE0

Frankfurt Radio Symphony Orchestra
Symphony No. 2 in c minor
Inbal (Teldec, 1988): 4102.IE0
Symphony No. 3 in d minor
Inbal (Teldec, 1982): 4103.IE0
Symphony No. 4 in E flat Major
Inbal (Teldec, 1982): 4104.IE0
Symphony No. 5 in B flat Major
Inbal (Teldec, 1987): 4105.IE0
Symphony No. 6 in A Major
Inbal (Teldec, 1988): 4106.IE0
Symphony No. 7 in E Major
Inbal (Teldec, 1985): 4107.IE0
Symphony No. 8 in c minor
Inbal (Teldec, 1982): 4108.IE0
Symphony No. 9 in d minor
Inbal (Teldec, 1987): 4109.IE0
Symphony No. 9 in d minor [Finale
only]
Inbal (Teldec, 1986): 4109.IE1
Goldman Band
Apollo March
Goldman (Decca, 1958): 4115.GR0
The Hague Philharmonic Orchestra
Symphony No. 7 in E Major
Schuricht (Preludio, 1964): 4107.SC1
Hague Residentie Orchestra
Symphony No. 4 in E flat Major
Otterloo (Epic, 1953): 4104.OW0
Hallé Orchestra
Symphony No. 4 in E flat Major
Macal (Classics for Pleasure, 1984):
4104.MC0
Hamburg New Symphony Orchestra
March in d minor
Walter (Family Records, 1960):
4096.WF0
Three Orchestral Pieces
Walter (Family Records, 1960):
4097.WF0

Hamburg Philharmonic Orchestra
    Symphony No. 4 in E flat Major
        Jochum (Telefunken, 1940): 4104.JE1
    Symphony No. 5 in B flat Major
        Jochum (Capitol, 1937): 4105.JE1
Hamburg Philharmonic State Orchestra
    Symphony No. 8 in c minor
        Jochum (Decca, 1948): 4108.JE0
    Symphony No. 9 in d minor
        Keilberth (Telefunken, 1956):
        4109.KJ0
Hastings Symphony
    Symphony No. 4 in E flat Major
        Tubbs (Allegro, 1954): 4104.TU0
Hilversum Radio Orchestra
    Symphony No. 4 in E flat Major
        Kempen (Telefunken, 1955): 4104.
        KE5
Japan Broadcasting Corporation Symphony Orchestra
    Symphony No. 8 in c minor
        Matacic (Denon, 1984): 4108.ML0
Japan Philharmonic Orchestra
    Symphony No. 1 in c minor
        Asahina (Victor, 1983): 4101.AX0
Leighton Lucas Orchestra
    Symphony No. 9 in d minor [Trio only]
        Lucas (EMI, 1948): 4109.LL0
Leipzig Gewandhaus Orchestra
    Symphony No. 1 in c minor
        Masur (Nippon Columbia, 1977):
        4101.MK0
        Neumann (Teldec, 1966): 4101.NV0
    Symphony No. 2 in c minor
        Masur (Nippon Columbia/Denon,
        1978): 4102.MK0
    Symphony No. 3 in d minor
        Masur (Denon, 1977): 4103.MS0
        Sanderling (Electrola, 1970): 4103.
        SA0

Leipzig Gewandhaus Orchestra
    Symphony No. 4 in E flat Major
        Konwitschny (Eurodisc, 1963): 4104.
        KQ3
        Masur (RCA, 1975): 4104.MK0
    Symphony No. 5 in B flat Major
        Konwitschny (Electrola, 1961): 4105.
        KZ0
        Masur (Vanguard, 1976): 4105.MK0
    Symphony No. 6 in A Major
        Bongartz (Philips, 1967): 4106.BH0
        Masur (Eurodisc, 1978): 4106.MK0
    Symphony No. 7 in E Major
        Konwitschny (Eterna, 1958): 4107.
        KW0
        Masur (Eterna, 1974): 4107.MK0
    Symphony No. 8 in c minor
        Masur (Eurodisc, 1978): 4108.MK0
    Symphony No. 9 in d minor
        Masur (Eurodisc, 1975): 4109.MK0
Leipzig Philharmonic Orchestra
    Symphony No. 5 in B flat Major
        Pflügler (Urania, 1955): 4105.PG0
Leipzig Radio Orchestra
    Symphony No. 5 in B flat Major
        Abendroth (Eterna, 1949): 4105.AH0
    Symphony No. 9 in d minor
        Abendroth (Eterna, 1951): 4109.AH0
    Symphony No. 8 in c minor
        Kegel (Magma, 1990): 4108.KH7
Leipzig Symphony Orchestra
    Symphony No. 4 in E flat Major
        Abendroth (Urania, 1949):
        4104.AH0
Leningrad Philharmonic Orchestra
    Symphony No. 4 in E flat Major
        Tchakarov (Melodiya, 1978):
        4104.TE0
    Symphony No. 8 in c minor
        Mravinsky (Artia, 1958): 4108.MZ7

Leningrad Philharmonic Orchestra
 Symphony No. 9 in d minor
  Mravinsky (Turnabout, 1980):
   4109.MY0
Linz Bruckner Symphony Orchestra
 Symphony No. 2 in c minor
  Jochum (Urania, 1943): 4102.JG0
 Symphony No. 6 in A Major
  Jochum (Urania, 1943): 4106.JG0
Ljubljana Symphony Orchestra
 Symphony No. 8 in c minor
  Nanut (Stradivari, 1989): 4108.NA0
London Philharmonic Orchestra
 March in d minor
  Schönzeler (Unicorn, 1970): 4096.
   SH0
 Three Orchestral Pieces
  Schönzeler (Unicorn, 1970):
   4097.SH0
 Symphony No. 8 in c minor
  Järvi (Chandos, 1986): 4108.JA0
  Tennstedt (Angel, 1982): 4108.TK0
London Symphony Orchestra
 Overture in g minor
  Shapirra (EMI Odeon, 1972): 4098.
   SE0
 Symphony No. 00 in f minor
  Shapirra (Odeon, 1972): 4099.SE0
 Symphony No. 4 in E flat Major
  Kertesz (London, 1965): 4104.KI0
Los Angeles Philharmonic Orchestra
 Symphony No. 4 in E flat Major
  Mehta (London, 1970): 4104.MN0
 Symphony No. 8 in c minor
  Mehta (London, 1974): 4108.MZ0
Minneapolis Symphony Orchestra
 Symphony No. 7 in E Major
  Ormandy (Victor, 1935): 4107.OE1

Moscow Radio Large Symphony Orches-
 tra
 Symphony No. 3 in d minor
  Rozhdestvensky (Westminster,
   1976): 4103.RG0
 Symphony No. 9 in d minor
  Rozhdestvensky (Westminster
   Gold, 1970): 4109.RG0
Munich Philharmonic Orchestra
 Symphony No. 4 in E flat Major
  Kempe (Acanta, 1976): 4104.KE0
 Symphony No. 5 in B flat Major
  Kempe (Columbia, 1975): 4105.KM0
  Knappertsbusch (Seven Seas, 1961):
   4105.KP1
 Symphony No. 7 in E Major
  Kabasta (Electrola, 1943): 4107.KA0
 Symphony No. 8 in c minor
  Knappertsbusch (Music Guild,
   1963): 4108.KP0
 Symphony No. 9 in d minor
  Hausegger (Past Masters, 1938):
   4109.HG0
Netherlands Philharmonic
 Symphony No. 3 in d minor
  Goehr (Concert Hall, 1954): 4103.
   GW0
New Philharmonia Orchestra
 Symphony No. 5 in B flat Major
  Klemperer (Angel, 1967): 4105.KO0
 Symphony No. 6 in A Major
  Klemperer (Angel, 1964): 4106.KO1
 Symphony No. 8 in c minor
  Klemperer (Angel, 1970): 4108.KO0
 Symphony No. 9 in d minor
  Klemperer (Angel, 1970): 4109.KL0
New York Philharmonic
 Symphony No. 9 in d minor
  Walter (Nuova Era, 1953): 4109.WB2
  Bernstein (Columbia, 1962):
   4109.BL0

Nomiuri Nippon Philharmonic Orchestra
Symphony No. 9 in d minor
Asahina (Victor, 1980): 4109.AT0
North German Radio Symphony Orchestra
Symphony No. 3 in d minor
Knappertsbusch (Discocorp, 1962): 4103.KN2
Symphony No. 6 in A Major
Wand (RCA Victor, 1988): 4106.WG1
Symphony No. 8 in c minor
Wand (EMI, 1987): 4108.WG2
Wand (RCA Victor, 1988): 4108.WG3
Symphony No. 9 in d minor
Wand (RCA Victor, 1987): 4109.WG1
Nuremburg Symphony Orchestra
Symphony No. 0 in d minor
Gelmini (Colosseum, 1975): 4100.GH0
Osaka Philharmonic Orchestra
Symphony No. 2 in c minor
Asahina (Victor, 1986): 4102.AX0
Symphony No. 7 in E Major
Asahina (Victor, 1975): 4107.AT1
Asahina (Victor, 1983): 4107.AT0
Symphony No. 8 in c minor
Asahina (Victor, 1980): 4108.AT1
Asahina (Bellaphon, 1988): 4108.AT0
Oslo Philharmonic Orchestra
Symphony No. 9 in d minor
Talmi (Chandos, 1985): 4109.TY0
Symphony No. 9 in d minor [sketch of Finale only]
Talmi (Chandos, 1985): 4143.TY0

Philadelphia Orchestra
Symphony No. 4 in E flat Major
Ormandy (Columbia, 1967): 4104.OE0
Symphony No. 5 in B flat Major
Ormandy (Columbia, 1965): 4105.OE0
Symphony No. 7 in E Major
Ormandy (RCA, 1968): 4107.OE0
Philharmonia Orchestra
Overture in g minor
Matacic (Angel, 1954): 4098.MA0
Symphony No. 0 in d minor [Scherzo only]
Matacic (Angel, 1954): 4100.ML0
Symphony No. 4 in E flat Major
Klemperer (Angel, 1963): 4104.KO0
Matacic (Angel, 1954): 4104.ML0
Symphony No. 7 in E Major
Klemperer (Angel, 1960): 4107.KO0
Philharmonic Symphony Orchestra
Symphony No. 8 in c minor
Paita (Lodia, 1982): 4108.PC0
Pittsburgh Symphony Orchestra
Overture in g minor
Steinberg (Command, 1968): 4098.SW0
Symphony No. 4 in E flat Major
Steinberg (Capitol, 1956): 4104.SW0
Symphony No. 7 in E Major
Steinberg (Command, 1968): 4107.SW0
Queen's Hall Orchestra
Overture in g minor
Wood (Decca, 1937): 4098.WH0
Radio France Philharmonic Orchestra
Overture in g minor
Janowski (Virgin Classics, 1990): 4098.JM0
Symphony No. 4 in E flat Major
Janowski (Virgin Classics, 1990): 4104.JM0

Salzburg Mozarteum Orchestra
Symphony No. 3 in d minor
Fekete (Remington, 1950): 4103.FZ0
Saxon State Orchestra
Symphony No. 4 in E flat Major
Böhm (Victor, 1936): 4104.BK1
Symphony No. 5 in B flat Major
Böhm (Victor, 1936): 4105.BK0
Schleswig-Holstein Music Festival Orchestra
Symphony No. 6 in A Major
Eschenbach (Eurodisc, 1988): 4106.
EC0
Shinsei Nihon Orchestra
Symphony No. 4 in E flat Major
Uno (Art Union, 1986): 4104.UK0
Slovene Philharmonic Orchestra
Symphony No. 7 in E Major
Matacic (Denon, 1984): 4107.ML1
South German Philharmonic Orchestra
Symphony No. 2 in c minor
Swarowsky (Ampex, 1970):
4102.SW0
Symphony No. 4 in E flat Major
Zsoltay (Mace, 1977): 4104.ZD0
Symphony No. 6 in A Major
Zsoltay (Mace, 1977): 4106.ZD0
Southwest German Radio Symphony Orchestra, Baden-Baden
Overture in g minor
Hager (Amati, 1988): 4098.HL0
Symphony No. 7 in E Major
Rosbaud (Turnabout, 1958):
4107.RH0
Staatskapelle Dresden
Symphony No. 1 in c minor
Jochum (EMI, 1978): 4101.JE1
Symphony No. 2 in c minor
Jochum (EMI, 1975): 4102.JE1
Symphony No. 3 in d minor
Jochum (EMI, 1977): 4103.JE1

Staatskapelle Dresden
Symphony No. 4 in E flat Major
Blomstedt (Denon, 1981): 4104.BH0
Jochum (EMI, 1975): 4104.JE3
Sinopoli (DG, 1987): 4104.SE0
Symphony No. 5 in B flat Major
Jochum (EMI, 1986): 4105.JE2
Symphony No. 6 in A Major
Jochum (Angel, 1978): 4106.JE1
Symphony No. 7 in E Major
Blomstedt (Denon, 1980): 4107.BH0
Jochum (Angel, 1976): 4107.JE1
Symphony No. 8 in c minor
Jochum (Angel, 1976): 4108.JE2
Symphony No. 9 in d minor
Jochum (Angel, 1978): 4109.JE2
Stuttgart Radio Symphony Orchestra
Symphony No. 9 in d minor
Celibidache (Rococo, 1970):
4109.CS0
Tokyo Metropolitan Symphony Orchestra
Symphony No. 3 in d minor
Asahina (Victor, 1984): 4103.AY0
Turin RAI Symphonic Orchestra
Symphony No. 9 in d minor
Celibidache (Hunt, 1969): 4109.CS0
Unidentified orchestra
Symphony No. 4 in E flat Major
Celibidache (Rococo, 1970): 4104.
CS0
Symphony No. 8 in c minor
Celibidache (Rococo, 1970): 4108.
CS0
Unidentified studio orchestra
Symphony No. 8 in c minor [excerpt
from Adagio]
Hoof (Mercury, 1980): 4108.HH0
USSR Academic Symphony Orchestra
Symphony No. 8 in c minor
Svetlanov (Melodiya, 1981):
4108.SV0

USSR Ministry of Culture Symphony
Symphony No. 4 in E flat Major
Rozhdestvensky (MCA, 1978):
4104.RG0
USSR Symphony Orchestra
Symphony No. 00 in f minor
Rozhdestvensky (Chant du Monde,
1983): 4099.RG0
Symphony No. 0 in d minor
Rozhdestvensky (Chant du Monde,
1983): 4100.RG0
Vienna Festival Orchestra
Symphony No. 6 in A Major
Swarowsky (Preludio, 1960):
4106.SS0
Vienna National Orchestra
Symphony No. 4 in E flat Major
Wallberg (Concert Hall, 1967):
4104.WA5
Symphony No. 8 in c minor
Wallberg (Concert Hall, 1968):
4108.WA5
Symphony No. 9 in d minor
Wallberg (Concert Hall, 1968):
4109.WA5
Vienna Orchestral Society
Symphony No. 1 in c minor
Adler (Unicorn, 1955): 4101.AF0
Vienna Philharmonia Orchestra
Overture in g minor
Adler (S.P.A., 1952): 4098.AF0
Symphony No. 3 in d minor
Adler (S.P.A., 1953): 4103.AF0
Symphony No. 9 in d minor
Adler (S.P.A., 1952): 4109.AL0
Vienna Philharmonic Orchestra
Symphony No. 1 in c minor
Abbado (London, 1969): 4101.AC0
Symphony No. 2 in c minor
Stein (London, 1973): 4102.SH0
Symphony No. 3 in d minor
Böhm (London, 1970): 4103.BK0

Vienna Philharmonic Orchestra
Symphony No. 3 in d minor
Knappertsbusch (London, 1954):
4103.KN1
Schuricht (Seraphim, 1966):
4103.SC0
Symphony No. 4 in E flat Major
Böhm (London, 1973): 4104.BK0
Furtwängler (DG, 1951): 4104.FW0
Furtwängler (Price-Less, 1951):
4104.FW1
Haitink (Philips, 1985): 4104.HB1
Knappertsbusch (London, 1955):
4104.KP1
Knappertsbusch (Nuova Era, 1960):
4104.KP2
Krauss (His Master's Voice, 1948):
4104.KQ5
Symphony No. 5 in B flat Major
Furtwängler (Rococo, 1951):
4105.FW2
Haitink (Philips, 1988): 4105.HB1
Klemperer (Hunt, 1989): 4105.KO1
Knappertsbusch (Decca, 1956):
4105.KP0
Maazel (London, 1974): 4105.MA0
Symphony No. 6 in A Major
Stein (London, 1972): 4106.SH0
Symphony No. 7 in E Major
Böhm (DG, 1976): 4107.BK1
Giulini (DG, 1986): 4107.GC0
Jochum (Telefunken, 1940): 4107.JE2
Knappertsbusch (Music & Arts,
1949): 4107.KP0
Solti (London, 1965): 4107.SG0
Szell (Rococo, 1960): 4107.SZ0
Symphony No. 8 in c minor
Böhm (DG, 1976): 4108.BK0
Furtwängler (DG, 1944): 4108.FW0
Furtwängler (Hunt, 1954): 4108.FW3
Giulini (DG, 1984): 4108.GC0

Vienna Philharmonic Orchestra
  Symphony No. 8 in c minor
    Karajan (Nuova Era, 1965): 4108.KH2
    Karajan (DG, 1988): 4108.KH3
    Knappertsbusch (BWS, 1961): 4108.KP5
    Schuricht (Angel, 1963): 4108.SC0
    Solti (London, 1966): 4108.SG0
  Symphony No. 9 in d minor
    Giulini (DG, 1988): 4109.GC1
    Mehta (London, 1965): 4109.MN0
    Schuricht (Seraphim, 1961): 4109.SC0
    Walter (Movimento Musica, 1953): 4109.WB0
Vienna State Opera Orchestra
  Symphony No. 7 in E Major
    Böhm (Vox, 1944): 4107.BK0
Vienna Symphony Orchestra
  Overture in g minor
    Otterloo (Epic, 1955): 4098.OW0
  Symphony No. 1 in c minor
    Andreae (Amadeo, 1953): 4101.AV1
  Symphony No. 2 in c minor
    Andreae (Amadeo, 1953): 4102.AV0
    Giulini (Odeon, 1974): 4102.GC0
  Symphony No. 3 in d minor
    Andreae (Epic, 1955): 4103.AV0
    Konrath (Victor, 1935): 4103.KO0

Vienna Symphony Orchestra
  Symphony No. 4 in E flat Major
    Klemperer (Vox, 1951): 4104.KO1
    Konwitschny (World Record Club, 1962): 4104.KQ1
  Symphony No. 6 in A Major
    Swoboda (Westminster, 1950): 4106.SW0
  Symphony No. 7 in E Major
    Otterloo (Epic, 1954): 4107.OW0
  Symphony No. 8 in c minor
    Horenstein (Turnabout, 1955): 4108.HJ0
  Symphony No. 9 in d minor
    Horenstein (Vox, 1953): 4109.HJ0
    Matacic (Polygram Vienna, 1983): 4109.ML1
Westphalian Symphony Orchestra, Recklinghausen
  Symphony No. 2 in c minor
    Reichert (Turnabout, 1971): 4102.RH0
  Symphony No. 6 in A Major
    Reichert (Vox, 1963): 4106.RH0
Zurich Tonhalle Orchestra
  Symphony No. 8 in c minor
    Kempe (Tudor, 1975): 4108.KM0

Annotator Index

Aldeborgh, David H.
  In jener letzten der Nächte (1985): 1017.JJ0
  Magnificat in B flat Major (1985): 1024.JJ0
  Missa Solemnis in B flat Major (1985): 1029.JJ0
  O du liebes Jesu Kind (1985): 1145.JJ0
Andry, Peter
  Symphony No. 8 in c minor (1973): 4108.KO0
Arnold, H. Ross
  Symphony No. 0 in d minor (1952): 4100.SH0
Auerbach-Schröder, Cornelia
  Christus factus est: 1011.GW0
  Locus iste (1963): 1023.GW0
  Os justi (1963): 1030.GO0
  Tantum ergo, D Major (1963): 1042.GW0
Batz, Karl
  Inveni David (1984): 1019.ZG0
Baxter, William C.
  Symphony No. 4 in E flat Major (1990): 4104.LJ0
  Symphony No. 7 in E Major (1989): 4107.LJ0
Bayliff, R.W.
  Symphony No. 5 in B flat Major (1980): 4105.SG0

Beaujean, Alfred
  Symphony No. 6 in A Major (1979): 4106.MK0
  Symphony No. 8 in c minor (1979): 4108.MK0
Biba, Otto
  Prelude and Fugue in c minor (1981): 3131.HU0
Birkner, Günter
  Symphony No. 4 in E flat Major (1979): 4104.FW0
  Symphony No. 8 in c minor (1979): 4108.FW0
  Symphony No. 9 in d minor (1979): 4109.FW0
Bollert, Werner
  Symphony No. 7 in E Major (1976): 4107.FW1
Brand, Joseph
  Symphony No. 2 in c minor (1975): 4102.SH0
  Symphony No. 5 in B flat Major (1974): 4105.MA0
  Symphony No. 5 in B flat Major (1980): 4105.SG0
Branscombe, Peter
  Symphony No. 4 in E flat Major (1986): 4104.MR0
  Symphony No. 6 in A Major (1988): 4106.MR0

Branscombe, Peter
Symphony No. 6 in A Major (1981): 4106.JE1
Symphony No. 7 in E Major (1987): 4107.GC0
Symphony No. 7 in E Major (1980): 4107.JE1
Symphony No. 9 in d minor (1989): 4109.GC1
Symphony No. 9 in d minor (1985): 4109.JE2

Bras, Jean-Yves
Ave Maria (1990): 1006.HA5
Christus factus est (1990): 1011.HP0
Locus iste (1990): 1023.HP0
Mass No. 2 in e minor (1990): 1027.HE0
Os justi (1990): 1030.HP0
Vexilla regis (1990): 1051.HP0
Æquale I (1990): 2114.EM0
Æquale II (1990): 2149.EM0

Braunstein, Joseph
Symphony No. 2 in c minor (1971): 4102.RH0
Symphony No. 5 in B flat Major (1978): 4105.MK0
Symphony No. 8 in c minor (1970): 4108.HJ0
Symphony No. 8 in c minor (1973): 4108.FW1
Symphony No. 9 in d minor (1956): 4109.JE0

Breckbill, David
Symphony No. 3 in d minor (1987): 4103.KN0
Symphony No. 6 in A Major (1987): 4106.KO0
Symphony No. 8 in c minor (1987): 4108.KP1

Bürgers, Irmelin
Symphony No. 7 in E Major (1989): 4107.DC0

Burkhardt, Peter
Symphony No. 3 in d minor (1982): 4103.KN2
Symphony No. 7 in E Major (1983): 4107.KP0
Symphony No. 9 in d minor (1986): 4109.KN0

Burns, Richard C.
Symphony No. 5 in B flat Major (1955): 4105.PG0

Calkin, Katherine
Symphony No. 3 in d minor (1976): 4103.RG0

Cardus, Neville
Symphony No. 5 in B flat Major (1982): 4105.FW0

Carner, Mosco
Overture in g minor (1956): 4098.MA0
Symphony No. 0 in d minor [Scherzo only] (1956): 4100.ML0
Symphony No. 4 in E flat Major (1956): 4104.ML0
Symphony No. 8 in c minor (1985): 4108.GC0

Carragan, William
Symphony No. 9 in d minor (1986): 4109.TY0
Symphony No. 9 in d minor [sketch of Finale only] (1986): 4143.TY0

Chapin, Victor
Ave Maria (1964): 1006.GH0
Locus iste (1964): 1023.GH0
Mass No. 2 in e minor (1964): 1027.GH0

Chisholm, Duncan
Symphony No. 7 in E Major (1986): 4107.CR0
Symphony No. 7 in E Major (1988): 4107.SG2

Chislett, W.A.
Ave Maria (1967): 1006.PW0
Christus factus est (1967): 1011.PW0
Locus iste (1967): 1023.PW0

Chislett, W.A.
  Os justi (1967): 1030.PW0
  Virga Jesse (1967): 1052.PW0
Clements, Andrew
  Symphony No. 4 in E flat Major (1988):
    4104.SE0
Colombeau, Christian
  Symphony No. 6 in A Major (1989):
    4106.SS0
Cooke, Deryck
  Symphony No. 1 in c minor (1973):
    4101.HB0
  Symphony No. 2 in c minor (1970):
    4102.HB0
  Symphony No. 5 in B flat Major (1972):
    4105.HB0
  Symphony No. 6 in A Major (1971):
    4106.HB0
  Symphony No. 8 in c minor (1968):
    4108.SG0
  Symphony No. 8 in c minor (1971):
    4108.HB0
  Symphony No. 8 in c minor (1974):
    4108.MZ0
  Symphony No. 9 in d minor (1965):
    4109.MN0
Crankshaw, Geoffrey
  Symphony No. 1 in c minor (1971):
    4101.AC0
Darrell, R.D.
  Symphony No. 8 in c minor [excerpt
    from Finale] (1956): 4108.ML5
Davies, Maxwell
  Mass No. 2 in e minor (1978): 1027.KL0
Dennison, Peter
  Afferentur regi (1974): 1001.GG0
  Ecce sacerdos (1974): 1013.GG0
  Inveni David (1974): 1019.GG0
  Os justi (1974): 1030.GG0
  Pange lingua et Tantum ergo (1974):
    1033.GG0

Diether, Jack
  Te Deum (1968): 1045.OE0
  Helgoland (1978): 1071.MW0
  Symphony No. 3 in d minor (1966):
    4103.SG0
  Symphony No. 4 in E flat Major (1986):
    4104.KP0
  Symphony No. 5 in B flat Major (1968):
    4105.OE0
  Symphony No. 5 in B flat Major (1976):
    4105.KM0
  Symphony No. 8 in c minor (1966):
    4108.SZ0
  Symphony No. 9 in d minor (1971):
    4109.BL0
  Symphony No. 9 in d minor (1986):
    4109.KN0
Dimpfel, Rolf-A.
  Symphony No. 1 in c minor (1982):
    4101.WG0
  Symphony No. 2 in c minor (1982):
    4102.WG0
  Symphony No. 3 in d minor (1981):
    4103.WG0
Dömling, Wolfgang
  Afferentur regi (1981): 1001.JE0
  Ave Maria (1981): 1006.JE0
  Christus factus est (1966): 1011.JE0
  Ecce sacerdos (1981): 1013.JE0
  Locus iste (1981): 1023.JE0
  Mass No. 2 in e minor (1981): 1027.JE0
  Os justi (1981): 1030.JE0
  Pange lingua et Tantum ergo (1981):
    1033.JE0
  Tota pulchra es (1981): 1046.JE0
  Vexilla regis (1981): 1051.JE0
  Virga Jesse (1981): 1052.JE0
Donat, Misha
  Symphony No. 9 in d minor (1989):
    4109.DC0

Gallois, Jean
  Symphony No. 00 in f minor (1986):
    4099.RG0
  Symphony No. 0 in d minor (1986):
    4100.RG0
Golding, Robin
  Symphony No. 7 in E Major (1966):
    4107.SG0
Goodwin, Noel
  Symphony No. 9 in d minor (1986):
    4109.TY0
  Symphony No. 9 in d minor [sketch of
    Finale only] (1986): 4143.TY0
  Symphony No. 8 in c minor (1990):
    4108.JA0
Guy, Rory
  Symphony No. 9 in d minor (1977):
    4109.GC0
Halbreich, Harry
  Os justi (1964): 1030.GE2
  Symphony No. 6 in A Major (1963):
    4106.RH0
Hall, George
  Symphony No. 6 in A Major (1980):
    4106.SG0
Hammond, Douglas
  Afferentur regi (1983): 1001.BM0
  Ave Maria (1983): 1006.BM0
  Christus factus es (1983): 1011.BM0
  Ecce sacerdos (1983): 1013.BM0
  Inveni David (1983): 1019.BM0
  Locus iste (1983): 1023.BM0
  Os justi (1983): 1030.BM0
  Pange lingua et Tantum ergo (1983):
    1033.BM0
  Tota pulchra es (1983): 1046.BM0
  Vexilla regis (1983): 1051.BM0
  Virga Jesse (1983): 1052.BM0
Hansen, Mathias
  Mass No. 2 in e minor (1990): 1027.RZ0
  Te Deum (1990): 1045.RH0

Harrison, Max
  Intermezzo (1978): 2113.AS0
Haselböck, Franz
  Fugue in d minor (1975): 3125.HF0
  Postlude in d minor (1975): 3126.HF0
  Prelude in E flat Major (1975): 3127.HF0
  Four Preludes in E flat Major (1975):
    3128.HF0
  Prelude in C Major (1975): 3129.HF0
  Prelude in d minor (1975): 3130.HF0
  Prelude and Fugue in c minor (1975):
    3131.HF0
Haylock, Julian
  Symphony No. 8 in c minor (1989):
    4108.SV0
Hecker, Joachim von
  Mass No. 2 in e minor (1973): 1027.RH0
Henderson, Robert
  Ave Maria (1968): 1006.AJ0
  Christus factus est (1968): 1011.AJ0
  Locus iste (1968): 1023.AJ0
  Virga Jesse (1968): 1052.AJ0
Hirano, Akira
  Symphony No. 4 in E flat Major (1984):
    4104.BH0
  Symphony No. 5 in B flat Major (1985):
    4105.ML0
  Symphony No. 7 in E Major (1984):
    4107.BH0
  Symphony No. 9 in d minor (1985):
    4109.ML0
Höcker, Karla
  Symphony No. 5 in B flat Major (1989):
    4105.FW1
Hodgson, Anthony
  Symphony No. 7 in E Major (1975):
    4107.HJ0
  Symphony No. 7 in E Major (1979):
    4107.SA0
Hoffmann-Erbrecht, Lothar
  Afferentur regi (1973): 1001.MJ0
  Ecce sacerdos (1973): 1013.MJ0

Hoffmann-Erbrecht, Lothar
Inveni David (1973): 1019.MJ0
Mass No. 2 in e minor (1973): 1027.MJ0
Hömberg, Johannes
Mass No. 2 in e minor [Kyrie only]
(1978): 1027.HJ0
Hoogen, Eckhardt van den
Symphony No. 6 in A Major (1989):
4106.WG1
Symphony No. 8 in c minor (1987):
4108.WG2
Symphony No. 8 in c minor (1989):
4108.WG3
Symphony No. 9 in d minor (1989):
4109.WG1
Horn, Erwin (b. 1940)
Organ works (1990): 3125.HO0, 3126.
HO0, 3127.HO0, 3128.HO0, 3129.
HW6, 3130.HO0, 3131.HO0
Symphony No. 00 in f minor [Scherzo
only]: 4099.HE0
Symphony No. 0 in d minor [Andante
only]: 4100.HE1
Symphony No. 6 in A Major [Adagio
only]: 4106.HE0
Huth, Andrew
Symphony No. 1 in c minor (1988):
4101.CR0
Symphony No. 9 in d minor (1986):
4109.SG0
Jacobson, Bernard
Requiem in d minor (1976): 1039.BH0
Jennings, Paul
Ave Maria (1967): 1006.PW0
Christus factus est (1967): 1011.PW0
Locus iste (1967): 1023.PW0
Os justi (1967): 1030.PW0
Virga Jesse (1967): 1052.PW0
Jochum, Eugen
Symphony No. 1 in c minor (1968):
4101.JE0

Jochum, Eugen
Symphony No. 2 in c minor (1968):
4102.JE0
Symphony No. 3 in d minor (1967):
4103.JE0
Symphony No. 4 in E flat Major (1968):
4104.JE0
Symphony No. 6 in A Major (1968):
4106.JE0
Symphony No. 7 in E Major (1968):
4107.JE0
Symphony No. 8 in c minor (1979):
4108.JE2
Keller, Hans
Symphony No. 8 in c minor (1973):
4108.KO0
Ketting, Knud
Afferentur regi (1989): 1001.GE0
Ave Maria (1989): 1006.GH3
Christus factus est (1989): 1011.GU0
Ecce sacerdos (1989): 1013.GE0
Locus iste (1989): 1023.GW3
Os justi (1989): 1030.GO0
Pange lingua et Tantum ergo (1989):
1033.GO0
Tota pulchra es (1989): 1046.GU0
Vexilla regis (1989): 1051.GU0
Virga Jesse (1989): 1052.GU0
Kennedy, Michael
Mass No. 3 in f minor (1989): 1028.DC0
Te Deum (1989): 1045.HB1
Symphony No. 3 in d minor (1986):
4103.CR0
Symphony No. 5 in B flat Major (1989):
4105.HB1
Kenton, Egon
String Quintet in F Major (1955):
2112.KQ0
Kirsch, Winfried
Mass No. 2 in e minor (1974): 1027.WH0

Klein, Hans-Günter
  Symphony No. 1 in c minor (1981):
    4101.BD0
  Symphony No. 2 in c minor (1981):
    4102.BD0
  Symphony No. 3 in d minor (1981):
    4103.BD0
Koch, Alois
  Afferentur regi (1985): 1001.FJ0
  Ave Maria (1985): 1006.FU0
  Christus factus est (1985): 1011.FJ0
  Ecce sacerdos (1985): 1013.FJ0
  Inveni David (1985): 1019.FJ0
  Locus iste (1985): 1023.FJ0
  Os justi (1985): 1030.FU0
  Pange lingua et Tantum ergo (1985):
    1033.FJ0
  Tota pulchra es (1985): 1046.FJ0
  Vexilla regis (1985): 1051.FJ0
  Virga Jesse (1985): 1052.FX0
  Æquale I (1985): 2114.FJ0
  Æquale II (1985): 2149.FJ0
Kohlhase, Thomas
  Te Deum (1985): 1045.KH1
  Symphony No. 5 in B flat Major (1979):
    4105.BD0
  Symphony No. 6 in A Major (1980):
    4106.KH0
Kolodin, Irving
  Te Deum (1951): 1045.JE0
  Symphony No. 8 in c minor (1948):
    4108.JE0
Kraemer, Uwe
  Symphony No. 4 in E flat Major (1984):
    4104.BD0
Krellmann, Hanspeter
  Symphony No. 5 in B flat Major (1977):
    4105.KH0
  Symphony No. 7 in E Major (1977):
    4107.KH1
  Symphony No. 8 in c minor (1976):
    4108.KH1

Krellmann, Hanspeter
  Symphony No. 9 in d minor (1976):
    4109.BD0
  Symphony No. 9 in d minor (1977):
    4109.KH1
Kroher, Ekkehart
  Symphony No. 1 in c minor (1985):
    4101.SW0
  Symphony No. 4 in E flat Major (1968):
    4104.HB0
  Symphony No. 7 in E Major (1980):
    4107.WG0
  Symphony No. 9 in d minor (1987):
    4109.SA0
Kross, Siegfried
  Psalm 150 (1980): 1038.BD0
  Helgoland (1980): 1071.BD0
  Symphony No. 7 in E Major (1980):
    4107.BD0
Kunze, Stefan
  Te Deum (1981): 1045.BD1
  Symphony No. 0 in d minor (1981):
    4100.BD0
  Symphony No. 1 in c minor (1982):
    4101.KH0
  Symphony No. 2 in c minor (1982):
    4102.KH0
  Symphony No. 3 in d minor (1981):
    4103.KH0
  Symphony No. 8 in c minor (1981):
    4108.BD0
Lang, Klaus
  Symphony No. 5 in B flat Major (1989):
    4105.FW1
Langevin, Paul-Gilbert
  String Quintet in F Major (1983):
    2112.OP0
  Symphony No. 8 in c minor (1984):
    4108.PC0
Lawton, Edward
  Overture in g minor (1952): 4098.AF0

Lawton, Edward
  Symphony No. 9 in d minor (1952):
  4109.AL0
Ledin, Victor
  Symphony No. 4 in E flat Major (1989):
  4104.RG0
Less, Helen H.
  Mass No. 3 in f minor (1953): 1028.GF0
Lewinski, Wolf-Eberhard von
  Symphony No. 8 in c minor (1979):
  4108.WG0
Lohmann, Heinz
  Fugue in d minor (1982): 3125.LH0
  Postlude in d minor (1982): 3126.LH0
  Prelude in E flat Major (1982): 3127.LH0
  Four Preludes in E flat Major (1982):
  3128.LH0
  Prelude in C Major (1982): 3129.LH0
  Prelude in d minor (1982): 3130.LH0
  Prelude and Fugue in c minor (1982):
  3131.LH0
Mann, William
  Symphony No. 4 in E flat Major (1972):
  4104.KA0
  Symphony No. 7 in E Major (1972):
  4107.KH0
  Symphony No. 7 in E Major (1985):
  4107.KO0
  Symphony No. 7 in E Major (1988):
  4107.SG1
Martin, D.R.
  Symphony No. 9 in d minor (1982):
  4109.WG0
Menuhin, Yehudi
  Symphony No. 5 in B flat Major (1989):
  4105.FW1
Miller, Gary W.
  Ave Maria (1983): 1006.MG0
Monson, Karen
  Symphony No. 9 in d minor (1977):
  4109.RG0

Nava, Alessandro [?]
  Symphony No. 8 in c minor (1989):
  4108.KH2
Neill, Edward D.R.
  Afferentur regi (1073): 1001.BG0
  Locus iste (1973): 1023.BG0
  Pange lingua et Tantum ergo (1973):
  1033.BG0
  Te Deum (1973): 1045.JA0
  Vexilla regis (1973): 1051.BG0
  Virga Jesse (1973): 1052.BG0
Nowak, Leopold
  String Quintet in F Major (1977):
  2112.VP0
  Intermezzo (1977): 2113.VP0
  Symphony No. 1 in c minor (1968):
  4101.JE0
  Symphony No. 2 in c minor (1968):
  4102.JE0
  Symphony No. 3 in d minor (1967):
  4103.JE0
  Symphony No. 3 in d minor (1971):
  4103.BK0
  Symphony No. 4 in E flat Major (1968):
  4104.JE0
  Symphony No. 6 in A Major (1968):
  4106.JE0
  Symphony No. 7 in E Major (1968):
  4107.JE0
Osborne, Richard
  Symphony No. 1 in c minor (1982):
  4101.KH0
  Symphony No. 2 in c minor (1982):
  4102.KH0
  Symphony No. 3 in d minor (1981):
  4103.KH0
  Symphony No. 5 in B flat Major (1977):
  4105.KH0
  Symphony No. 6 in A Major (1978):
  4106.BD0
  Symphony No. 6 in A Major (1980):
  4106.KH0

Sargeant, Winthrop
Symphony No. 6 in A Major (1972): 4106.ST0
Symphony No. 7 in E Major (1969): 4107.OE0
Sauer, Ralph
Locus iste (1976): 1023.LA0
Pange lingua et Tantum ergo (1976): 1033.LA0
Vexilla regis (1976): 1051.LA0
Schimpf, Sigurd
Mass No. 3 in f minor (1988): 1028.FK0
Schmidt, H.C.
Mass No. 2 in e minor [Kyrie only] (1978): 1027.HJ0
Scholz, Horst-Günther
Mass No. 1 in d minor (1973): 1026.JE0
Scholz, Rudolf
Fugue in d minor: 3125.FA0
Postlude in d minor: 3126.FA0
Prelude in E flat Major: 3127.FA0
Four Preludes in E flat Major: 3128.FA0
Prelude in C Major: 3129.FA0
Prelude in d minor: 3130.FA0
Prelude and Fugue in c minor: 3131.FA0
Schönzeler, Hans-Hubert
Mass No. 2 in e minor (1976): 1027.BD0
Mass No. 3 in f minor (1973): 1028.BD0
Requiem in d minor (1971): 1039.SH0
March in d minor (1971): 4096.SH0
Three Orchestral Pieces (1971): 4097.SH0
Overture in g minor (1972): 4098.SE0
Symphony No. 00 in f minor (1972): 4099.SE0
Symphony No. 4 in E flat Major (1977): 4104.MK0
Symphony No. 4 in E flat Major (1984): 4104.MC0
Schönzeler, Hans-Hubert
Symphony No. 7 in E Major (1989):

4107.MA0
Schuhmacher, Gerhard
Ave Maria (1988): 1006.GH2
Christus factus est (1988): 1011.GH1
Locus iste (1988): 1023.GH2
Os justi (1988): 1030.GE3
Virga Jesse (1988): 1052.GH1
Schultze, Wolfgang
Symphony No. 4 in E flat Major (1986): 4104.MR0
Schumann, Karl
Symphony No. 4 in E flat Major (1972): 4104.KA0
Symphony No. 4 in E flat Major (1986): 4104.HB1
Symphony No. 7 in E Major (1972): 4107.KH0
Symphony No. 7 in E Major (1989): 4107.DC0
Symphony No. 8 in c minor (1989): 4108.KR0
Symphony No. 8 in c minor (1981): 4108.HB1
Symphony No. 9 in d minor (1968): 4109.KH0
Symphony No. 9 in d minor (1982): 4109.HB1
Selvini, Michele
Symphony No. 8 in c minor (1989): 4108.FW3
Sheridan, Hope
Ave Maria (1975): 1006.ME0
Os justi (1975): 1030.MX0
Siegmund-Schultze, Walther
Symphony No. 7 in E Major (1976): 4107.MK0
Simpson, Robert
Libera me, Domine (1986): 1022.BM0
Mass No. 2 in e minor (1986): 1027.BM0
Psalm 112 (1987): 1035.BM0
Psalm 114 (1987): 1036.BM0
Psalm 150 (1980): 1038.BD0

Simpson, Robert
　Requiem in d minor (1987): 1039.BE0
　Te Deum (1981): 1045.BD1
　Helgoland (1980): 1071.BD0
　Æquale I (1986): 2114.BM0
　Æquale II (1986): 2149.BM0
　Symphony No. 0 in d minor (1981):
　　4100.BD0
　Symphony No. 4 in E flat Major (1982):
　　4104.BK0
　Symphony No. 4 in E flat Major (1990):
　　4104.CR0
　Symphony No. 7 in E Major (1980):
　　4107.BD0
　Symphony No. 8 in c minor (1981):
　　4108.BD0
Selvini, Michele
　Symphony No. 5 in B flat Major (1989):
　　4105.SM0
Slapak, Kamil
　Symphony No. 7 in E Major (1968):
　　4107.ML0
Smith, Warren Storey
　Symphony No. 1 in c minor (1955):
　　4101.AF0
Stanley, Charles
　Symphony No. 4 in E flat Major (1967):
　　4104.HH0
　Symphony No. 4 in E flat Major (1959):
　　4104.KO1
　Symphony No. 4 in E flat Major (1987):
　　4104.FW1
Steinbeck, Wolfram
　Symphony No. 4 in E flat Major (1988):
　　4104.SE0
　Symphony No. 7 in E Major (1987):
　　4107.GC0
Stone, Kurt
　Symphony No. 9 in d minor (1973):
　　4109.HJ0

Stone, Kurt
　Symphony No. 9 in d minor (1984):
　　4109.MY0
Stone, Peter Eliot
　Symphony No. 4 in E flat Major (1981):
　　4104.KR0
Tank, Ulrich
　Symphony No. 7 in E Major (1989):
　　4107.MA0
Thalmann, Joachim
　Christus factus est (1982): 1011.WT0
　Locus iste (1982): 1023.WT0
Uno, Isao
　Symphony No. 8 in c minor (1986):
　　4108.ML0
Veinus, Abraham
　Symphony No. 9 in d minor (1978):
　　4109.HG0
Velly, Jean-Jacques
　Symphony No. 4 in E flat Major (1988):
　　4104.SE0
　Symphony No. 7 in E Major (1987):
　　4107.GC0
Vidal, Pierre
　Symphony No. 8 in c minor (1985):
　　4108.GC0
Vyslouzil, Jiri
　Overture in g minor (1988): 4098.PL0
　Symphony No. 7 in E Major (1988):
　　4107.PL0
Wagner, Manfred
　Symphony No. 3 in d minor (1983):
　　4103.IE0
　Symphony No. 4 in E flat Major (1983):
　　4104.IE0
　Symphony No. 5 in B flat Major (1988):
　　4105.IE0
　Symphony No. 8 in c minor (1985):
　　4108.GC0
　Symphony No. 9 in d minor [Finale
　　only] (1988): 4109.IE1

Wand, Günter
  Symphony No. 9 in d minor (1989): 4109.WG1
Warrack, John
  Te Deum (1985): 1045.KH1
  Symphony No. 8 in c minor (1989): 4108.KH3
Watson, Derek
  Mass No. 2 in e minor (1974): 1027.NR0
  Symphony No. 4 in E flat Major (1982): 4104.TK0
  Symphony No. 8 in c minor (1983): 4108.TK0
Weille, F.B.
  Overture in g minor (1970): 4098.SW0
  Symphony No. 7 in E Major (1970): 4107.SW0
Werner-Jensen, Arnold
  Symphony No. 6 in A Major (1978): 4106.BD0

Wilson, Conrad
  Te Deum (1967): 1045.HB0
  Symphony No. 3 in d minor (1965): 4103.HB0
  Symphony No. 7 in E Major (1967): 4107.HB0
Worbs, Hans Christoph
  Te Deum (1989): 1045.HB1
  Symphony No. 5 in B flat Major (1989): 4105.HB1
  Symphony No. 5 in B flat Major (1989): 4105.JE2
  Symphony No. 7 in E Major (1986): 4107.IE0
  Symphony No. 7 in E Major (1979): 4107.HB1
  Symphony No. 9 in d minor (1987): 4109.IE0

Chronology

1909
Locus iste
  Anonymous, Vienna Hofmusik-
    kapelle: 1023.AA0
1924
Symphony No. 7 in E Major
  Fried, Berlin State Opera Orchestra:
    4107.FO0
Symphony No. 8 in c minor [Adagio
  only]
  Klemperer, Berlin State Opera Or-
    chestra: 4108.KO1
1925
Ave Maria
  Kalt, St. Hedwig's Cathedral Choir:
    1006.KA0
Mass No. 1 in d minor
  Kalt, St. Hedwig's Cathedral Choir:
    1026.KP0
1928
Christus factus est
  Schauerte, Paderborn Cathedral
    Choir: 1011.SW1
Te Deum
  Gatz, Berlin Staatskapelle: 1045.GF0
Symphony No. 7 in E Major
  Horenstein, Berlin Philharmonic
    Orchestra: 4107.HJ0

1929
Tota pulchra es
  Berberich, Munich Cathedral Choir:
    1046.BL0
1930
Mass No. 2 in e minor
  Odermath, Gregorius-Chor and
    Orchestra of the Liebfrauen-
    kirche, Zürich: 1027.OH0
Tota pulchra es
  Messner, Salzburg Cathedral Choir:
    1046.MJ0
1931
Ave Maria
  Berberich, Munich Cathedral Choir:
    1006.BL0
Locus iste
  Berberich, Munich Cathedral Choir:
    1023.BE0
Mass No. 2 in e minor [excerpts]
  Berberich, Munich Cathedral Choir:
    1027.BL0
Os justi
  Berberich, Munich Cathedral Choir:
    1030.BL0
Pange lingua et Tantum ergo
  Habel, St. Stephen's Cathedral
    Choir of Vienna: 1033.HF0

1931
  Tantum ergo, D Major
    Berberich, Munich Cathedral Choir:
    1042.BL0
  Vexilla regis
    Habel, St. Stephen's Cathedral
    Choir of Vienna: 1051.HF0
  Virga Jesse
    Habel, St. Stephen's Choir of
    Vienna: 1052.HA0
1935
  Mass No. 1 in d minor
    Anonymous, Basilica Chorus:
    1026.AA0
  Symphony No. 3 in d minor [Scherzo
    only]
    Konrath, Vienna Symphony Or-
    chestra: 4103.KO0
  Symphony No. 7 in E Major
    Ormandy, Minneapolis Symphony
    Orchestra: 4107.OE1
1936
  Symphony No. 4 in E flat Major
    Böhm, Saxon State Orchestra:
    4104.BK1
  Symphony No. 5 in B flat Major
    Böhm, Saxon State Orchestra:
    4105.BK0
1937
  Overture in g minor
    Wood, Queen's Hall Orchestra:
    4098.WH0
  Symphony No. 5 in B flat Major
    Jochum, Hamburg Philharmonic
    Orchestra: 4105.JE1
1938
  Mass No. 2 in e minor
    Rehmann, Berlin Symphony Or-
    chestra: 1027.RE0

1938
  Mass No. 2 in e minor
    Thurn, Hamburg State Opera Or-
    chestra: 1027.TM0
  Symphony No. 9 in d minor
    Hausegger, Munich Philharmonic
    Orchestra: 4109.HG0
1939
  Symphony No. 7 in E Major
    Schuricht, Berlin Philharmonic Or-
    chestra: 4107.SC0
1940
  Ave Maria
    Hoch, Strasbourg Cathedral Choir:
    1006.HL0
  Symphony No. 4 in E flat Major
    Jochum, Hamburg Philharmonic
    Orchestra: 4104.JE1
  Symphony No. 7 in E Major
    Jochum, Vienna Philharmonic Or-
    chestra: 4107.JE2
1942
  Symphony No. 5 in B flat Major
    Furtwängler, Berlin Philharmonic
    Orchestra: 4105.FW0
    Furtwängler, Berlin Philharmonic
    Orchestra: 4105.FW1
  Symphony No. 7 in E Major
    Furtwängler, Berlin Philharmonic
    Orchestra: 4107.FW3
1943
  Symphony No. 2 in c minor
    Jochum, Linz Bruckner Symphony
    Orchestra: 4102.JG0
  Symphony No. 6 in A Major
    Jochum, Linz Bruckner Symphony
    Orchestra: 4106.JG0
  Symphony No. 7 in E Major
    Kabasta, Munich Philharmonic Or-
    chestra: 4107.KA0

1943
Symphony No. 9 in d minor
Schuricht, Berlin Municipal Orchestra: 4109.SC1
1943/44
Symphony No. 4 in E flat Major
Knappertsbusch, Berlin Philharmonic Orchestra: 4104.KP0
1944
Symphony No. 7 in E Major
Böhm, Vienna State Opera Orchestra: 4107.BK0
Symphony No. 8 in c minor
Furtwängler, Vienna Philharmonic Orchestra: 4108.FW0
Symphony No. 9 in d minor
Furtwängler, Berlin Philharmonic Orchestra: 4109.FW0
1945
Afferentur regi
Rehmann, Aachen Cathedral Choir: 1001.RT0
1947
Symphony No. 7 in E Major
Beinum, Concertgebouw Orchestra, Amsterdam: 4107.BE1
1948
Ave Maria
Forster, St. Hedwig's Cathedral Choir: 1006.FE5
Mauersberger, Dresden Kreuzchor: 1006.MA5
Ave regina coelorum
Rehmann, Aachen Cathedral Choir: 1008.RT0
Locus iste
Schrems, Regensburg Cathedral Choir: 1023.SW1
Os justi
Forster, St. Hedwig's Cathedral Choir: 1030.FK0

1948
Os justi
Holliday, Hamline Choir: 1030.HR0
Mauersberger, Dresden Kreuzchor: 1030.MR0
Tantum ergo
Rehmann, Aachen Cathedral Choir: 1042.RT0
Te Deum
Jochum, Munich Radio Symphony Orchestra: 1045.JE0
Virga Jesse
Arndt, Berlin Motet Choir: 1052.AR0
Faure, William Faure Kammerchor: 1052.FW0
Mauersberger, Dresden Kreuzchor: 1052.MR0
Herbstlied
Schrems, Regensburg Cathedral Choir: 1073.ST0
String Quintet in F Major
Prisca Quartet: 2112.PQ0
Strub Quartet: 2112.SQ0
March in d minor
Mayer, Berlin Municipal Orchestra: 4096.ML0
Three Orchestral Pieces
Mayer, Berlin Municipal Orchestra: 4097.ML0
Overture in g minor
Mayer, Berlin Municipal Orchestra: 4098.ML0
Symphony No. 0 in d minor [Scherzo only]
Zaun, Berlin State Opera Orchestra: 4100.ZF0
Symphony No. 1 in c minor [Scherzo only]
Zaun, Berlin Symphony Orchestra: 4101.ZF0

1948

Symphony No. 2 in c minor [Scherzo only]
  Zaun, Berlin Symphony Orchestra: 4102.ZF0
Symphony No. 4 in E flat Major
  Krauss, Vienna Philharmonic Orchestra: 4104.KQ5
Symphony No. 5 in B flat Major
  Anonymous, Dol Dauber Orchestra: 4105.AA0
Symphony No. 8 in c minor
  Jochum, Hamburg Philharmonic State Orchestra: 4108.JE0
Symphony No. 9 in d minor [Trio only]
  Lucas, Leighton Lucas Orchestra: 4109.LL0

1949

Te Deum
  Messner, Salzburg Festival Orchestra and Chorus: 1045.MZ5
Symphony No. 4 in E flat Major
  Abendroth, Leipzig Symphony Orchestra: 4104.AH0
Symphony No. 5 in B flat Major
  Abendroth, Leipzig Radio Orchestra: 4105.AH0
Symphony No. 7 in E Major
  Furtwängler, Berlin Philharmonic Orchestra: 4107.FW0
  Knappertsbusch, Vienna Philharmonic Orchestra: 4107.KP0
Symphony No. 8 in c minor
  Furtwängler, Berlin Philharmonic Orchestra: 4108.FW1
  Furtwängler, Berlin Philharmonic Orchestra: 4108.FW2

1950

Psalm 112
  Swoboda, Vienna Symphony Orchestra: 1035.SH0a

1950

Psalm 150
  Swoboda, Vienna Symphony Orchestra: 1038.SH0a
Um Mitternacht
  Schneider, Stuttgart Liederkreis: 1090.SW0
String Quintet in F Major
  Vienna Philharmonic Quintet: 2112.VP1
Symphony No. 3 in d minor
  Fekete, Salzburg Mozarteum Orchestra: 4103.FZ0
  Rubahn, Berlin Symphony Orchestra: 4103.RG1
Symphony No. 6 in A Major
  Swoboda, Vienna Symphony Orchestra: 4106.SW0
Symphony No. 9 in d minor
  Knappertsbusch, Berlin Philharmonic Orchestra: 4109.KN0
  Knappertsbusch, Berlin Philharmonic Orchestra: 4109.KN1
  Knappertsbusch, Bavarian Radio Symphony Orchestra: 4109.KN3

1951

Symphony No. 1 in c minor
  Andreae, Austrian State Symphony Orchestra: 4101.AV0
Symphony No. 4 in E flat Major
  Furtwängler, Vienna Philharmonic Orchestra: 4104.FW0
  Furtwängler, Vienna Philharmonic Orchestra: 4104.FW1
  Klemperer, Vienna Symphony Orchestra: 4104.KO1
Symphony No. 5 in B flat Major
  Furtwängler, Vienna Philharmonic Orchestra: 4105.FW2
Symphony No. 7 in E Major
  Furtwängler, Berlin Philharmonic Orchestra: 4107.FW1

1951
  Symphony No. 7 in E Major
    Furtwängler, Berlin Philharmonic
    Orchestra: 4107.FW2
  Symphony No. 9 in d minor
    Abendroth, Leipzig Radio Orches-
    tra: 4109.AH0
1952
  Te Deum
    Karajan, Vienna Symphony Orches-
    tra: 1045.KH2
  Overture in g minor
    Adler, Vienna Philharmonia Or-
    chestra: 4098.AF0
  Symphony No. 0 in d minor
    Spruit, Concert Hall Symphony
    Orchestra: 4100.SH0
  Symphony No. 4 in E flat Major
    Konwitschny, Czech Philharmonic
    Orchestra: 4104.KQ0
  Symphony No. 7 in E Major
    Jochum, Berlin Philharmonic Or-
    chestra: 4107.JE3
  Symphony No. 8 in c minor
    Knappertsbusch, Berlin Philhar-
    monic Orchestra: 4108.KP2
  Symphony No. 9 in d minor
    Adler, Vienna Philharmonia Or-
    chestra: 4109.AL0
1953
  Mass No. 3 in f minor
    Grossmann, Vienna State Philhar-
    monia: 1028.GF0
  Te Deum
    Walter, New York Philharmonic:
    1045.WB0
  Symphony No. 1 in c minor
    Andreae, Vienna Symphony Or-
    chestra: 4101.AV1
  Symphony No. 2 in c minor
    Andreae, Vienna Symphony Or-
    chestra: 4102.AV0

1953
  Symphony No. 3 in d minor
    Adler, Vienna Philharmonia: 4103
    .AF0
  Symphony No. 4 in E flat Major
    Otterloo, Hague Residentie Orches-
    tra: 4104.OW0
  Symphony No. 7 in E Major
    Beinum, Concertgebouw Orchestra,
    Amsterdam: 4107.BE0
  Symphony No. 9 in d minor
    Horenstein, Vienna Symphony Or-
    chestra: 4109.HJ0
    Walter, Vienna Philharmonic Or-
    chestra: 4109.WB0
    Walter, New York Phiharmonic:
    4109.WB2
1954
  Te Deum
    Jochum, Bavarian Radio Symphony
    Orchestra: 1045.JE2
  Overture in g minor
    Matacic, Philharmonia Orchestra:
    4098.MA0
  Symphony No. 0 in d minor [Scherzo
  only]
    Matacic, Philharmonia Orchestra:
    4100.ML0
  Symphony No. 3 in d minor
    Goehr, Netherlands Philharmonic:
    4103.GW0
    Knappertsbusch, Bavarian State
    Orchestra: 4103.KN0
    Knappertsbusch, Vienna Philhar-
    monic Orchestra: 4103.KN1
  Symphony No. 4 in E flat Major
    Matacic, Philharmonia Orchestra:
    4104.ML0
    Tubbs, Hastings Symphony:
    4104.TU0

1954
Symphony No. 7 in E Major
Otterloo, Vienna Symphony Orchestra: 4107.OW0
Symphony No. 8 in c minor
Furtwängler, Vienna Philharmonic Orchestra: 4108.FW3
1955
Ave Maria
Rehmann, Aachen Cathedral Choir: 1006.RT0
Mass No. 2 in e minor
Forster, Berlin Philharmonic Orchestra: 1027.FK0
Te Deum
Forster, Berlin Philharmonic Orchestra: 1045.FK0
Walter, Vienna Philharmonic Orchestra: 1045.WB1
Herbstlied
Rehmann, Aachen Cathedral Choir: 1073.RT0
Um Mitternacht
Kühbacher, Vienna Choir Boys: 1089.KR0
String Quintet in F Major
Koeckert Quartet: 2112.KQ0
Overture in g minor
Otterloo, Vienna Symphony Orchestra: 4098.OW0
Symphony No. 1 in c minor
Adler, Vienna Orchestral Society: 4101.AF0
Symphony No. 2 in c minor
Konwitschny, Berlin Radio Symphony Orchestra: 4102.KO0
Symphony No. 3 in d minor
Andreae, Vienna Symphony Orchestra: 4103.AV0
Symphony No. 4 in E flat Major
Kempen, Hilversum Radio Orchestra: 4104.KE5

1955
Symphony No. 4 in E flat Major
Knappertsbusch, Vienna Philharmonic Orchestra: 4104.KP1
Symphony No. 5 in B flat Major
Pflügler, Leipzig Philharmonic Orchestra: 4105.PG0
Symphony No. 8 in c minor
Beinum, Concertgebouw Orchestra, Amsterdam: 4108.BE0
Horenstein, Vienna Symphony Orchestra: 4108.HJ0
Knappertsbusch, Bavarian State Orchestra: 4108.KP1
1956
Locus iste
Rehmann, Aachen Cathedral Choir: 1023.RT0
Tota pulchra es
Wasner, Trapp Family Singers: 1046.WF0
String Quintet in F Major
Vienna Konzerthaus Quartet: 2112. VK0
Intermezzo
Vienna Konzerthaus Quartet: 2113. VK0
Symphony No. 4 in E flat Major
Steinberg, Pittsburgh Symphony Orchestra: 4104.SW0
Symphony No. 5 in B flat Major
Knappertsbusch, Vienna Philharmonic Orchestra: 4105.KP0
Symphony No. 8 in c minor [excerpt from Finale]
Boston Symphony Orchestra, bass Wagner tuba in F solo: 4108.ML5
Symphony No. 9 in d minor
Beinum, Concertgebouw Orchestra, Amsterdam: 4109.BE0

1956
- Symphony No. 9 in d minor
  - Jochum, Bavarian Radio Symphony Orchestra: 4109.JE0
  - Keilberth, Hamburg State Philharmonic Orchestra: 4109.KJ0

1957
- Mass No. 1 in d minor
  - Adler, Radio Vienna Chorus and Orchestra: 1026.AC0
- Symphony No. 8 in c minor
  - Karajan, Berlin Philharmonic Orchestra: 4108.KH0

1958
- Ave Maria
  - Froschauer, Singverein der Gesellschaft der Musikfreunde: 1006.FH0
  - Lippe, St. Hedwig's Cathedral Choir: 1006.LA0
  - Meyer, Vienna Choir Boys: 1006.ME1
- Locus iste
  - Froschauer, Singverein der Gesellschaft der Musikfreunde: 1023.FH0
- Tantum ergo, D Major
  - Hans, Haselbach [Choir]: 1042.WH0
- Apollo March
  - Goldman, Goldman Band: 4115.GR0
- Symphony No. 4 in E flat Major
  - Jochum, Bavarian Radio Symphony Orchestra: 4104.JE1
- Symphony No. 5 in B flat Major
  - Jochum, Bavarian Radio Symphony Orchestra: 4105.JE0
- Symphony No. 7 in E Major
  - Klemperer, Berlin Philharmonic Orchestra: 4107.KO1
  - Konwitschny, Gewandhaus Orchestra, Leipzig: 4107.KW0

1959
- Symphony No. 7 in E Major
  - Rosbaud, Southwest German Radio Orchestra, Baden-Baden: 4107.RH0
- Symphony No. 8 in c minor
  - Mravinsky, Leningrad Philharmonic Orchestra: 4108.MZ7
- Symphony No. 9 in d minor
  - Knappertsbusch, Bavarian State Orchestra: 4109.KN2

1959
- Symphony No. 5 in B flat Major
  - Beinum, Concertgebouw Orchestra, Amsterdam: 4105.BE0
- Symphony No. 9 in d minor
  - Walter, Columbia Symphony Orchestra: 4109.WB1

1960
- Ave Maria
  - Fries, Les Rossignols de Bruxelles: 1006.FF0
  - Gillesberger, Vienna Academy Chamber Choir: 1006.GH1
  - Herzog, Göttinger Boys' Choir: 1006.HE0
  - Peloquin, Peloquin Chorale: 1006.PC0
  - Smith, Keighly Vocal Union: 1006.SW4
  - Wormsbächer, Bergedorfer Chamber Choir: 1006.WH0
- Christus factus est
  - Gillesberger, Vienna Academy Chamber Choir: 1011.GH0
- Locus iste
  - Gillesberger, Vienna Kammerchor: 1023.GH1
  - Klausing, Palestrina-Kreis: 1023.KF0

1960
Os justi
Clausing, Palestrina-Kreis: 1030.CF0
Gillesberger, Vienna Academy
Chamber Choir: 1030.GE0
Virga Jesse
Gillesberger, Vienna Academy
Chamber Choir: 1052.GH0
Um Mitternacht
Anonymous, Essen Schubertbund:
1090.AA0
Fugue in d minor
Roizman: 3125.RL0
Postlude in d minor
Roizman: 3126.RL0
March in d minor
Walter, Hamburg New Symphony
Orchestra: 4096.WF0
Three Orchestral Pieces
Walter, Hamburg New Symphony
Orchestra: 4097.WF0
Symphony No. 4 in E flat Major
Knappertsbusch, Vienna Philhar-
monic Orchestra: 4104.KP2
Walter, Columbia Symphony Or-
chestra: 4104.WB0
Symphony No. 6 in A Major
Swarowsky, Vienna Festival Or-
chestra: 4106.SS0
Symphony No. 7 in E Major
Klemperer, Philharmonia Orches-
tra: 4107.KO0
Szell, Vienna Philharmonic Orches-
tra: 4107.SZ0
1961
Erinnerung
Demus: 2117.DJ0
Symphony No. 4 in E flat Major
Hollreiser, Bamberg Symphony
Orchestra: 4104.HH0

1961
Symphony No. 5 in B flat Major
Knappertsbusch, Munich Philhar-
monic Orchestra: 4105.KP1
Konwitschny, Leipzig Gewandhaus
Orchestra: 4105.KZ0
Symphony No. 6 in A Major
Klemperer, Concertgebouw Or-
chestra, Amsterdam: 4106.KO0
Symphony No. 7 in E Major
Walter, Columbia Symphony Or-
chestra: 4107.WB0
Symphony No. 8 in c minor
Knappertsbusch, Vienna Philhar-
monic Orchestra: 4108.KP5
Symphony No. 9 in d minor
Schuricht, Vienna Philharmonic
Orchestra: 4109.SC0
1962
Ave Maria
Arndt, Berlin Handel Chorus:
1006.AR0
Christus factus est
Gönnenwein, Stuttgart Madrigal
Choir: 1011.GW0
Locus iste
Gönnenwein, Stuttgart Madrigal
Choir: 1023.GW0
Mass No. 3 in f minor
Forster, Berlin Symphony Orches-
tra: 1028.FK0
Jochum, Bavarian Radio Symphony
Orchestra: 1028.JE0
Os justi
Gönnenwein, Stuttgart Madrigal
Choir: 1030.GO0
Tantum ergo, D Major
Gönnenwein, Stuttgart Madrigal
Choir: 1042.GW0
Symphony No. 3 in d minor
Knappertsbusch, North German
Radio Orchestra: 4103.KN2

1962

Symphony No. 4 in E flat Major
Konwitschny, Vienna Symphony Orchestra: 4104.KQ1
Symphony No. 9 in d minor
Bernstein, New York Philharmonic: 4109.BL0

1963

Symphony No. 3 in d minor
Haitink, Concertgebouw Orchestra, Amsterdam: 4103.HB0
Symphony No. 4 in E flat Major
Klemperer, Philharmonia Orchestra: 4104.KO0
Konwitschny, Leipzig Gewandhaus Orchestra: 4104.KQ3
Symphony No. 6 in A Major
Keilberth, Berlin Philharmonic Orchestra: 4106.KJ0
Reichert, Westphalian Symphony Orchestra: 4106.RH0
Symphony No. 7 in E Major
Knappertsbusch, Cologne Radio Symphony Orchestra: 4107.KP1
Symphony No. 8 in c minor
Knappertsbusch, Munich Philharmonic Orchestra: 4108.KP0
Kubelik, Bavarian Radio Symphony Orchestra: 4108.KR0
Schuricht, Vienna Philharmonic Orchestra: 4108.SC0

1964

Ave Maria
Gillesberger, Vienna Kammerchor: 1006.GH0
Locus iste
Gillesberger, Vienna Kammerchor: 1023.GH0
Mass No. 2 in e minor
Gillesberger, Vienna State Opera Orchestra: 1027.GH0

1964

Os justi
Gillesberger, Vienna Academy Chamber Choir: 1030.GE2
Symphony No. 5 in B flat Major
Jochum, Concertgebouw Orchestra, Amsterdam: 4105.JE2
Symphony No. 6 in A Major
Klemperer, New Philharmonia Orchestra: 4106.KO1
Symphony No. 7 in E Major
Jochum, Berlin Philharmonic Orchestra: 4107.JE0
Schuricht, The Hague Philharmonic Orchestra: 4107.SC1
Symphony No. 8 in c minor
Jochum, Berlin Philharmonic Orchestra: 4108.JE1
Symphony No. 9 in d minor
Haitink, Concertgebouw Orchestra, Amsterdam: 4109.HB0
Jochum, Berlin Philharmonic Orchestra: 4109.JE1

1965

Afferentur regi
Bertola, Coro Polifonico Italiano: 1001.BG0
Ave Maria
Möller, Obernkirchen Children's Choir: 1006.MT1
In jener letzten der Nächte
Möller, Obernkirchen Children's Choir: 1017.ME0
Locus iste
Bertola, Coro Polifonico Italiano: 1023.BG0
Pange lingua et Tantum ergo
Bertola, Coro Polifonico Italiano: 1033.BG0
Te Deum
Jochum, Berlin Philharmonic Orchestra: 1045.JE1

1965
Vexilla regis
Bertola, Coro Polifonico Italiano: 1051.BG0
Virga Jesse
Bertola, Coro Polifonico Italiano: 1052.BG0
String Quintet in F Major
Amadeus Quartet: 2112.AQ0
Symphony No. 1 in c minor
Jochum, Berlin Philharmonic Orchestra: 4101.JE0
Symphony No. 4 in E flat Major
Haitink, Concertgebouw Orchestra, Amsterdam: 4104.HB0
Jochum, Berlin Philharmonic Orchestra: 4104.JE0
Kertesz, London Symphony Orchestra: 4104.KI0
Symphony No. 5 in B flat Major
Ormandy, Philadelphia Orchestra: 4105.OE0
Symphony No. 7 in E Major
Solti, Vienna Philharmonic Orchestra: 4107.SG0
Symphony No. 8 in c minor
Karajan, Vienna Philharmonic Orchestra: 4108.KH2
Symphony No. 9 in d minor
Mehta, Vienna Philharmonic Orchestra: 4109.MN0
1966
Afferentur regi
Jochum, Chorus of the Bavarian Radio: 1001.JE0
Ave Maria
Jochum, Chorus of the Bavarian Radio: 1006.JE0
Pitz, New Philharmonia Chorus: 1006.PW0

1966
Christus factus est
Jochum, Chorus of the Bavarian Radio: 1011.JE0
Pitz, New Philharmonia Chorus: 1011.PW0
Ecce sacerdos
Jochum, Chorus of the Bavarian Radio: 1013.JE0
Inveni David
Koekelkoeren, Maastreechter Staar: 1019.KM0
Locus iste
Jochum, Chorus of the Bavarian Radio: 1023.JE0
Pitz, New Philharmonia Chorus: 1023.PW0
Os justi
Jochum, Chorus of the Bavarian Radio: 1030.JE0
Pitz, New Philharmonia Chorus: 1030.PW0
Pange lingua et Tantum ergo
Jochum, Chorus of the Bavarian Radio: 1033.JE0
Te Deum
Haitink, Concertgebouw Orchestra, Amsterdam: 1045.HB0
Ormandy, Philadelphia Orchestra: 1045.OE0
Tota pulchra es
Jochum, Chorus of the Bavarian Radio: 1046.JE0
Vexilla regis
Jochum, Chorus of the Bavarian Radio: 1051.JE0
Virga Jesse
Jochum, Chorus of the Bavarian Radio: 1052.JE0
Pitz, New Philharmonia Chorus: 1052.PW0

1966

Symphony No. 0 in d minor
Haitink, Concertgebouw Orchestra, Amsterdam: 4100.HB0

Symphony No. 1 in c minor
Neumann, Leipzig Gewandhaus Orchestra: 4101.NV0

Symphony No. 2 in c minor
Jochum, Bavarian Radio Symphony Orchestra: 4102.JE0

Symphony No. 3 in d minor
Schuricht, Vienna Philharmonic Orchestra: 4103.SC0
Szell, Cleveland Orchestra: 4103.SG0
Szell, Cleveland Orchestra: 4103.SG0a

Symphony No. 4 in E flat Major
Leinsdorf, Boston Symphony Orchestra: 4104.LE0

Symphony No. 6 in A Major
Jochum, Bavarian Radio Symphony Orchestra: 4106.JE0

Symphony No. 7 in E Major
Haitink, Concertgebouw Orchestra, Amsterdam: 4107.HB0
Rudolf, Cincinnati Symphony Orchestra: 4107.RM0

Symphony No. 8 in c minor
Solti, Vienna Philharmonic Orchestra: 4108.SG0

Symphony No. 9 in d minor
Karajan, Berlin Philharmonic Orchestra: 4109.KH0

1967

Ave Maria
Alldis, John Alldis Choir: 1006.AJ0

Christus factus est
Alldis, John Alldis Choir: 1011.AJ0
Guest, Berkshire Boy Choir: 1011.GW1

1967

Locus iste
Alldis, John Alldis Choir: 1023.AJ0

Te Deum
Wallberg, Vienna National Orchestra: 1045.WA0

Virga Jesse
Alldis, John Alldis Choir: 1052.AJ0

String Quartet in c minor
Keller Quartet: 2111.KQ0

String Quintet in F Major
Keller Quartet: 2112.KE0

Intermezzo
Keller Quartet: 2113.KQ0

Symphony No. 3 in d minor
Jochum, Bavarian Radio Symphony Orchestra: 4103.JE0

Symphony No. 4 in E flat Major
Ormandy, Philadelphia Orchestra: 4104.OE0
Wallberg, Vienna National Orchestra: 4104.WA5

Symphony No. 5 in B flat Major
Klemperer, New Philharmonia Orchestra: 4105.KO0

Symphony No. 6 in A Major
Bongartz, Leipzig Gewandhaus Orchestra: 4106.BH0

1968

Ave regina coelorum
Loré, Petit Chanteurs de la Notre-Dame de la de la Joie: 1008.L_0

Overture in g minor
Steinberg, Pittsburgh Symphony Orchestra: 4098.SW0

Symphony No. 5 in B flat Major
Klemperer, Vienna Philharmonic Orchestra: 4105.KO1

Symphony No. 7 in E Major
Matacic, Czech Philharmonic Orchestra: 4107.ML0

1968
  Symphony No. 7 in E Major
    Ormandy, Philadelphia Orchestra:
    4107.OE0
  Steinberg, Pittsburgh Symphony
    Orchestra: 4107.SW0
  Symphony No. 8 in c minor
    Wallberg, Vienna National Orches-
    tra: 4108.WA5
  Symphony No. 9 in d minor
    Wallberg, Vienna National Orches-
    tra: 4109.WA5
1969
  Ave Maria
    Thomas, Silver Ring Choir of Bath:
    1006.TK0
  Te Deum
    Barenboim, New Philharmonia Or-
    chestra: 1045.BD0
  String Quintet in F Major
    Melos Quartet: 2112.MQ0
  Symphony No. 1 in c minor
    Abbado, Vienna Philharmonic Or-
    chestra: 4101.AC0
  Symphony No. 2 in c minor
    Haitink, Concertgebouw Orchestra,
    Amsterdam: 4102.HB0
  Symphony No. 6 in A Major
    Steinberg, Boston Symphony Or-
    chestra: 4106.ST0
  Symphony No. 8 in c minor
    Haitink, Concertgebouw Orchestra,
    Amsterdam: 4108.HB0
  Symphony No. 9 in d minor
    Celibidache, Turin RAI Symphonic
    Orchestra: 4109.CS0
1970
  Ave Maria
    Kramm, Münster Madrigal Choir:
    1006.KH0
    Pernoud, La Psallette de Geneve:
    1006.PP0

1970
  Ave regina coelorum
    Pernoud, La Psallette de Geneve:
    1008.PP0
  Christus factus est
    Pernoud, La Psallette de Geneve:
    1011.PP0
  Os justi
    Kramm, Münster Madrigal Choir:
    1030.KH0
    Pernoud, La Psallette de Geneve:
    1030.PP0
  Requiem in d minor
    Schönzeler, London Philharmonic
    Orchestra: 1039.SH0
  Te Deum
    Bernardi, Leipzig Bach Festival Or-
    chestra: 1045.BL0
  Tota pulchra es
    Pernoud, La Psallette de Geneve:
    1046.PP0
  Virga Jesse
    Brandstetter, Bach Choir Hannover:
    1052.BM1
  March in d minor
    Schönzeler, London Philharmonic
    Orchestra: 4096.SH0
  Three Orchestral Pieces
    Schönzeler, London Philharmonic
    Orchestra: 4097.SH0
  Symphony No. 2 in c minor
    Swarowsky, South German Phil-
    harmonic Orchestra: 4102.SW0
  Symphony No. 3 in d minor
    Böhm, Vienna Philharmonic Or-
    chestra: 4103.BK0
    Sanderling, Leipzig Gewandhaus
    Orchestra: 4103.SA0
  Symphony No. 4 in E flat Major
    Celibidache, unidentified orchestra:
    4104.CS0

1970
Symphony No. 4 in E flat Major
Karajan, Berlin Philharmonic Orchestra: 4104.KA0
Mehta, Los Angeles Philharmonic Orchestra: 4104.MN0
Symphony No. 6 in A Major
Haitink, Concertgebouw Orchestra, Amsterdam: 4106.HB0
Symphony No. 8 in c minor
Celibidache, unidentified orchestra: 4108.CS0
Klemperer, New Philharmonia Orchestra: 4108.KO0
Szell, Cleveland Orchestra: 4108.SZ0
Symphony No. 9 in d minor
Celibidache, Stuttgart Radio Symphony Orchestra: 4109.CS0
Klemperer, New Philharmonia Orchestra: 4109.KL0
Rozhdestvensky, Moscow Radio Large Symphony Orchestra: 4109.RG0

1971
Ave Maria
Martini, Darmstadt Junge Kantorei: 1006.MA0
Christus factus est
Martini, Darmstadt Junge Kantorei: 1011.MJ0
Locus iste
Martini, Junge Kantorei, Darmstadt: 1023.MJ0
Mass No. 2 in e minor
Gönnenwein, Southwest German Radio Orchestra: 1027.GW0
Jochum, Bavarian Radio Symphony Orchestra: 1027.JE0
Os justi
Martini, Junge Kantorei, Darmstadt: 1030.MJ0

1971
Pange lingua et Tantum ergo
Martini, Junge Kantorei, Darmstadt: 1033.MJ0
Tota pulchra es
Martini, Junge Kantorei, Darmstadt: 1046.MJ0
Æquale I
Berlin Trombone Quartet: 2114.BE0
Postlude in d minor
Davies: 3126.DH0
Prelude in d minor
Davies: 3130.DH0
Symphony No. 2 in c minor
Reichert, Westphalian Symphony Orchestra, Recklinghausen: 4102.RH0
Symphony No. 5 in B flat Major
Haitink, Concertgebouw Orchestra, Amsterdam: 4105.HB0
Symphony No. 7 in E Major
Karajan, Berlin Philharmonic Orchestra: 4107.KH0

1972
Ave Maria
Gillesberger, Vienna Choir Boys: 1006.GH2
Christus factus est
Gillesberger, Vienna Choir Boys: 1011.GH1
Locus iste
Gillesberger, Vienna Choir Boys: 1023.GH2
Mass No. 2 in e minor
Rilling, Bach-Collegium Stuttgart: 1027.RH0
Mass No. 3 in f minor
Barenboim, New Philharmonia Orchestra: 1028.BD0
Os justi
Gillesberger, Vienna Choir Boys: 1030.GE3

1972
Virga Jesse
Gillesberger, Vienna Choir Boys: 1052.GH1
Overture in g minor
Shapirra, London Symphony Orchestra: 4098.SE0
Symphony No. 00 in f minor
Shapirra, London Symphony Orchestra: 4099.SE0
Symphony No. 1 in c minor
Haitink, Concertgebouw Orchestra, Amsterdam: 4101.HB0
Symphony No. 4 in E flat Major
Barenboim, Chicago Symphony Orchestra: 4104.BD0
Symphony No. 6 in A Major
Stein, Vienna Philharmonic Orchestra: 4106.SH0

1973
Afferentur regi
Guest, Choir of St. John's College, Cambridge: 1001.GG0
Martini, Junge Kantorei, Darmstadt: 1001.MJ0
Ecce sacerdos
Guest, Choir of St. John's College, Cambridge: 1013.GG0
Martini, Junge Kantorei, Darmstadt: 1013.MJ0
Inveni David
Guest, Choir of St. John's College, Cambridge: 1019.GG0
Martini, Junge Kantorei, Darmstadt: 1019.MJ0
Mass in C Major
Riedelbauch: 1025.RW0
Mass No. 1 in d minor
Jochum, Bavarian Radio Symphony Orchestra: 1026.JE0

1973
Mass No. 2 in e minor
Martini, Vienna Symphony: 1027.MJ0
Norrington, Philip Jones Wind Ensemble: 1027.NR0
Wormsbächer, Hamburg State Philharmonic Orchestra: 1027.WH0
Os justi
Guest, Choir of St. John's College, Cambridge: 1030.GG0
Pange lingua et Tantum ergo
Guest, Choir of St. John's College, Cambridge: 1033.GG0
Psalm 146
Riedelbauch, Nuremberg Symphony Orchestra: 1037.RW0
Requiem in d minor
Beuerle, Werner Keltsch Instrumental Ensemble: 1039.BH0
String Quintet in F Major
Kammermusiker Zürich: 2112.KA0
Symphony No. 2 in c minor
Stein, Vienna Philharmonic Orchestra: 4102.SH0
Symphony No. 4 in E flat Major
Böhm, Vienna Philharmonic Orchestra: 4104.BK0
Symphony No. 5 in B flat Major
Matacic, Czech Philharmonic Orchestra: 4105.ML0

1974
Ave Maria
Bradshaw, Saltarello Choir: 1006.BR0
Schrems, Regensburger Domspatzen: 1006.SW1
Christus factus est
Bradshaw, Saltarello Choir: 1011.BR0

1974
Locus iste
   Bradshaw, Saltarello Choir: 1023.
   BR0
Mass No. 2 in e minor
   Barenboim, English Chamber Or-
   chestra. 1027.BD0
Os justi
   Bradshaw, Saltarello Choir: 1030.
   BR0
Virga Jesse
   Bradshaw, Saltarello Choir: 1052.
   BR0
   Schrems, Regensburger Dom-
   spatzen: 1052.SW1
String Quintet in F Major
   Heutling Quartet: 2112.HQ0
   Vienna Philharmonia Quintet:
   2112.VP0
Intermezzo
   Vienna Philharmonia Quintet:
   2113.VP0
Symphony No. 2 in c minor
   Giulini, Vienna Symphony Orches-
   tra: 4102.GC0
Symphony No. 3 in d minor
   Maazel, Berlin Radio Symphony
   Orchestra: 4103.ML0
Symphony No. 5 in B flat Major
   Maazel, Vienna Philharmonic Or-
   chestra: 4105.MA0
   Wand, Cologne Radio Symphony
   Orchestra: 4105.WG0
Symphony No. 7 in E Major
   Masur, Leipzig Gewandhaus Or-
   chestra: 4107.MK0
Symphony No. 8 in c minor
   Mehta, Los Angeles Philharmonic
   Orchestra: 4108.MZ0

1975
Ave Maria
   Meyer, Vienna Academy Kammer-
   chor: 1006.ME0
   Mittergradnegger, Klagenfurt Mad-
   rigal Chorus: 1006.MT0
Os justi
   Meyer, Vienna Academy Kammer-
   chor: 1030.MX0
Te Deum
   Janigro, Angelicum Orchestra of
   Milan: 1045.JA0
Fugue in d minor
   Forer: 3125.FA0
   Haselböck: 3125.HF0
Postlude in d minor
   Forer: 3126.FA0
   Haselböck: 3126.HF0
Prelude in E flat Major
   Forer: 3127.FA0
   Haselböck: 3127.HF0
Four Preludes in E flat Major
   Forer: 3128.FA0
   Haselböck: 3128.HF0
Prelude in C Major
   Forer: 3129.FA0
   Haselböck: 3129.HF0
Prelude in d minor
   Forer: 3130.FA0
   Haselböck: 3130.HF0
Prelude and Fugue in c minor
   Forer: 3131.FA0
   Haselböck: 3131.HF0
Symphony No. 0 in d minor
   Gelmini, Nuremburg Symphony
   Orchestra: 4100.GH0
Symphony No. 2 in c minor
   Jochum, Staatskapelle Dresden:
   4102.JE1
Symphony No. 4 in E flat Major
   Jochum, Staatskapelle Dresden:
   4104.JE3

1975
Symphony No. 4 in E flat Major
Masur, Leipzig Gewandhaus Orchestra: 4104.MK0
Symphony No. 5 in B flat Major
Kempe, Munich Philharmonic Orchestra: 4105.KM0
Symphony No. 7 in E Major
Asahina, Osaka Philharmonic Orchestra: 4107.AT1
Karajan, Berlin Philharmonic Orchestra: 4107.KH1
Symphony No. 8 in c minor
Karajan, Berlin Philharmonic Orchestra: 4108.KH1
Kempe, Zurich Tonhalle Orchestra: 4108.KM0
Symphony No. 9 in d minor
Barenboim, Chicago Symphony Orchestra: 4109.BD0
Karajan, Berlin Philharmonic Orchestra: 4109.KH1
Masur, Leipzig Gewandhaus Orchestra: 4109.MK0
1976
Ave Maria
Günther, Rhenish Choral Society: 1006.GH5
Schweizer, Pforzheim Motettenchor: 1006.SW3
Christus factus est
Schweizer, Pforzheim Motettenchor: 1010.SR0
Ecce sacerdos
Günther, Rhenish Youth Choir: 1013.GH0
Locus iste
Günther, Rheinische Singgemeinschaft: 1023.GW5
Los Angeles Philharmonic Trombone Ensemble: 1023.LA0

1976
Mass No. 2 in e minor
Mehta, Vienna Philharmonic Orchestra: 1027.MZ0
Os justi
Günther, Männergesangverein Concordia Hamm: 1030.GH0
Schweizer, Pforzheim Motettenchor: 1030.SZ0
Pange lingua et Tantum ergo
Günther, Rheinische Singgemeinschaft: 1033.GH0
Los Angeles Philharmonic Trombone Ensemble: 1033.LA0
Requiem in d minor
Günther, Rhenish Symphony Orchestra: 1039.GH0
Tantum ergo, D Major
Günther, Rheinische Singgemeinschaft: 1042.GW5
Te Deum
Karajan, Berlin Philharmonic Orchestra: 1045.KH0
Mehta, Vienna Philharmonic Orchestra: 1045.MZ0
Te Deum ["In te, Domine, speravi" only]
Stephani, Philharmonia Hungarica: 1045.SM0
Vexilla regis
Los Angeles Philharmonic Trombone Ensemble: 1051.LA0
Trösterin Musik
Günther, Männergesangverein Concordia Hamm: 1088.GH0
Um Mitternacht
Günther: 1090.GI0
Hostias
Günther, Männergesangverein Concordia Hamm: 1999.GH0

1976
Æquale I
  P. Schreckenburger Posaunen-
    ensemble: 2114.SP0
Quadrille
  Wikman: 2121.WS0
Fugue in d minor
  Ruegenberg: 3125.RH0
Prelude in E flat Major
  Ruegenberg: 3127.RH0
Symphony No. 3 in d minor
  Rozhdestvensky, Moscow Radio
    Large Symphony Orchestra:
    4103.RG0
Symphony No. 4 in E flat Major
  Karajan, Berlin Philharmonic Or-
    chestra: 4104.KA1
  Kempe, Munich Philharmonic Or-
    chestra: 4104.KE0
  Wand, Cologne Radio Symphony
    Orchestra: 4104.WG0
Symphony No. 5 in B flat Major
  Karajan, Berlin Philharmonic Or-
    chestra: 4105.KH0
  Masur, Leipzig Gewandhaus Or-
    chestra: 4105.MK0
Symphony No. 6 in A Major
  Wand, Cologne Radio Symphony
    Orchestra: 4106.WG0
Symphony No. 7 in E Major
  Böhm, Vienna Philharmonic Or-
    chestra: 4107.BK1
  Jochum, Staatskapelle Dresden:
    4107.JE1
Symphony No. 8 in c minor
  Böhm, Vienna Philharmonic Or-
    chestra: 4108.BK0
  Jochum, Staatskapelle Dresden:
    4108.JE2
  Wand, Cologne Gürzenich Orches-
    tra: 4108.WG1

1976
Symphony No. 9 in d minor
  Giulini, Chicago Symphony Orches-
    tra: 4109.GC0
1977
Asperges me
  Breitschaft, Limburger Dom-Sing-
    knaben: 1004.BM0
Ave Maria
  Breitschaft, Limburger Dom-Sing-
    knaben: 1006.BM1
Christus factus est
  Breitschaft, Limburger Dom-Sing-
    knaben: 1011.BT0
In S. Angelum custodem
  Breitschaft, Limburger Dom-Sing-
    knaben: 1018.BM0
Locus iste
  Breitschaft, Limburger Dom-Sing-
    knaben: 1023.BT0
Mass No. 2 in e minor
  Kron, Bruckner Chorus of Linz:
    1027.KL0
Os justi
  Breitschaft, Limburger Dom-Sing-
    knaben: 1030.BT0
Pange lingua et Tantum ergo
  Breitschaft, Limburger Dom-Sing-
    knaben: 1033.BM5
Tantum ergo, D Major
  Breitschaft, Limburger Dom-Sing-
    knaben: 1042.BM0
Vexilla regis
  Breitschaft, Limburger Dom-Sing-
    knaben: 1051.BM5
Helgoland
  Morris, Symphonica of London:
    1071.MW0
Symphony No. 1 in c minor
  Masur, Leipzig Gewandhaus Or-
    chestra: 4101.MK0

1977

Symphony No. 3 in d minor
  Jochum, Staatskapelle Dresden:
  4103.JE1
  Masur, Leipzig Gewandhaus Or-
  chestra: 4103.MS0
Symphony No. 4 in E flat Major
  Zsoltay, South German Philhar-
  monic: 4104.ZD0
Symphony No. 5 in B flat Major
  Barenboim, Chicago Symphony
  Orchestra: 4105.BD0
Symphony No. 6 in A Major
  Barenboim, Chicago Symphony
  Orchestra: 4106.BD0
  Zsoltay, South German Philhar-
  monic: 4106.ZD0
Symphony No. 7 in E Major
  Sanderling, Danish Radio Sym-
  phony Orchestra: 4107.SA0
Prelude and Fugue in c minor
  Forer: 3131.FA0

1978

Mass No. 2 in e minor [Kyrie only]
  Hömberg, Pro Musica Köln:
  1027.HJ0
Intermezzo
  Alberni String Quartet: 2113.AS0
Symphony No. 0 in d minor
  Märzendorfer, Austrian Broadcast
  Symphony Orchestra: 4100.ME0
Symphony No. 1 in c minor
  Jochum, Staatskapelle Dresden:
  4101.JE1
Symphony No. 2 in c minor
  Masur, Leipzig Gewandhaus Or-
  chestra: 4102.MK0
Symphony No. 4 in E flat Major
  Rozhdestvensky, USSR Ministry of
  Culture Symphony: 4104.RG0

1978

Symphony No. 4 in E flat Major
  Tchakarov, Leningrad Philhar-
  monic Symphonic Orchestra:
  4104.TE0
Symphony No. 6 in A Major
  Jochum, Staatskapelle Dresden:
  4106.JE1
  Masur, Leipzig Gewandhaus Or-
  chestra: 4106.MK0
Symphony No. 7 in E Major
  Haitink, Concertgebouw Orchestra,
  Amsterdam: 4107.HB1
  Solti, Chicago Symphony Orches-
  tra: 4107.SG2
Symphony No. 8 in c minor
  Masur, Leipzig Gewandhaus Or-
  chestra: 4108.MK0
Symphony No. 9 in d minor
  Jochum, Staatskapelle Dresden:
  4109.JE2
  Wand, Cologne Radio Symphony
  Orchestra: 4109.WG0

1979

Ave Maria
  Hellmann, Bach Choir of Mainz:
  1006.HD0
Christus factus est
  Hellmann, Bach Choir of Mainz:
  1011.HD0
Locus iste
  Hellmann, Bach Choir of Mainz:
  1023.HD0
Os justi
  Hellmann, Bach Choir of Mainz:
  1030.HD0
Psalm 150
  Barenboim, Chicago Symphony
  Orchestra: 1038.BD0
Virga Jesse
  Hellmann, Bach Choir of Mainz:
  1052.HD0

1979

Helgoland
  Barenboim, Chicago Symphony
  Orchestra: 1071.BD0
Symphony No. 0 in d minor
  Barenboim, Chicago Symphony
  Orchestra: 4100.BD0
Symphony No. 4 in E flat Major
  Kubelik, Bavarian Radio Symphony
  Orchestra: 4104.KR0
Symphony No. 6 in A Major
  Karajan, Berlin Philharmonic Or-
  chestra: 4106.KH0
  Solti, Chicago Symphony Orches-
  tra: 4106.SG0
Symphony No. 7 in E Major
  Barenboim, Chicago Symphony
  Orchestra: 4107.BD0
Symphony No. 8 in c minor
  Wand, Cologne Radio Symphony
  Orchestra: 4108.WG0

1980

Fugue in d minor
  Galard: 3125.GJ0
Postlude in d minor
  Galard: 3126.GJ0
Four Preludes in E flat Major
  Galard: 3128.GJ0
Prelude in C Major
  Galard: 3129.GJ0
Prelude in d minor
  Galard: 3130.GJ0
Prelude and Fugue in c minor
  Galard: 3131.GJ0
Symphony No. 2 in c minor
  Mandeal, Cluj-Napoca Symphony
  Orchestra: 4102.MC0
Symphony No. 3 in d minor
  Karajan, Berlin Philharmonic Or-
  chestra: 4103.KH0
  Kubelik, Bavarian Radio Symphony
  Orchestra: 4103.KR0

1980

Symphony No. 3 in d minor
  Mandeal, Cluj-Napoca Symphony
  Orchestra: 4103.ML5
Symphony No. 5 in B flat Major
  Solti, Chicago Symphony Orches-
  tra: 4105.SG0
Symphony No. 6 in A Major
  Rögner, Berlin Symphony Orches-
  tra: 4106.RH5
Symphony No. 7 in E Major
  Blomstedt, Staatskapelle Dresden:
  4107.BH0
  Wand, Cologne Radio Symphony
  Orchestra: 4107.WG0
Symphony No. 8 in c minor
  Asahina, Osaka Philharmonic Or-
  chestra: 4108.AT1
  Barenboim, Chicago Symphony
  Orchestra: 4108.BD0
  Rögner, Berlin Radio Symphony
  Orchestra: 4108.RH0
Symphony No. 8 in c minor [excerpt
  from Adagio]
  Hoof, unidentified studio orches-
  tra: 4108.HH0
Symphony No. 9 in d minor
  Asahina, Nomiuri Nippon Philhar-
  . monic Orchestra: 4109.AT0
  Matacic, Czech Philharmonic Or-
  chestra: 4109.ML0
  Mravinsky, Leningrad Philhar-
  monic Orchestra: 4109.MY0

1981

Afferentur regi
  Reichel, Zürcher Bach-Kantorei:
  1001.RT5
Ave Maria
  Reichel, Zürcher Bach-Kantorei:
  1006.RT5

1981

Christus factus est
Reichel, Zürcher Bach-Kantorei: 1011.RE5

Ecce sacerdos
Reichel, Zürcher Bach-Kantorei: 1013.RH0

Locus iste
Reichel, Zürcher Bach-Kantorei: 1023.RT5

Os justi
Reichel, Zürcher Bach-Kantorei: 1030.RE5

Pange lingua et Tantum ergo
Reichel, Zürcher Bach-Kantorei: 1033.RH0

Te Deum
Barenboim, Chicago Symphony Orchestra: 1045.BD1

Tota pulchra es
Reichel, Zürcher Bach-Kantorei: 1046.RH0

Vexilla regis
Reichel, Zürcher Bach-Kantorei: 1051.RH0

Virga Jesse
Reichel, Zürcher Bach-Kantorei: 1052.RH0

Prelude and Fugue in c minor
Humer: 3131.HU0

Symphony No. 1 in c minor
Barenboim, Chicago Symphony Orchestra: 4101.BD0
Karajan, Berlin Philharmonic Orchestra: 4101.KH0
Wand, Cologne Radio Symphony Orchestra: 4101.WG0

Symphony No. 2 in c minor
Barenboim, Chicago Symphony Orchestra: 4102.BD0
Karajan, Berlin Philharmonic Orchestra: 4102.KH0

1981

Symphony No. 2 in c minor
Wand, Cologne Radio Symphony Orchestra: 4102.WG0

Symphony No. 3 in d minor
Barenboim, Chicago Symphony Orchestra: 4103.BD0
Wand, Cologne Radio Symphony Orchestra: 4103.WG0

Symphony No. 4 in E flat Major
Blomstedt, Staatskapelle Dresden: 4104.BH0
Solti, Chicago Symphony Orchestra: 4104.SG0
Tennstedt, Berlin Philharmonic Orchestra: 4104.TK0

Symphony No. 6 in A Major
Sawallisch, Bavarian State Orchestra: 4106.SA0

Symphony No. 8 in c minor
Haitink, Concertgebouw Orchestra, Amsterdam: 4108.HB1
Svetlanov, U.S.S.R. Academic Symphony Orchestra: 4108.SV0

Symphony No. 9 in d minor
Haitink, Concertgebouw Orchestra, Amsterdam: 4109.HB1

1982

Afferentur regi
Best, Corydon Singers: 1001.BM0

Ave Maria
Best, Corydon Singers: 1006.BM0

Christus factus es
Best, Corydon Singers: 1011.BM0

Christus factus est
Westphalian Trombone Quartet: 1011.WT0

Ecce sacerdos
Best, Corydon Singers: 1013.BM0

Inveni David
Best, Corydon Singers: 1019.BM0

1982

Locus iste
Best, Corydon Singers: 1023.BM0
Westphalian Trombone Quartet: 1023.WT0
Os justi
Best, Corydon Singers: 1030.BM0
Pange lingua et Tantum ergo
Best, Corydon Singers: 1033.BM0
Tota pulchra es
Best, Corydon Singers: 1046.BM0
Vexilla regis
Best, Corydon Singers: 1051.BM0
Virga Jesse
Best, Corydon Singers: 1052.BM0
String Quintet in F Major
Soloists of the Orchestra of Paris: 2112.OP0
Fugue in d minor
Lohmann: 3125.LH0
Postlude in d minor
Lohmann: 3126.LH0
Prelude in E flat Major
Lohmann: 3127.LH0
Four Preludes in E flat Major
Lohmann: 3128.LH0
Prelude in C Major
Lohmann: 3129.LH0
Prelude in d minor
Lohmann: 3130.LH0
Prelude and Fugue in c minor
Lohmann: 3131.LH0
Symphony No. 3 in d minor
Inbal, Frankfurt Radio Symphony Orchestra: 4103.IE0
Symphony No. 4 in E flat Major
Inbal, Frankfurt Radio Symphony Orchestra: 4104.IE0
Symphony No. 8 in c minor
Inbal, Frankfurt Radio Symphony Orchestra: 4108.IE0

1982

Symphony No. 8 in c minor
Paita, Philharmonic Symphony Orchestra: 4108.PC0
Symphony No. 8 in c minor
Tennstedt, London Philharmonic Orchestra: 4108.TK0

1983

Ave Maria
Miller, New York City Gay Men's Chorus: 1006.MG0
Mass No. 3 in f minor
Asahina, Osaka Philharmonic Orchestra: 1028.AT0
String Quintet in F Major
Kocian Quartet: 2112.KO0
Symphony No. 00 in f minor
Rozhdestvensky, USSR Symphony Orchestra: 4099.RG0
Symphony No. 0 in d minor
Rozhdestvensky, USSR Symphony Orchestra: 4100.RG0
Symphony No. 1 in c minor
Asahina, Japan Philharmonic Orchestra: 4101.AX0
Symphony No. 7 in E Major
Asahina, Osaka Philharmonic Orchestra: 4107.AT0
Rögner, Berlin Radio Symphony Orchestra: 4107.RE0
Symphony No. 9 in d minor
Matacic, Vienna Symphony Orchestra: 4109.ML1
Rögner, Berlin Radio Symphony Orchestra: 4109.RE0

1984

Afferentur regi
Fuchs, Zurich Chamber Choir: 1001.FJ0
Schäfer, Freiburg Vocal Ensemble: 1001.SW0

1984

Ave Maria
Fuchs, Zurich Chamber Choir: 1006.
FU0
Schäfer, Freiburg Vocal Ensemble:
1006.SW0
Christus factus est
Fuchs, Zurich Chamber Choir: 1011.
FJ0
Schäfer, Freiburg Vocal Ensemble:
1011.SW0
Ecce sacerdos
Fuchs, Zurich Chamber Choir: 1013.
FJ0
Schäfer, Freiburg Vocal Ensemble:
1013.SW0
In jener letzten der Nächte
Jürgens: 1017.JJ0
Inveni David
Fuchs, Zurich Chamber Choir: 1019.
FJ0
Zapf, Bavaria-Blechsolisten Mün-
chen: 1019.ZG0
Locus iste
Fuchs, Zurich Chamber Choir: 1023.
FJ0
Schäfer, Freiburg Vocal Ensemble:
1023.SW0
Magnificat in B flat Major
Jürgens, Israel Chamber Orchestra:
1024.JJ0
Missa Solemnis in B flat Major
Jürgens, Israel Chamber Orchestra:
1029.JJ0
Os justi
Boles, Choir of St. Paul's Episcopal
Church: 1030.BO0
Fuchs, Zurich Chamber Choir:
1030.FU0
Schäfer, Freiburg Vocal Ensemble:
1030.SW0

1984

Pange lingua et Tantum ergo
Fuchs, Zurich Chamber Choir: 1033.
FJ0
Schäfer, Freiburg Vocal Ensemble:
1033.SW0
Te Deum
Karajan, Vienna Philharmonic Or-
chestra: 1045.KH1
Tota pulchra es
Fuchs, Zurich Chamber Choir: 1046.
FJ0
Schäfer, Freiburg Vocal Ensemble:
1046.SW0
Vexilla regis
Fuchs, Zurich Chamber Choir: 1051.
FJ0
Schäfer, Freiburg Vocal Ensemble:
1051.SW0
Virga Jesse
Fuchs, Zurich Chamber Choir: 1052.
FX0
Schäfer, Freiburg Vocal Ensemble:
1052.SW0
O du liebes Jesu Kind
Jürgens: 1145.JJ0
Æquale I
Fuchs, Slokar Trombone Quartet:
2114.FJ0
Æquale II
Fuchs, Slokar Trombone Quartet:
2149.FJ0
Symphony No. 1 in c minor
Sawallisch, Bavarian State Orches-
tra: 4101.SW0
Symphony No. 3 in d minor
Asahina, Tokyo Metropolitan Sym-
phony Orchestra: 4103.AY0
Symphony No. 4 in E flat Major
Macal, Hallé Orchestra: 4104.MC0

1984

Symphony No. 4 in E flat Major
Rögner, Berlin Radio Symphony Orchestra: 4104.RH0
Symphony No. 5 in B flat Major
Rögner, Berlin Symphony Orchestra: 4105.RH0
Symphony No. 7 in E Major
Chailly, Berlin Radio Symphony Orchestra: 4107.CR0
Matacic, Slovene Philharmonic Orchestra: 4107.ML1
Symphony No. 8 in c minor
Giulini, Vienna Philharmonic Orchestra: 4108.GC0
Matacic, Japan Broadcasting Corporation Symphony Orchestra: 4108.ML0
Symphony No. 9 in d minor
Sawallisch, Bavarian State Orchestra: 4109.SA0

1985

Afferentur regi
Flämig, Dresdner Kreuzchor: 1001. FA5
Gronostay, Denmark Radio Choir: 1001.GE0
Ave Maria (I)
Flämig, Dresdner Kreuzchor: 1005. FA5
Ave Maria (II)
Flämig, Dresdner Kreuzchor: 1006. FA0
Gronostay, Denmark Radio Choir: 1006.GH3
Christus factus est
Flämig, Dresdner Kreuzchor: 1011 .FA5
Gronostay, Denmark Radio Choir: 1011.GU0

1985

Ecce sacerdos
Flämig, Dresdner Kreuzchor: 1013. FA5
Gronostay, Denmark Radio Choir: 1013.GE0
Inveni David
Flämig, Dresdner Kreuzchor: 1019.FA5
Libera me, Domine
Best, English Chamber Orchestra Wind Ensemble: 1022.BM0
Flämig, Dresdner Kreuzchor: 1022.FA5
Locus iste
Flämig, Dresdner Kreuzchor: 1023. FA0
Gronostay, Denmark Radio Choir: 1023.GW3
Mass No. 2 in e minor
Best, English Chamber Orchestra Wind Ensemble: 1027.BM0
Os justi
Flämig, Dresdner Kreuzchor: 1030. FA5
Gronostay, Denmark Radio Choir: 1030.GO0
Pange lingua et Tantum ergo
Flämig, Dresdner Kreuzchor: 1033. FA5
Gronostay, Denmark Radio Choir: 1033.GO0
Tantum ergo, D Major
Flämig, Dresdner Kreuzchor: 1042. FA5
Tota pulchra es
Flämig, Dresdner Kreuzchor: 1046. FA0
Gronostay, Denmark Radio Choir: 1046.GU0

1985
  Vexilla regis
    Flämig, Dresdner Kreuzchor: 1051.FA5
    Gronostay, Denmark Radio Choir: 1051.GU0
  Virga Jesse
    Flämig, Dresdner Kreuzchor: 1052.FA5
    Gronostay, Denmark Radio Choir: 1052.GU0
  Æquale I
    Best, English Chamber Orchestra Wind Ensemble: 2114.BM0
  Æquale II
    Best, English Chamber Orchestra Wind Ensemble: 2149.BM0
  Symphony No. 3 in d minor
    Chailly, Berlin Radio Symphony Orchestra: 4103.CR0
  Symphony No. 4 in E flat Major
    Haitink, Vienna Philharmonic Orchestra: 4104.HB1
    Muti, Berlin Philharmonic Orchestra: 4104.MR0
  Symphony No. 7 in E Major
    Inbal, Frankfurt Radio Symphony Orchestra: 4107.IE0
  Symphony No. 9 in d minor
    Solti, Chicago Symphony Orchestra: 4109.SG0
    Talmi, Oslo Philharmonic Orchestra: 4109.TY0
  Symphony No. 9 in d minor [sketch of Finale only]
    Talmi, Oslo Philharmonic Orchestra: 4143.TY0
1986
  Ave Maria
    Garbers, Herrenhäuser Chorgemeinschaft: 1006.GA5

1986
  Ave Maria
    Hausmann, Capella Vocale St. Aposteln, Cologne: 1006.HA5
    Matkowitz, Heinrich-Schütz-Kreis Berlin: 1006.MA2
    Wilhelm, Stuttgarter Hymnus-Chorknaben: 1006.WG0
  Christus factus est
    Beringer, Windsbacher Knabenchor: 1011.BK0
    Hahn, St. Jakobschor Rothenburg: 1011.HA5
    Rilling, Figuralchor Stuttgart: 1011.RH0
    Sonnenschmidt, Bezirkskantorei Pirmasens: 1011.SW5
  Locus iste
    Beringer, Windsbacher Knabenchor: 1023.BF0
    Garbers, Herrenhäuser Chorgemeinschaft: 1023.GA5
    Hahn, St. Jakobschor Rothenburg: 1023.HA5
    Itai, Israel Kibbutz Choir: 1023.IA0
    Mattmann, Trinity Church Choir, Bern: 1023.MT0
    Raabe, Gerson Raabe Brass Ensemble: 1023.RG0
  Missa Solemnis in B flat Major
    Günther, BRT Symphony Orchestra, Brussels: 1029.GH0
    Hausmann, Capella Vocale St. Aposteln, Cologne: 1029.HE0
  Os justi
    Beringer, Windsbacher Knabenchor: 1030.BL5
    Hahn, St. Jakobschor Rothenburg: 1030.HA5
    Harrassowitz, Bach-Chor St. Lorenz Nürnberg: 1030.HA5

1986

Os justi
  Hausmann, Capella Vocale St.
  Aposteln, Cologne: 1030.HA5
  Rilling, Gächinger Kantorei Stutt-
  gart: 1030.RH0
  Sonnenschmidt, Bezirkskantorei
  Pirmasens: 1030.SZ5
Requiem in d minor
  Ermert, Siegerland-Orchester: 1039.
  EH0
Tantum ergo, D Major
  Hahn, St. Jakobschor Rothenburg:
  1042.HH0
  Wilhelm, Stuttgarter Hymnus-
  Chorknaben: 1042.WG0
Te Deum
  Helbich, Bremen Bach Orchestra:
  1045.HW0
Tota pulchra es
  Hausmann, Capella Vocale St.
  Aposteln, Cologne: 1046.HE0
Virga Jesse
  Hausmann, Capella Vocale St.
  Aposteln, Cologne: 1052.HA5
String Quintet in F Major [Adagio only]
  Horn: 2112.HW5
Erinnerung
  Howard: 2117.HL0
Fugue in d minor
  Knitl: 3125.KI0
Prelude in C Major
  Bovet: 3129.BG0
  Horn: 3129.HW5
Prelude in C Major
  Kuhlman: 3129.KW0
Prelude in d minor
  Knitl: 3130.KI0
Prelude and Fugue in c minor
  Kaufmann: 3131.KE0

1986

Overture in g minor
  Pesek, Czech Philharmonic Orches-
  tra: 4098.PL0
Symphony No. 0 in d minor [Scherzo
  only]
  Horn: 4100.HE0
Symphony No. 2 in c minor
  Asahina, Osaka Philharmonic:
  4102.AX0
Symphony No. 2 in c minor [Scherzo
  only]
  Horn: 4102.HE0
Symphony No. 4 in E flat Major
  Uno, Shinsei Nihon Orchestra:
  4104.UK0
Symphony No. 5 in B flat Major
  Albert, Bavarian State Youth Or-
  chestra, Augsburg: 4105.AW0
  Jochum, Staatskapelle Dresden:
  4105.JE2
Symphony No. 7 in E Major
  Giulini, Vienna Philharmonic Or-
  chestra: 4107.GC0
  Pesek, Czech Philharmonic Orches-
  tra: 4107.PL0
  Solti, Chicago Symphony Orches-
  tra: 4107.SG1
Symphony No. 7 in E Major [Adagio
  only]
  Horn: 4107.HW0
Symphony No. 8 in c minor
  Järvi, London Philharmonic Orches-
  tra: 4108.JA0
  Suitner, Berlin Radio Symphony
  Orchestra: 4108.SO0
Symphony No. 9 in d minor [Finale
  only]
  Inbal, Frankfurt Radio Symphony
  Orchestra: 4109.IE1

1987

Afferentur regi
Zanotelli, Philharmonisches Vocal-
ensemble Stuttgart: 1001.ZH0
Ave Maria
Bader, St. Hedwig's Cathedral
Choir, Berlin: 1006.BA5
Rinscheid, Singkreis Wehbach:
1006.RT5
Zanotelli, Philharmonisches Vocal-
ensemble Stuttgart: 1006.ZH0
Mass for Holy Thursday
Peerik, Ensemble Vocal Raphael:
1009.PJ0
Christus factus est
Zanotelli, Philharmonisches Vocal-
ensemble Stuttgart: 1011.ZH0
Ecce sacerdos
Zanotelli, Philharmonisches Vocal-
ensemble Stuttgart: 1013.ZH0
Inveni David
Zanotelli, Philharmonisches Vocal-
ensemble Stuttgart: 1019.ZH0
Libera me, Domine
Zanotelli, Philharmonisches Vocal-
ensemble Stuttgart: 1022.ZH0
Locus iste
Peerik, Ensemble Vocal Raphael:
1023.PJ0
Rinscheid, Singkreis Wehbach:
1023.RT5
Zanotelli, Philharmonisches Vocal-
ensemble Stuttgart: 1023.ZH0
Os justi
Zanotelli, Philharmonisches Vocal-
ensemble Stuttgart: 1030.ZH0
Pange lingua et Tantum ergo
Zanotelli, Philharmonisches Vocal-
ensemble Stuttgart: 1033.ZH0
Psalm 112
Best, English Chamber Orchestra:
1035.BM0

1987

Psalm 114
Best, Corydon Singers: 1036.BM0
Requiem in d minor
Best, English Chamber Orchestra:
1039.BE0
Tota pulchra es
Zanotelli, Philharmonisches Vocal-
ensemble Stuttgart: 1046.ZH0
Vexilla regis
Zanotelli, Philharmonisches Vocal-
ensemble Stuttgart: 1051.ZH0
Virga Jesse
Zanotelli, Philharmonisches Vocal-
ensemble Stuttgart: 1052.ZH0
Symphony No. 1 in c minor
Chailly, Berlin Radio Symphony
Orchestra: 4101.CR0
Inbal, Frankfurt Radio Symphony
Orchestra: 4101.IE0
Symphony No. 4 in E flat Major
Sinopoli, Staatskapelle Dresden:
4104.SE0
Symphony No. 5 in B flat Major
Inbal, Frankfurt Radio Symphony
Orchestra: 4105.IE0
Symphony No. 7 in E Major
Davis, Bavarian Radio Symphony
Orchestra: 4107.DC0
Symphony No. 8 in c minor
Wand, North German Radio Sym-
phony Orchestra: 4108.WG2
Symphony No. 9 in d minor
Inbal, Frankfurt Radio Symphony
Orchestra: 4109.IE0
Wand, North German Radio Sym-
phony Orchestra: 4109.WG1

1988

Ave Maria
Böck, Concentus Vocalis Wien: 1006.
BM0h

1988

Christus factus est
Böck, Concentus Vocalis Wien: 1011.
BO0
Locus iste
Valen, Valen Choir: 1023.VS0
Mass No. 2 in e minor
Rögner, Berlin Radio Symphony
Orchestra: 1027.RZ0
Mass No. 3 in f minor
Davis, Bavarian Radio Symphony
Orchestra: 1028.DC0
Os justi
Böck, Concentus Vocalis Wien:
1030.BN0
Te Deum
Haitink, Vienna Philharmonic Or-
chestra: 1045.HB1
Rögner, Berlin Radio Symphony
Orchestra: 1045.RH0
Tota pulchra es
Böck, Concentus Vocalis Wien:
1046.BO0
Eichorn, Jugendkantorei Wetzlar:
1046.EJ0
Virga Jesse
Böck, Concentus Vocalis Wien:
1052.BM0h
String Quartet in c minor
Bamberg Cathedral Quartet:
2111.BQ0
Prelude in d minor
Wachowski: 3130.WG0
Overture in g minor
Chailly, Berlin Radio Symphony
Orchestra: 4098.CR0
Overture in g minor
Hager, Southwest German Radio
Symphony Orchestra: 4098.HL0
Symphony No. 0 in d minor
Chailly, Berlin Radio Symphony
Orchestra: 4100.CR0

1988

Symphony No. 2 in c minor
Inbal, Frankfurt Radio Symphony
Orchestra: 4102.IE0
Symphony No. 4 in E flat Major
Chailly, Concertgebouw Orchestra:
4104.CR0
Symphony No. 5 in B flat Major
Haitink, Vienna Philharmonic Or-
chestra: 4105.HB1
Symphony No. 6 in A Major
Eschenbach, Schleswig-Holstein
Music Festival Orchestra:
4106.EC0
Inbal, Radio Symphony Orchestra
Frankfurt: 4106.IE0
Muti, Berlin Philharmonic Orches-
tra: 4106.MR0
Wand, North German Radio Sym-
phony Orchestra: 4106.WG1
Symphony No. 7 in E Major
Maazel, Berlin Philharmonic Or-
chestra: 4107.MA0
Symphony No. 8 in c minor
Asahina, Osaka Philharmonic Or-
chestra: 4108.AT0
Karajan, Vienna Philharmonic Or-
chestra: 4108.KH3
Wand, North German Radio Sym-
phony Orchestra: 4108.WG3
Symphony No. 9 in d minor
Dohnányi, Cleveland Orchestra:
4109.DC0
Giulini, Vienna Philharmonic Or-
chestra: 4109.GC1

1989

Ave Maria
Herreweghe, La Chapelle Royale:
1006.HA5
Christus factus est
Herreweghe, La Chapelle Royale:
1011.HP0

1989
  Locus iste
    Herreweghe, La Chapelle Royale:
    1023.HP0
  Mass No. 2 in e minor
    Herreweghe, Ensemble Musique
    Oblique: 1027.HE0
  Os justi
    Herreweghe, La Chapelle Royale:
    1030.HP0
  Vexilla regis
    Herreweghe, La Chapelle Royale:
    1051.HP0
  Æquale I
    Herreweghe, Ensemble Musique
    Oblique: 2114.EM0
  Æquale II
    Herreweghe, Ensemble Musique
    Oblique: 2149.EM0
  Symphony No. 7 in E Major
    López-Cobos, Cincinnati Sympho-
    ny Orchestra: 4107.LJ0
  Symphony No. 8 in c minor
    Nanut, Ljubljana Symphony Or-
    chestra: 4108.NA0
1990
  Christus factus est
    Graham, Grace Church Choir: 1011.
    GR0
  Locus iste
    Graham, Grace Church Choir: 1023.
    GR0
  Os justi
    Graham, Grace Church Choir: 1030.
    GR0
  String Quintet in F Major
    Sonare Quartet: 2112.SO0

1990
  Intermezzo
    Sonare Quartet: 2113.SO0
  Four Preludes in E flat Major
    Horn, Klais organ: 3128.HO0
  Fugue in d minor
    Horn: 3125.HO0
  Prelude in E flat Major
    Horn: 3127.HO0
  Prelude in d minor
    Horn: 3130.HO0
  Prelude in C Major
    Horn: 3129.HW6
  Prelude and Fugue in C Major
    Horn: 3131.HO0
  Postlude in d minor
    Horn: 3126.HO0
  Overture in g minor
    Janowski, Radio France Philhar-
    monic Orchestra: 4098.JM0
  Symphony No. 00 in f minor [Scherzo
    only]
    Horn: 4099.HE0
  Symphony No. 0 in d minor [Andante
    only]
    Horn: 4100.HE1
  Symphony No. 4 in E flat Major
    Janowski, Radio France Philhar-
    monic Orchestra: 4104.JM0
    López-Cobos, Cincinnati Sym-
    phony Orchestra: 4104.LJ0
  Symphony No. 6 in A Major [Adagio
    only]
    Horn: 4106.HE0
  Symphony No. 8 in c minor
    Kegel, Leipzig Radio Symphony
    Orchestra: 4108.KH7